Dianora Della Torre Arrigoni

COLOUR in PAINTING:
materials and spirituality

Translated by
Margot Kerr

C ONTENTS

Introduction   p.6

1) The search for colour

Nature's gift

The palette of the artists of Altamira and Lascaux

2) Ancient Egypt   12

The importance of colour in Ancient Egypt

Natural colours

New pigments from chemical technology

Lake pigments

The preparation of colours

3) Ancient Mesopotamia   24

The invention of glass

Blue and gold: sacred and royal colours

4) Classical Antiquity   31

3

A colourful past

Pompeian colours

5) The medieval palette 47

Divine light in colour

Sources of raw materials

The contribution of the Alchemists

The early medieval treatises on colours

The purple codices

The palette of early medieval codices

Imitation of precious materials

Illuminated manuscripts

The colours in "De Arte Illuminandi"

The blues in medieval painting

The Book of Art of Cennino Cennini

In Cennino's workshop

Cennino's colours

6) The traditional palette of the late 15th century Florence 121

Ghirlandaio's workshop

Purchasing pigments in Florence

7) The city of colour   128

Colour in Renaissance Venice

The 'vendecolori' of Venice

8) Antwerp's golden age   147

The great art market of Northern Europe

Antwerp's most famous adoptive son

9) The Baroque palette   152

10) The eighteenth century palette   159

11) Between two centuries   169

A wave of new pigments

Monet's and Cezanne's palettes

A new vision of colour

12) A palette without limits   192

Revolutionary new materials

American Expressionism

INTRODUCTION

This text comes from the desire to respond to a cultural expectation of many fine art lovers who are aware of the crucial importance that the materials have always had in creating a work of art. It is rather surprising to see how the history of art materials is regularly overlooked by any art history textbook. If it is true on the one hand that the materials by themselves are not enough to create a masterpiece, it is also true that the limits or the potential of painting materials available in every period have reduced or enhanced the possibilities of the artist and his expressive power.

In total agreement with Philip Ball's words when he says that "Use of color in art is determined at least as much by the artist's personal inclinations and cultural context as by the materials at hand" (Bright Earth, p.7), I have tried to write down a concise survey of the history of colour, both from a material and a spiritual side; a history that goes from prehistoric cave painters up to today's artists; a path along which chemistry, history of art, the meaning of colour in different eras and the technique of the use of colour by some great masters intertwine and interact.

An initial reading to enable one to understand better a painting when looking at it, a stimulus for further readings and in depth study.

1) THE SEARCH FOR COLOUR

Nature's gift

To go back with certainty to the moment in which man began to use the first colouring substances is still impossible; nevertheless it wouldn't seem a rash conjecture that the quest for colour and the attraction for dyed materials has accompanied human beings ever since their appearance; the most antique and certain evidence of the use of the first pigments goes back to the Paleolithic period; the Neanderthal man, the first who began to bury their deceased, painted the corpses with red ochres; with the appearance of the Cro-Magnon man, the coloured ochres became of current use; the red ochres were placed on the skull and on the chest of the deceased, as findings of about 30,000 years ago prove; then the bodies began to be laid on solid layers of red earth; this was a widespread custom in a really vast geographical area: burials of this type have been found in many parts of Europe and are present in the prehistory of other peoples in other continents. It is more than probable that already at that time, man had associated red to the colour of blood which in turn was associated to life and that this custom may have been used for magic-ritual purposes. In France, in the cave of Arcy-sur-Cure there is a layer of ten to twenty centimetres composed of a red-violet ochre; it is not known why this enormous quantity of colour was accumulated; it is, however, unquestionable proof of the importance that colour or all that had the power to colour, had for prehistoric man; in the same cave, numerous finds were discovered, dating back to 40,000 years before and revealing the abundant use of yellow ochre; according to some historians, the capacity to transform yellow ochre into red ochre through the process known as calcination (that is, burning yellow ochre to a temperature of about 200° and so removing the

8

water from the limonite which then transforms into hematite) goes back to this period; on the site of Troubat (High Pyrenees), inhabited between 11,000 and 6,500 B.C., blocks of hematite were found, which, from the results of the analysis, are formed of 25% calcined goethite (an iron bearing hidroxide mineral): the Paleolithic man, therefore, had discovered that fire was also an extraordinary and powerful means for the transformation of materials.

During the whole superior Paleolithic, rock paintings in caves appeared in Europe; whatever the main purpose of these paintings was, they reveal a very rich palette and a conscious artistic technique.

The palette of the artists of Altamira and Lascaux

The caves of Altamira in Spain and of Lascaux in France are certainly the most famous and the paintings in them done by the Magdalenian men about 15,000 years ago are the most photographed and reproduced in worldwide publishing.

The artists who painted the roof and walls of these caves deliberately manipulated the natural materials at their disposal for artistic purposes. The pigments used are the fruit of a knowledgeable use to obtain colours that are resistant and alive. By drawing on natural resources, the artists of the Upper Paleolithic created an incredibly vast range of colours; in the prehistoric deposits of the Frankish-cantabric region, about fifteen different colours were identified, nearly all of mineral origin. Earths, ochres and coloured minerals were used uninterruptedly throughout history; used by all civilizations, earths lend themselves to decorations, from bodily ones to wall paintings. Their excellent colour stability explains their wide and prolonged use; their colours are not brilliant, but offer a wide range of hues and shades which give complete freedom of artistic expression. Most of the natural earths get their own colour from the presence of iron minerals which can be found in abundance in the superficial layer of the earth crust with a great variety of colours: yellow and red ochre, green earths, brown earths and iron hydroxides in their pure state, more or less. Iron and oxygen, in fact, can combine under the form of oxides, in very different ratios; the colours of the resultant compounds of the various combinations vary from yellow to violet through a wide range of reds and browns: these compounds are commonly known as "ochres". Technically, by the term "ochre" one means only the product extracted from the ochre sands through a process which entails the pulverization and the separation in water of the quartzitic granules of the clay and the coloured oxide: whilst the former, heavier, deposit on the base, the latter, lighter, float on the surface; once the liquid has been collected and the water evaporated, what remains is "ochre".

Ochres are produced from the oxidization of materials containing iron; this process of oxidization is carried out in the same place in which they are found.

Amongst the iron oxides, hematite and limonite are the most important. Hematite, in the form of rocky mineral, is black with metallic reflections; when it is scraped for pulverizing it assumes a dark red colour; this explains the origin of its name which derives from the Greek "haimatites" (= bloodstone). According to the size of the granules the hematite powder assumes colours varying from violet-purple to red, to orange. The colour of the mineral limonite varies from yellow to yellow brown and confers the coloration typical of yellow ochres. Ochre possesses a series of positive characteristics which have enabled its use in all artistic techniques and as a colorant in dyeing, either alone or with other substances which favour its fixation on fibres; it was used in textile printing until recent times. Every different type of ochre can be blended with all the whites, it resists light and exposure to the air and to dampness; it can be worked with any type of binding and therefore can be used in all pictorial techniques: watercolour, fresco, tempera painting, oil. Ochre was the favourite yellow pigment of Raphael and of Titian. Also, it can be found in rocks of all geological eras since its formation did not take place in one particular geological era. In Europe, it particularly abounds in France, Spain and Italy. When various quantities of manganese oxide are present in limonite, we have brown earth pigments, known to us as raw sienna and umber. The brown earths, unlike the ochres which are very soon sided by other yellow and red pigments, were the only source for the brown pigments: resistant to light, inert when mixed with other pigments, they can be used in all pictorial techniques. Raw sienna is composed of hydrated iron oxide, manganese oxide, clay, and water; umber differs from raw sienna because it has a greater quantity of manganese oxide and a smaller quantity of iron oxide and water; its composition varies a lot, according to its place of origin.

In the cave paintings of Lascaux and Altamira, some pigments based on iron and manganese oxide were identified, but as there is no precise information as to the proportion of the components, it is impossible to ascertain if it is one earth or the other. Umber, however, was certainly used, since it was identified amongst the pigments preserved in the cavity of a big shell in Altamira. For the whites, marly limestone or lime powder was used, for the blacks, natural manganese dioxide and charcoal* have been used, with which the contours of the figures were outlined, and used initially for monochrome paintings. The colouring materials, pulverized with bone or slate pestles, were made into a paste with water and animal fats. The Magdalenian artists already practiced the blending of colours and had discovered the important use of additives, neutral substances that enhance the chromatic properties of the pigments and increase their duration and stability; in many rock paintings the pigments were mixed with clay, talcum, potassic or granite feldspar, minerals that are common in nature and that help to give special characteristics to the pictorial materials, such as a certain iridescence to the painted surface, when it's used on biotite, a black mica to be found in granite.

In all the prehistoric paintings, one can notice the absence of two colours, blue and green; for the former one should not be amazed, given the rarity of blue minerals; but for the latter their absence seems strange given the fairly abundant presence of green earths in the region of the painted caves and their stability; some historians put forward the theory that the lack of brightness in the colours of green earths made their use unpopular in surroundings where there could only be torchlight; others think that the greens could be of vegetable origin which would explain their lack of preservation in that all pigments of vegetable extraction are easily perishable.

From the study of materials and their technical elaboration, it emerges that the artists of the prehistoric age aspired even then to surpass the simple representation of the concrete; they constantly extended their palette, they intervened on the pictorial material to elaborate it and to obtain special effects, using a series of auxiliary materials to control the final result of their work. 1

* The name **carbon black** is generally used as a generic name for those blacks that are made from the partial burning or carbonizing of oil, wood, vegetables and other organic matter. Best prepared from vine clippings, fruit pits, or small twigs, which are partially burned, and then ground.
There are lots of varieties of names, each of which reflects a traditional method for producing a particular kind of carbon black:
Charcoal black or wood black produced by carbonizing beechwood
Vine black was traditionally produced by charring desiccated grape vines and stems. Lamp black was traditionally produced by collecting soot, also known as lampblack, from oil lamps.

2)   ANCIENT EGYPT

The importance of colour in Ancient Egypt

Amongst the ancient civilizations, Egypt distinguished itself because of its wide use of colour and its exuberant chromatism: from the external and internal decorations and frescoes, to the statues, to the everyday objects, the Egyptians coloured everything. For thousands of years, the Egyptians dedicated ability and effort to create the artists' colours, more than any other civilization west of the Nile. The importance that colour assumed in the Egyptian civilization was not, however, only an artistic propensity in itself, but the consequence of what art meant and of the powers that the Egyptians attributed to it.

" *One of the most striking aspects of Egyptian painting is its mundanity, in the literal sense. It is, to the good fortune of anthropologists, a documentary art. Here are people going about their daily duties: fishing, washing, building, hunting, taking offerings to the pharaoh. The overall impression is of a calm, orderly society. The world of the Egyptians does not necessarily conform to this harmonious image; rather, the artist depicted an ideal, a wish that chaos should yield to order and reason. And art was an instrumental means to this end, since it was invested with the magic power to transform the world. The completion of a work of art was accompanied by a ritual through which it acquired this divine influence.*

"The social importance of Egyptian art was reflected in the culture's systematic accumulation of bright pigments." 1

And as in all societies strongly linked to religion, colour, and certain colours in particular, was charged with symbolic strength and magic-ritual powers; every colour was associated with a precious stone and a divinity: the colour, like the same stone, ended

13

up being considered as substance and materialization of the same divinity that it represented.

"In fact, colours were considered a subtle force, a ring of connection between sky and earth and unity was found in the mysterious harmony between the world in high where the gods lived and the world in low, that of men, who believed that this connection was proved by the rainbow, a real bridge of coloured light between the spiritual sphere and the material one, incarnated in the Greek myth of the goddess Iris (...), the luminous and incorporeal colours of the rainbow substantiated on earth (...) particularly in the precious stones which represented the purest and most brilliant aspect (...)

"At times, when such precious material was not available, vitreous pastes and enamels replaced the precious stones and their colour was a guarantee of the magic powers of the amulets. The esoteric use of colours, carriers so full of magic and symbolic virtues, was reserved to a narrow circle of people and regulated by strict and immutable rules: the polychrome decoration of the temples and the production of stuccoed and inlaid statues, of wall and panel paintings, of ceramics, of amulets and sacred objects were carried out in the temples, which constituted the first centres of development of artistic culture, inseparable from the magic-religious context. In this way, the colours had a decorative, symbolic and magic use, at the same time (...) Colours were considered to be indicative signs of the essence, and not of the appearance, of things, as testified by the Egyptian word used for "colour" which also means "to be", (...) the Egyptian culture was founded on the strength of images and on the word written or pronounced in the right way; hieroglyphic writing was entrusted to two types of ink: one of which was black with positive value, and one red with negative value, kept for corrections or for the writing of names referring to negative entities or facts; at times, the

hieroglyphics were engraved in stone and painted with coloured enamels or filled with insertions of precious stones or vitreous pastes, in which every colour stood out and strengthened the value of the meaning. The use of single colours in the sanctuaries, in architecture, in sculptures and in the manufacture of each object, depended on its religious, symbolic and magic values and therefore it was subject to the rules for worship established in the temples".2
A very significant example of the application of colour for magic-religious purposes can be found in the rubrics that follow the chapters in the Book of the Dead; they also explain the correct way to repeat the prayers and they advise it to be done in the presence of precise colours. This is the origin of the importance given to the manufacture of colours and to their application, above all in religious paintings, in which the palette was restricted to six basic colours, each one of which had a precise use and magic power; therefore, mixing them or putting one layer on top of another would have deprived them of their symbolic strength and of their deep significance; this explains the use of self-colours and pure colours in juxtaposition with each other; the balance of the chromatism in Egyptian religious paintings remains unsurpassed. The preparation of colours for religious paintings and the finished product were subject to the supervision of the priests, many of whom were also skilful alchemists and, often, the actual artificers of the pigments. 3

Natural colours

Many of the raw materials recorded in the manufacture of colours were obtainable from nature. The red and yellow ochres were the mineral pigments most widely used since the Predynastic period; in some of the western desert oases and around Assuan, there were abundant deposits of red ochre; the use of red ochre is the most widely used and the most common, compared to that of the other reds, and in all civilizations, traces can be found in paintings, dyes and cosmetics. In Egypt, it was also used to obtain red ink for the writing on papyruses, mixing it with Arabic gum or honey; however, it is probable that the Egyptians, who were exceptional experimenters, also made use of artificial red ochre, obtained from the calcinations of yellow ochre. Madder and kermes were used, not only for dyes, but also to prepare lakes for painting, as we shall see further on. Various species of Madder (*Rubia tinctorum*) are spread in the whole Mediterranean area; their colourant principles, alizarin and pseudo-purpurin, are contained in their roots; the dye is extracted by boiling the roots in water.

'Kermes' is the generic term with which one indicates various species of scale insects of the superfamily Coccoidea distributed in an area which extends from the regions of Spain, Southern France, North Africa, to areas of the East, Eastern Europe and the Middle East. The word 'kermes' comes from the Indo-European root *krmih= larvae, insect, and from this root derive in turn the Persian 'kirmiz' = worm, the Armenian 'karmir' = red, the Turkish 'kirmizi' = red, the French 'cramoisi', the English 'crimson', the Italian words 'cremexe, cremesino, chermisi, cremisi'.

In the western Mediterranean areas full of *Quercus coccifera* forests, they gathered the *Kermes vermilio* Planchon, designated by the Latin name of 'granum' or 'coccus' (Eng. grain) - from Gr. Kókkos = berry - that testifies that in the ancient Roman world kermes was believed to be of vegetable origin, a belief that, for many people, lasted for a long time. 4

Orpiment, a beautiful bright yellow, similar to the colour of gold, was supplied by a native mineral made of arsenic tri-sulphide; in its pure state, it shows up in the form of brilliant, flexible scales, from which a golden-yellow powder is obtained; the very root word of the name reveals the shade of its colour: in fact, it derives from the Latin "auripigmentum" which means "gold-coloured pigment".

Orpiment is very toxic and alters easily if mixed with compounds of copper and lead as the sulphur that they emit reacts to the copper or the lead, changing into copper sulphate or lead sulphate, both of which are black. On the other hand, it can be mixed with no problem with ultramarine – a blue pigment with a Lapis lazuli base, with ochre, as with all iron oxides, and with many organic pigments, including lakes. In spite of its various defects, among which some masters complain of its hardness and the difficulty in grinding it, orpiment was used a lot for the beauty and brilliance of its colour. In Egypt, its use has been certified since the XVIII dynasty (XVI-XIV century B.C.); in the classic age, Pliny and Vitruvius spoke about it, and in the Middle Ages, it began to be prepared artificially too, by fusing together sulphur and realgar, an arsenic sulfide that, in the ore deposits, is often to be found associated with orpiment so giving the latter a colour tending towards orange.

However, it was the Venetian artists, as we shall see further on, who made great use of it, often combining it with realgar; the raw mineral arrived from the ore deposits of Eastern Europe or central Asia, and Venice was particularly skilled in washing and purifying it.

Malachite (basic copper carbonate) was finely ground for the preparation of green pigments; malachite has been certified since the most antique phase of the Predynastic period when copper ore deposits were discovered in the eastern desert and in the Sinai peninsula; the Egyptians used it as a cosmetic, both on their person and in paintings, to underline the eyes; because of the beneficial magic powers that were attributed to it, it has been found in many tombs in the form of worked stone and as raw or ground mineral in linen bags. In non-religious painting, where the blending and superposition of colours was permitted, the Egyptians also used a green pigment composed of yellow ochre and Egyptian blue: one pigment with a natural base, ochre, and one with an artificial base, Egyptian blue, created in turn by the same artificers.

The different hues and shades of colour were obtained by varying the quantity of yellow ochre and adding chalk for the lighter and more delicate tones.

The most common natural, black pigments were those already used by the men of Altamira and Lascaux, that is , carbonaceous and natural manganese dioxide products; a black used in cosmetics, painting and medicine was the famous "bistre", obtained by grinding lead sulphate finely on a stone and mixing it with water and Arabic gum.

In a palette conserved in the Egyptian Museum of Turin, two brown earths are present, and their composition corresponds to those of sienna and umber; this should not amaze us, because, as we have already seen, they belong to the most antique and important pigments in history. 5

New pigments from chemical technology

The great variety and diversity of supports on which to apply colour led the Egyptians to refine their techniques admirably; thanks to their enormous predisposition for experimentation, the Egyptians acquired a really vast experience in chemical technology and immense ideas in practical chemistry, and an extraordinary mastery in manipulating and transforming nature's products: they knew the chemistry of the metallic oxides, vitriols and many other substances which they used in the manufacture of glass, and this is even more surprising if one considers that the transformation agents at their disposal were nothing else but fire and some very bland acids and alkalis such as vinegar and urine. Heat can modify the composition or chemical structure of a mineral and cause changes in colour; the Egyptians, thanks to their great mastery in managing fire, were able to put together the first synthetic material in history, later named Caeruleum aegyptium by the Romans and then Egyptian blue or Alexandria frit: this second name was given to it both by the name of the city (that presumably became a large centre of production), and because, on the basis of research of some chemicals in the XIX century, it is maintained that it was a "frit", a term used to describe those substances of a vitreous nature, obtained by melting, that are used in the surface finishing of ceramic products, for example enamels; in actual fact, it was discovered later that Egyptian blue is a crystalline compound and not a vitreous substance. This light blue pigment, which goes back to the IV dynasty, 2500 B:C., is a copper calcium silicate; it was certainly the fruit of a conscious mixture of the natural minerals which form it: copper, calcium and silica, cooked in a furnace at a temperature of about 830°C; the heat caused a change in colour from green to blue; the pigment was obtained by grinding the cooked paste into powder; different shades of colour could be had with different grades of grinding, as the bigger the ground granules are, the darker and more intense is the tone of colour, whilst the finer the ground powder of the pigment, the lighter and more delicate is the tone. In the classic era, Vitruvius was to give a precise and detailed account of the manufacture of ancient Caeruleum aegyptium, a description that permitted various chemists of the 19th century to reproduce it in the laboratory and clarify its characteristics. According to this description, the raw materials used were: copper mineral (probably malachite), sand and sodium carbonate (impure for calcium carbonate, iron carbonate, etc.) which for mixture and cooking gave way to the Egyptian blue in the form of spherules. This pigment was undoubtedly the object of production on a vast scale and of considerable exportations also towards the Roman world, until the Romans too, were able to produce it by themselves; first Pompeii (hence also the name of

Pompeian azure) and then Pozzuoli were to become the main centres of manufacture. 6

The knowledge of the reaction of certain elements to others led the ancient Egyptians to create many other artificial colours: amongst the yellows, the yellow known as lead antimonate was obtained through the use of synthetic reactants, in other words, obtained from the chemical transformation of minerals, that is lead carbonate or lead oxide and antimony oxide. Antimony yellow – called Naples yellow from the start of its introduction into Europe in the second half of the XVIII century and then Egyptian yellow after its discovery amongst the pigments of ancient Egypt - can vary in colour from lemon yellow to orange yellow; it was also used as a pigment for ceramic and glass both in Mesopotamia and in Egypt. Another artificial yellow produced by the ancient Egyptians and found in a palette which goes back to 400 B.C. is yellow lead oxide, which is obtained from the calcination of lead white; it is to be considered as an intermediary product between the preparation of lead white and that of red lead: at a temperature of about 300°C, the lead white frees the carbonate dioxide; the oxide residual presents itself in the form of a powder of a sulphur yellow colour and of a very light consistency. The pigment has a pale yellow colour tone with a good covering power and lightfastness; also in this case, the principal transformation agent was fire: from a primary product, lead white, (in turn, the fruit of chemical transformations), two different pigments at two different temperatures could be obtained. From the VI century onwards (about 2250 B.C.), the preparation of an artificial green frit began; this was done at a temperature of between 900° and 1150°C, through the fusion of copper minerals with silica and natron powder, or sodium carbonate, available in abundance in various places in Egypt; they were actually the same ingredients as those used for Egyptian blue, but with more sodium and less copper. The use of ancient Egyptian green has been certified up to the Third intermediate period (1070-660 B.C.), and until now, it has been found only on Egyptian territory. In some tombs which go back to 1700 B.C. and 1550 B.C., greens have been recognized which were obtained by mixing ancient Egyptian blue with a variable quantity of yellow ochre and with the addition of chalk for the lighter shades. A green-blue obtained chemically was verdigris, which, strangely, appeared much later compared to other artificial colours and most probably through contact with Mesopotamia, where it was already known; the procedure for obtaining it was similar to that used for lead white, that is, by corroding the copper mineral with vinegar vapour; the Greek writer Theophrastus (IV century B.C.) says that the copper was placed above the wine sediment and the rust that formed above the copper lamellas was used as colour.

The corrosive action of vinegar acid on lead, was the means to obtain lead white which is a basic lead carbonate and it can be considered the only artificial white of ancient times; the most ancient process to make lead white (called ceruse in antiquity) is that described by Theophrastus, Pliny and Vitruvius; Pliny mentions two methods to obtain the pigment, one by immersion of lead into vinegar, the other by exposing lead to vinegar vapours. According to Theophrastus description, " *lead is placed in earthen vessels over sharp vinegar, and after it has acquired some thickness of a sort of rust, which it commonly does in about ten days, they open the vessels and scrape it off, as it were, in a sort of foulness; they then place the lead over vinegar again, repeating over and over again the same method of scraping it till it has wholly dissolved. What has been scraped off they then beat to powder and boil for a long time, and what at last subsides to the bottom of the vessel is ceruse.*" 7

The medieval process generally was that of exposing lead to strong vinegar vapours.

The fortune of ceruse in the artist's palette was very long; widely used in all pictorial techniques, absolute protagonist in oil paintings until the end of the 19th century when it was partly replaced by new, synthetic products. It is interesting to note that the presence of sulphurous vapours causes the darkening of colour, as, under their action, the lead carbonate which is white, changes into lead sulphur which is black and this is the reason why ceruse was not preserved, for example, amongst the Pompeian colours, given the abundant presence of sulphurous vapours in the volcanic emissions. All lead compounds have toxicity in common and the fact that they darken if they come into contact with other pigments containing sulphur, such as realgar, orpiment, both with an arsenic sulphur base, cinnabar, artificial cinnabar or vermilion.

The action of the heat produced another artificial colour: by cooking the ceruse in the oven, that is from the calcination of lead white, a beautiful brilliant red tending towards orange, could be obtained, red lead, the pigment even now known as minium, named 'miniun secondarium' by the Latins, or 'cerussa usta', a term which clearly referred to the process used for the manufacture of the pigment, in order to distinguish it from minium, or natural cinnabar. This red lead, amalgamated with Arabic gum, a resinous secretion soluble in water and obtained from Cutch (*Acacia catechu*), supplied the Egyptians with one of the most beautiful red inks. Red lead, too, like all lead compounds, is sensitive to the action of sulphurs and it easily darkens when exposed to air, for the transformation into lead sulphide, which is black. Nevertheless, red, above all, was the colour in the manuscripts and decorated codices on which the action of the air and light had no influence and in which the pigments are preserved, unchanged.

An artificial black that had a lot of success in the history of pigments and inks was lampblack, which was obtained from the incomplete combustion of organic substances rich in carbon; this is the atramentum of the Latins, the preparation of which Pliny gives a detailed description. (see chap. 4) 8

Lake pigments

The Egyptians also made use of coloured lakes, even though it is impossible to date with certainty when they began to use them.
In ancient times, the lakes were prepared by colouring the powder of an inorganic mineral substance, a white clay, with a natural, organic dyeing substance of a vegetable or animal nature; they were used as such in paintings, or to imitate, adulterate or falsify other colours. They were used for a long time in all of the Mediterranean world, and, in the classical era, Pozzuoli became the most famous and qualified centre of production. We don't know exactly when the Egyptians began using them, according to some, fairly late, during the Greek-Macedonian period. Those lakes had an excellent covering power and therefore they were suitable for conferring bright and decisive colours on materials such as wood and stone; the Egyptians certainly made use of madder lake too; a special lake, which had a lot of success for quite a few centuries, was the lake from cloth clippings: the remains of cloth dyed with kermes were re-boiled in an alkaline solution, generally wood ash, to dissolve the dye again.
"The dye was then extracted from the hot alkaline solution by adding alum, which precipitates fine-grained alumina (hydrated aluminium oxide) when the solution is cooled. The dye is absorbed onto the surfaces of the alumina particles, which dry to a dark red powder." 9

The preparation of the colours and the inks

The Egyptians practiced both tempera and fresco painting; the term 'tempera' derives from the Latin 'temperare', which means "to mix", as the pigments, in order to be spread out on a support, need to be mixed, or tempered, in a binding medium; fresco technique consists of spreading the colours on a layer of wet sand and lime with which the wall to be painted is covered.

The raw materials used for the colour were ground with pestles inside mortars and the powder was generally compressed in cloths, then scraped and re-powdered; the powder was mixed with adhesives and water to obtain the pigment ready for application; the most common adhesives were Arabic gum, egg white, and animal glue, obtained by boiling pieces of skin and thickening the liquid obtained. In order to make the colours more brilliant, loose beeswax was spread on the painting or on a single colour to make it stand out above the others.

The Egyptians applied the varnishing on mural paintings, as on wooden objects, and also on fabrics, especially linen. The varnishing is a thin, transparent, uncoloured layer, which is useful above all to preserve and protect the colour; it is quite possible that the early varnishes were natural oleoresin fluids, applied with a brush whilst hot; according to some experts, in the composition of the varnishing, there could be gum extracted by cutting the bark of the Arabic acacia, already used in the preparation of papyrus and linen bandages for binding the mummies. [10]

3) ANCIENT MESOPOTAMIA

The invention of glass

In ancient times, the chemical technology acquired for the production of colours, developed as a result of a wider industry of the transformation of raw materials into substances for the creation of objects necessary in everyday life: the manufacture of glass, the glazing of ceramics, the production of soap. The most antique glass known, goes back to about 2500 B.C.; it was found in Mesopotamia and was probably the secondary result of experiments in another sector, the manufacture of coloured glass for ceramics. Glass was obtained by the fusion of sand and soda, at about 2,500°C; numerous furnaces were discovered following the archaeological digs, the earthenware ovens go back to 4000 B.C.; the so-called "Egyptian ceramic" was a blue, glassy substance, produced in Mesopotamia a long time before it became an Egyptian industry: steatite ornaments enamelled in blue were produced since about 4500 B.C., by dusting the surface of the rock and heating it, in the presence of copper minerals such as azurite or malachite; it can happen that, during the cooking of the ceramic, the sand fuses with the ashes, which have a high soda content, and that, once the furnace has cooled, the ceramic craftsmen have found lumps of coarse glass inside. The addition of a small amount of lime will soon improve the quality; this is the recipe from an antique, cuneiform text: *"Take sixty portions of sand, one hundred and eighty portions of ashes of marine plants, five portions of chalk, heat it all together and you will obtain glass"*. 1

Blue and Gold: sacred and royal colours

In Mesopotamia, as in Egypt, colour had decorative, symbolic and magic functions.

The ancient peoples of Mesopotamia showed a marked preference for the coloured enamels which they used to cover objects, statues, palaces; the splendour and the magnificence of Babylon was also due to its colours: its walls were covered with lapis lazuli blue enamel and on it, raised, there were decorations and sacred animals enamelled in yellow and orange ochre.

"The chemical analysis of the monuments has revealed that the blue enamel was manufactured artificially, while that of the sculptures was obtained by finely mincing the lapis lazuli and then mixing it with a fatty material. Even the fortified walls that surrounded and defended the cities were covered with tiles of blue enamel, as was the temple, the royal palace and the cell that Nebuchadnezzar had built on the top of the main ziggurat, and which he wanted gleaming with light-blue bricks. The Babylonian kings had wanted sumptuous kingdoms on earth, like the magnificent dwellings they imagined for their gods, covering them with the colour of lapis lazuli, whose sacredness and preciousness had been sanctified by religious use too. The particles of pyrites incorporated in the stone gave the illusion of seeing a piece of starry sky and its colour invited one to meditate on blue things, bringing one beyond the sensitive experience and leading one to divine and superior places. The profusion of this colour was also to be found among the sacred furnishings and the treasures in the temples, in which it was always associated with gold; as far as the Babylonians were concerned, all the divine objects in the heavens were like this (…) In the Mesopotamian cities, the constant ostentation of this colour had, as well as the mystical function which we spoke about, also a magic and talismanic aim (…) For the ancients, it represented the materialization of some specific functions of divinity, especially present in precious stones, that

were therefore used, for magic reasons, in sacred rites, and for talismanic purposes in everyday use; amongst all those ranging in colour between light blue and dark blue, the ancients held a great respect for lapis lazuli and turquoise. In Mesopotamia, lapis lazuli was the precious, earthly image of the starry sky, of Anu and of all the cosmic and astral gods, and as such it was considered to be a strong, life-bestowing substance. It was probably believed to be the actual essence of the gods (…) the power that was believed to be inherent in the actual lapis lazuli was certainly beneficial and had the strength to draw upon itself the protection of the celestial hierarchies related to the gift of life; because of this virtue, Gilgames chose it when he ordered a statue from the smith in memory of his dead friend, Enkidu:

Smith (… …)
Worker of metal, Kabsar goldsmith, make my friend!
He made a statue of his friend (… …)
(….) of lapis lazuli is your chest, of gold your body.

Marduk, the very powerful Babylonian god who had absorbed all the attributes of the other Mesopotamian deities, had his representation in the precious azure of the lapis lazuli, with which his pictures were realized." 2
The Egyptians, too, attributed the same values and magic powers to lapis lazuli and the colour blue; the colour azure-blue had great importance for the Middle-Eastern peoples; among the Hebrews, Egyptians, Babylonians, sacredness and regality were always expressed by the inseparable coupling of azure-blue and gold, different from what happened among the peoples of Indo-European origin for whom, for a space of many centuries, red (nearly always combined with gold) was the colour of power and regality. Gold and the yellow-gold colour that represents it have always had the

same symbolic connotations and the same values: the light of the sun, that symbolized the cosmic order in the ancient cosmogony, was the material concentration of the divine light; the divinities linked to the splendour of the sun were defined in gold; gold was considered to be of the same substance as the gods, a symbol, therefore, of divine virtue and eternity and, consequently, used almost exclusively for that which was sacred; for this reason, gold was initially reserved only for kings and high priests, to underline their own divine origin. The kings' palaces and the sacred buildings were covered with gold, and the gold that profusely adorned the king's person affirmed his divine descent and symbolized sacredness and power. Among the funeral dress of the royal tombs of Ur (third millennium B.C.) a series of splendid handmade articles in gold and semi-precious stones give us an idea of the artistic refinement of the goldsmiths of the most ancient Mesopotamian dynasties and testify the symbolic value of blue and gold; in the museum of Baghdad the so-called "Dagger of Ur" is in gold, with a handle of lapis lazuli; the sheath, in gold filigree, is considered to be one of the masterpieces of goldsmith's art of all time, along with some jewels in lapis lazuli and gold. Two rampant 'rams', from Ur, southern Iraq, about 2600-2400 BC (one is conserved in the British Museum, the other is now in the University of Pennsylvania Museum in Philadelphia) belong to the same tomb; the two statuettes, 50cm. tall, have a wooden core covered in gold leaf; the horns and the snout details are in lapis lazuli.
The ram's head and legs are covered in gold leaf, its ears are copper (now green), its twisted horns and the fleece on its shoulders are of lapis lazuli, and its body fleece is made of shell. Its genitals are gold. The tree is covered in gold leaf, with golden flowers, the whole supported on a small rectangular base decorated with a mosaic of shell, red limestone and lapis lazuli. 3

Archaeological finds have shown that the use of lapis lazuli, as a precious and sacred stone, existed in Mesopotamia since 4000 B.C.; lapis lazuli is a rock formed by the joining together of numerous minerals among which is lazulite which gives the colour blue; it doesn't have a uniform colour and it is often veined with gold and silver, that are constituted by pyrite and calcite respectively: in antique times, they were often mistaken for gold. It's name derives from medieval Latin lapis lazuli ("stone of làzulum") from the Persian lazward = azure. The richest deposits were to be found in remote areas, very difficult to reach, corresponding to parts of present day Afghanistan; its provisioning had extremely high costs and the pigment, the "Ultramarine" of the Middle Ages, remained absolutely the most expensive. The procedure for extracting from the ground stone a pigment that conserves the same shade of colour as the stone, is extremely long and complicated and was perfected only in the classical epoch; Pliny (1st century A.D.) calls it Caeruleum scythicum. Perhaps it was due to the fact that, initially, the colour of the pigment did not live up to expectations (because of the excessive impurities that remained in the mineral powder, and which gave a greyish hue) that the Egyptians, who were so disposed towards painting, tried to create an artificial blue that met their demands and they succeeded perfectly: in this way, under the 4th dynasty, around 2500 B.C., the famous Egyptian blue was born, the Caeruleum aegyptium of the Latins, the result of a mixture of copper mineral (probably malachite), calcium and silica, cooked in a furnace where the high temperature also caused a change of colour. This beautiful azure-blue would have an immense fortune in the antique world and in the classical era; towards 1500 B.C., through contacts with the ancient Egyptian world, it also reached Mesopotamia, where even now, it appears that enamelling is preferred to painting. The author of "Ninive" tells us that among the archaeological finds, he discovered a block of azure colour that weighed about one kilo; the artist tried to make use of that colour to reproduce, (in watercolour and in shade as close as possible to the original), the decorations of one of the walls covered with enamelled tiles, but each attempt was useless; in fact, as was then discovered during a chemical analysis, the azure block was lapis lazuli in powder for the manufacture of the enamels and it could not, therefore, be used for painting in watercolours. The azure-blue and the yellow enamels were the most frequently used; a lovely synthesis of yellow was the antimony yellow, largely used by the Assyrians and Babylonians for glazing the ceramics; in the palace of King Sargon the second, at Khorsabad, a pigment lump of antimony yellow was found among other pigments; it had probably gone missing in the classical era, as it was not discovered amongst the yellows that were identified in the Pompeian paintings; it was reintroduced in the 18th century under the name of Naples yellow and, later on, Egyptian yellow, following its discovery among the pigments of ancient Egypt; it is difficult to know with certainty who was really the first artificer of this artificial yellow: some authoritative experts attribute the invention to the Mesopotamian peoples, while others, just as authoritative, maintain that it was the Egyptians, famous for their great skill and experience in practical chemistry, to create it; the same dilemma concerns the use of Minium (red lead), the Cerussa usta (burnt lead white) of the Romans. Minium is obtained from the calcination of lead white; in fact, both in Egypt and in Mesopotamia, the production and the use of lead white are testified by various sources in contemporary periods; therefore, it is possible that, finding oneself in front of the great masters of chemical experimentation in both cases, the creation of minium came about in an independent way and more or less at the same time; Brunello assumes that minium appeared in Egypt much later, by means of Thoutmes the Third, who had brought it with him after his conquests in Asia in the age of the New Reign (around 1400 B.C.) and it is also referred that, according to others, minium was introduced in Egypt in the Roman era. 4

The passion for enamelled objects and palaces was conserved in successive eras, until the arrival of the Arabs, who in turn, assimilated the taste for enamelled ceramic and for blue and gold.

4) THE CLASSICAL ANTIQUITY

A colourful past

The Greek-Roman world inherited the patrimony of Cretan, Oriental and Ancient Egyptian knowledge; the classic Greek writers, Theophrastus (IV century B.C.) and Dioscorides (I cent. A.D.) and the Latin writers, Vitruvius (I cent. B.C.) and Pliny (I cent. A.D.) are one of the principal sources on the origin and techniques of the preparation of colours for painting and dyeing, on their characteristics and methods of recognition, and on the most current falsifications and imitations. Although no other Mediterranean civilization has equalled the polychrome vivacity of the Ancient Egyptians, neither the Greeks nor the Romans were lacking in sensibility and taste for colour; their palettes were limited, at times, because of technical reasons, limited availability of suitable materials, and pre-conceived dogmatic-theoretic prejudice tied to the metaphysics of the colours elaborated by the philosophers.

Philip Ball tells us that *"The Greeks and the Romans showed a taste for interior decoration that would look decidedly bold and modern today (…) The classical Greek painter Apelles was admired by Titian the prime colorist of the Renaissance, yet Apelles reputedly employed just four colors. (…) There is ample reason to suppose that most, if not all, of the pigments known to the Egyptians were available also to the Greek painters; yet, both Pliny and Cicero insist that four-colour painting was a strong tradition during the heyday of classical Greek art, around the fourth century B.C. (…) Pliny names several renowned four-color artists from this period: the preeminent Apelles, along with Aetion, Melanthius, and Nicomachus; Cicero's list has a slightly longer reach, including the early-fifth -century painter Polignotos as well* as Zeuxi and Timanthes, from the early fourth century. The tradition of limiting the palette seems to have begun in the mid-fifth century B.C., when Empedocles was refining the idea of the four elements, and Democritus was postulating atoms. Nietzsche proposed rather contentiously that the Greek painters avoided blue and green because <they dehumanize nature more than any other colour>. But the real reason is probably more practical than metaphysical. During the fifth century B.C. the Greek artists began to paint three-dimensionally, using a 'chiaroscuro' ("highlight and shadow") technique to depict depth. This development might have motivated the four-color technique, as a means of bringing color under control while artists worked out how to manage light and dark. As Renaissance artists were to discover, the larger the palette, the more difficult it is to achieve harmony of hue and tone so that no one color stands out jarringly from the others; by restricting the range of hues, and moreover by rendering them in low-keyed earth pigments, rather than bright ones, it becomes easier to master a three-dimensional world of light and shadow. Once this system was in place, it may have metamorfosed from a technical necessity into an aesthetic principle. Pliny makes no bones about his preference for "austere" over "florid" colors (...) Yet pure, bright colors were not shunned in decorative arts. They were used by the Greeks to adorn buildings, as evident in the reds and yellows of Olynthus, dating from the fifth to fourth centuries B.C. Egyptian blue frit has been found in wall paintings at Knossos in Crete dating from before 2100 B.C., on buildings from the Mycenaean period of ancient Greece (around 1400 B.C.), and on artifacts throughout the waxing and waning of Greek civilization. Theophrastus says that an artificial blue pigment was imported from Egypt suggesting that the Greeks did not know how (or did not bother) to make it. The Etruscans used Egyptian blue in the sixth century B.C., as did the Romans who succeeded them. It is found not only on the walls of Pompeii, but also unused in the city's color shops, as well as in the tombs of Roman painters.(...) Chemistry ignited when West met East in the crucible of Hellenistic Alexandria, bringing the logical worldview of classical Greece into contact with the Eastern penchant for practical experimentation. By the same token, the use of color in Western art became more inventive and more gorgeous when Alexander's empire found new aesthetics and new materials in the East.

The bright red mineral cinnabar (mercury sulphide), for example, was used as a pigment in China long before it appear in the West. Even the Egyptian may have been ignorant of it, and evidence of it in Greek art before Theophrastus' time is rare. Indigo was imported from India: the Greeks called it indikon, and Vitruvius tells how the Romans used it as an artist's pigment in the first century B.C. (...) But perhaps more significant than the infusion of new "florid" pigments was the brightly hued artistic aesthetic of Persia and India, contrasting with the austerity of the Greeks. It was this influence that led to the gorgeous riches of Byzantine art, later to inspire the Europeans toward bolder use of color when it was brought to the West in the Crusades.

The Hellenistic culture had a more relaxed attitude towards color mixing, based on empiricism rather than misconceived dogma. Alexander of Aphrodisias in the third century A.D. explained how (contrary to Aristotle's belief) green could be made from yellow and blue, and violet from blue and red. But, he said, these "artificial"(mixed) colors are no match for the corresponding pure hues seen in nature. And indeed they are not, for mixing requires good primaries to avoid a loss in brilliance. Limitations of materials were restricting the artist's capabilities. (...)

The Greek penchant for idealization and intellectual abstraction led to the notion that mixed colors are inferior both to "pure" natural pigments and the "true" colors of nature. So there was

little point in attempting to match artists' colors to nature's by mixing them together. (...)
This practice was discouraged by classical scholars:<Mixing produces conflict>, says Plutarch in the first century A.D. It was common to refer to the blending of pigments as "deflowering".(...) There was also a technical inhibition toward mixing. Because the available pigments were not pure primary colors, mixing resulted in a diminution of tone toward grayness or brownness and so was indeed a degrading process. (...) It is hard to say to what extent the Greek dislike of pigment mixing motivated by theoretical prejudice and to what extent practical experience- the loss of brilliance- played a part. Either way, it accentuated the painter's dependence on materials." 1

Archaeological studies and discoveries have, for a long time, disproved the stereotyped idea of an achromatic and candid classical antiquity - especially the Greek and Roman one.

"From what does this very mistaken and deeply-rooted vision derive? The Enlightenment had already zeroized colour from the point of view of its symbolic use, but above all, with the advent of Neoclassicism and with the affirmation and diffusion of Napoleonic white, great damage was caused to the artistic heritage, baring it forever of its antique, original colours: in the name of culture, an operation of cleaning, levigation and shining was begun, on the antique remains, on architecture and sculptures, with the aim of enhancing the aulic whiteness of the materials; this was presumed to be the distinctive symbol of classical antiquity and from that moment on, it became a categorical imperative for every imaginable representation. In actual fact, this questionable restoration work was the fruit of a centuries-old mistake: a great many Hellenistic sculptures which were made in white marble and with empty eyes – unlike the originals in polychrome – were believed to be authentic for centuries, only to be subsequently

35

revealed as copies of statues from the classical period, produced by sculptors from the Hellenistic age on the request of foreign admirers, above all the Romans. Therefore, these copies represented the sole testimony of a large part of Greek sculpture and generated the aforesaid misunderstanding." 2

"The walls of Pompeii were colored to a degree that we might now consider gaudy, adorned with brilliant vermilion and polished to a high gloss. The Greeks painted much of their stonework, from pillars to reliefs to statues. Figures were depicted on rich grounds of red, yellow, blue, and black. As this became evident to the archaeologists in the early nineteenth century, Western architects presented brightly colored reconstructions of how the temples – the pallid stone of their surfaces now laid bare - would have looked in their heyday. (...)

The belief, prevalent until the mid-Victorian era, that Greek sculpture was left in a chalky whiteness rather than being colored, is probably the most famous example of modern misconception about classical art derived from a misguided aesthetic bias (the supposed "purity" of white). To the Greeks there was nothing sacred about plain stone that need preserve in from an enlivening lick of paint. Nor they were subtle about it: beards were deep blue (...) and if we can judge from Roman statues and relief, gods often had bright red faces." 3

The virtual reconstructions of today, based on the results of archaeological research, show us finally a series of bright, polychrome 'polis' (or Greek city-states): temples richly-adorned with colour, brightly coloured costumes and objects, painted or covered with enamels and stucco work. Yellow, red and light blue are the colours that recur together most frequently, in the wall paintings of the temples, as in the fabrics depicted, for example, in the frescoes of Knossos.

In the Homeric poems (IX – VIII A.D.), there are frequent references to the colours of the garments and palaces: the light blue of the adornments in Alcinoo's palace – and it must surely have been "Egyptian blue" (caeruleum aegyptium)- the purple cloths draped over the thrones, the vivid colours of Nausicaa's garments, the purple cloaks belonging to Nestor and Telemachus, the Queen of the Feaci who works with purple yarn; and Homer refers to the skill possessed by the women of Caria and Lidia, in colouring ivory with purple. Plutarch (about 46/50 A.D. – 120 A.D.) recounts that when Alexander the Great arrived at Susa, he found about 25 kilos of materials from Hermione, a city in Argolide that was famous for the dyeing of fabrics with murex purple: nearly two hundred years old, those materials still conserved an intact freshness of colour. We know of other important centres for murex purple dyeing: Melibea in Thessaly, the city of Boulis in Phocis, where more than half of the population was engaged in murex fishing, and, in the Peloponnesus, Corinth, where, imitating the Phoenicians, they inscribed the murex shell on some coins. A clear prevalence for the use of red tones, in the dyeing of fabrics, emerges from these testimonials. 4

"(…) *therefore, in the Classical Age, dyeing a fabric meant, for the most part, changing its original colour, a colour to be found in the wide range of red tones (from pale ochre to the deepest purple, passing through all the yellow oranges, vermilions, flesh tones, garnet reds, etc.) Most of the materials used in red dyes enter deeply into the fibre of the fabric, they resist the effects of time better than other colours and they produce rich, luminous nuances.*" 5

Practical motives associated with others of a different nature, tied to magic-religious symbols and to the philosophic-metaphysical theory on colours that had been elaborated in the Western world, were to make red become the colour of royalty and power, and also, in the Christian era, of the resurrection and the blood of Christ.

The Pompeian colours

The ashes of the volcan Vesuvius have preserved an incredible amount of objects of the past, which are of an extraordinary and unique importance; the archaeological finds have given back two cities, Herculaneum and Pompeii, almost exactly as they were at the moment of the eruption, in 79 A.D. Villas and houses have emerged from the ashes, with interiors that are amazingly frescoed in vivid and brilliant colours; in the artisans' workshops, there was an incredible amount of artistic materials, among which there was an endless number of pigments, that has allowed us to analyze and understand the exact nature of the colours used in painting at that time, so filling in the passages (not clear at times) of some of the much-copied information that the authors of that era, and particularly Pliny, have left us, on the pigments used and on their preparation. The great variety and quantity of powdered colours that were found in the workshops of the Pompeian merchants has permitted the analysis of unaltered colours, just as they were in their original state, ready for use.

There was a very vast range of colours, including many natural colours, prevalently of mineral origin and for which a process of extraction and purification was necessary; the natural colours of vegetable and organic origin were inferior in number. Amongst the natural whites, Paraetonium was considered the most suitable to use on plaster, because of its resistance and smoothness; Pliny shows a very imaginative side of his nature: he says that it is composed of "sea foam consolidated with mud"; in any case, it has a marine origin, as paraetonium is a limestone mixed with phosphatic marine debris; it was doubtlessly the most precious background colour because of the qualities already mentioned: it was an excellent colour stabilizer and it exalted the colours used on it; the white clays were used in painting as white colours, or else they were used as a background in mural painting, for the dilution of colours, or as an inorganic base for the creation of lakes; amongst the calcareous clays, we recall Melinum, - already used by the Greek painter Apelles -, and Selinusia; among the siliceous clays Cimolia and Eretria, used, above all, as a background for wall paintings; Creta argentaria, which is a fossil flour, or in other words, a blend of microscopic remains of siliceous seaweed (diatoms), mixed with sand, organic substances, carbonate of calcium, iron oxide; Pliny describes it in his chapter on clays, where he says that its name derives from the fact that it is used to shine silver; argentaria clay has great absorption power and this is why it was used in the preparation of lakes, among which there was the precious Purpurissum. Amongst the natural azures, Pliny mentions Caeruleum Shythicum and Caeruleum Cyprium, saying that the latter was preferred to the former, and this is understandable due to the fact that Sythicum was composed of lapis lazuli, which completely discolours on contact with acids, whilst azurite – which Cyprium is composed of, proved to be much more stable; in actual fact, also azurite - a copper-based carbonate - changes with time, into malachite, which is the most stable form of copper-based carbonate; a transformation that is, nevertheless, very slow, taking decades or centuries; the result can be observed today in some of the medieval murals, where the blue of the sky has become green. Indigo, on the contrary, being an organic substance and therefore easily alterable, has not been conserved in any Pompeian painting, but anyhow we know of its use in painting, thanks to Pliny's information.

Amongst the greens, Creta viridis (green earth) has been recognized: this clay in its best quality came from Smyrna, according to Vitruvius; under the name of appianum, a green pigment which was obtained from the creta viridis, was designed and was used above all to falsify a much more precious green, obtained from a copper mineral, malachite, which in antique times, was called by the name of "armenium" and "chrysocolla". Chrysocolla means "gold glue" and this term was used to indicate both the operation of the gold welding, for which this mineral was used, and the products used for this operation. Chrysocolla was a widely-used colour about which the writers give lots of information; Theophrastus says that chrysocolla was present in the gold mines in large quantities and it was even more abundant in the copper mines; Pliny puts chrysocolla among the florid colours, or in other words, among those colours which, being prestigious and costing more, were supplied to the painter by the purchaser; he says that it is a liquid that flows in the wells of the goldmines, that the best one is to be found in the copper mines, and this must be the malachite that is the copper mineral, chrysocolla in its rarest form.

Pliny also says that there was a way to obtain chrysocolla artificially and that it consisted of slowly pouring water into the metallic vein during the whole winter, until the month of June, and then letting it dry up for the two successive months; however, this chrysocolla was considered to be of a much more inferior quality to the natural one. Copper minerals in their various forms comprised the greens most widely-used by the ancients; therefore they had an elevated cost and were subject to falsifications and imitations.

The natural red colours were supplied by "rubricae", that is to say, by the various types of ochre; the most prestigious was the Sinopis pontica, originally from the city of Sinope, in Pontus, and which was traded in various types, depending on the depth of colour. Minium (mercuric red sulfide), later called Cinnabar, is a mineral that, according to what Pliny says, came entirely from the mines in Spain, and reached Rome as a native mineral, since it could be purified and cooked only in the capital; Pliny, who puts it among the florid colours, also describes its manufacture: the mineral, which has a scarlet colour, is ground, and the grainy powder is subjected to several washes, to purify it of the various residues; some use the powder from the first wash, but the best one is that obtained from the second wash. Cinnabar, without special precautions, cannot be used in fresco because it becomes changed and decomposed by the lime; the atmospheric agents, particularly the light, blacken it; to get round this difficulty, the Roman technique made use of wax and added oils, which, spread on the wall painting, neutralized the causticity of the lime, so preventing it from acting on the cinnabar and altering it. As well as this, the wax (already used for this purpose by the ancient Egyptians) prevented the atmospheric agents from acting on the colours, as it constituted a waterproof, external coat of protection.

Amongst the pigments found in Pompeii and analysed by Selim Augusti, there were some in the form of hard, stony, compact pieces, of a vivid red colour, partly covered in yellow, which, once pulverized, give a powder of a beautiful red-orange colour, in a warm tone.

They are colours created from Realgar (an arsenic sulphide), called "sandaracha" by the Romans, and partly covered on the outside by Orpiment.

These two colours are both native minerals, of the same chemical composition (arsenic sulphide), that are often to be found combined in their mines. Realgar is fairly widespread in nature, but rarely in large quantities, as it tends to turn into orpiment, which constitutes the more stable form, and is to be found, naturally, in fair considerable masses. Vitruvius says that orpiment originates from the mines of Pontus and Pliny writes that orpiment and 'sandaracha' are substances of the same nature and that orpiment is roasted in an earthen vase until it changes colour: and in fact the orpiment, heated up in a closed recipient, turns into realgar.

Pliny speaks about an organic pigment called Cinnabaris Indicus; it corresponds to Dragon's blood, a natural product obtained from the resin of *Dracaena draco*. Yet, in Pliny's time, the true origin was not known and it was believed to be, according to the same Pliny's account, derived from a mixture of elephant's and dragon's blood, following the mortal fight that these two animals engaged in, every time they met; Pliny talks about it with a wealth of details, as if he had really been an eye witness to such battles; speaking about pigment, he affirms that there is nothing else that improves the colour of blood in painting, and he puts it among the florid colours. Dragon's blood, too, is easily decomposable, as it is a substance of vegetable origin, and it has not preserved in any Pompeian painting. The sap from *Dracaena draco* dries into a brownish-red gum resin.

The natural yellows were created from various kinds of yellow ochres and from orpiment; the most prestigious type of ochre was Sil Atticum, of a lovely golden-yellow shade, that was subject to a lot of falsifications. Artificial colours were just as numerous; their manufacture took place on a large scale, in classical antiquity; Pozzuoli was a very important centre of production and exportation. All the colours were traded in the form of powders or small, compact lumps.

There were different methods of preparation for artificial colours; some were obtained by mixing natural or artificial colours, others by cooking or calcining a natural product; in other cases, the raw materials were treated with liquid products of an acid nature; lastly, by fixing a dye of an organic nature on an inert, mineral substance, lakes were obtained.

During the mixing, which was a dry process or in other words without the intervention of liquids, two or more natural or artificial colours were blended with each other, without this causing any chemical reaction. As well as the colours traditionally obtained by mixing, like for example, the greens that were obtained from the blending of yellow and blue, very special mixtures were prepared; Sandyx was a red colour, obtained from a mixture of Rubrica (red earth) and 'Cerussa usta' (Red lead); Syricum was a red obtained from a mixture of Sinopis (red ochre) and Sandyx where the red lead strengthened the colour of the ochre, so giving it a warmer tone; Leucophorum was a glue that was used for fixing gold on wood, and it was a mixture of Sinopis Pontica, Sil Lucidum from Gaul (a type of yellow ochre) and Melinum (a white clay); white clay was used in variable quantities, along with another colour, to obtain a series of shades varying from light to dark. Other colours were subjected to calcination, a process already widely practiced in Egypt and Mesopotamia; with this method, the aforementioned Cerussa usta and Minium secondarium were obtained: the chemical effect of the heat turned the Cerussa (lead white), a carbonate with a lead base, into lead oxide of a red colour. Another nice red obtained through cooking was the 'Ocra usta' or artificial red ochre, obtained from the calcination of Sil, the natural, yellow ochre. Atramentum or lampblack was produced in large quantities; it was needed, in painting, for black and for the preparation of inks; Vitruvius and Pliny give a detailed description of the manufacturing procedure: resin, resinous wood, or wine dregs were burnt in an oven; through a narrow opening, the thick smoke from the combustion was channelled into a room with perfectly smooth walls; on the cold walls of the room, soot or lampblack was deposited, which was then scraped away and gathered; it was then dried in the sun and mixed with Arabic gum, to be used as ink, or with gluten (a vegetable glue used as a medium in tempera painting) for mural painting.

A black mentioned by Pliny, that corresponds to Ivory black, is Elephantinum, obtained by calcining the residues of ivory particles in closed vases; this pigment presents itself in the form of a fine, velvety powder.

Of the colours obtained for paste and cooking, the most famous and prestigious one is Caeruleum aegyptium or Egyptian blue, which was discovered in large quantities in the Pompeian workshops, and in various grades of colour; obtained by mixing with white clay, it is in different consistencies: in the form of spherules of about 2 cm in diameter and in a very fine powder, or in bigger granules. This colour, because of its beauty and inalterability, was first imported and then manufactured in Pozzuoli, and this is why it is also mentioned under the name of "Pompeian blue" or caeruleum Vestorianum – from the name of Vestorio, who was the first person to begin manufacturing it, at Pozzuoli. 6

Vitruvius tells us that the sand is ground with natural sodium carbonate, the Egyptian "natron", until it is reduced to a powder as fine as flour, and it is then mixed with Cyprus copper, reduced to filings, and soaked, to make it agglomerate. Small balls are obtained from this doughy mass and left to dry. Once dried, they are put into an earthenware vase in a very hot oven, until caeruleum is formed. 7

At Pompeii, Egyptian blue was present in a wide range of shades, from the darkest, in a coarser powder, to the lightest, in a very fine powder; this belies what was stated by some authors, on the fact that Egyptian blue was always prepared in coarse powders, while all the other colours were prepared in fine powders; therefore, because of the excessive difference in the size of the particles, Egyptian blue could not have been mixed with other pigments nor diluted with pulverized white clay for use in tempera painting, as its coarse particles would have been deposited and only the clay would have remained in the painting. Augusti's investigations and analysis have shown that, on the contrary, there were numerous samples of blue colours diluted with clay at Pompeii and that Egyptian blue was used , in mural painting, in the same way as all the other colours. Various types of caeruleum existed, of different costs and qualities; Pliny refers to Coelon, of a very light blue colour, very prestigious and expensive, which was obtained from the lightest part of the Egyptian blue, by grinding the pure blue very finely; in fact, as already said, the finer the ground particles are, the lighter and more delicate is the colour of the pigment; Pliny also talks about Lomentum, which is lighter and more costly than the ordinary caeruleum, and which is prepared by washing Egyptian blue, pounding it into a fine powder, and then adding clay.

Two colours that had a lot of success in painting and that were prepared through wet process, or in other words, due to the effect of liquids of an acid nature, were cerussa, or lead white, (lead carbonate) and Aerugo, or Verdigris (basic copper acetate), obtained by exposing the lead and copper to vinegar vapours, as already described in chapter 2. Vinegar was also needed to dissolve the impurities of the various colours, both natural and artificial. Augusti's analysis have not, however, revealed traces of cerussa at Pompeii and this, in truth, seems very strange for such an important colour; but we know that the action of the sulphurous vapours turns the white lead carbonate into black lead sulphate, and as sulphurous vapours are exhaled abundantly from volcanoes, cerussa could not have remained unaltered in Pompeii.

Then, some colours were the by-product of other industries; for example, the Spuma argenti (silver foam) of which Pliny spoke, was a by-product of the metallurgical industry; it has to do with Litargirium (Litharge), a lead oxide that is obtained in plenitude during the extraction of the silver from the argentiferous lead; its colour varies from red to yellow; Pliny says that it is prepared by founding the mineral and making it flow out, from a higher recipient to a lower one, then removing it from this through iron strainers and putting it back onto the flame to make it lighter; therefore "silver foam" indicates the froth of the smelting material; litharge, too, was obtained from the scum of the smelting material. Pozzuoli was specialized in the extraction of colouring materials from vegetables and it was renowned for the great variety of lakes that it produced. As we have already seen, the antique lakes were the result of a "dyeing" carried out on the powder of a natural mineral, usually a white clay, by means of a vegetable or animal colouring juice. From analyses conducted on colours discovered in Pompeii, Selim Augusti has singled out two of these antique lakes, a violet lake and a yellow one; the first is the precious Purpurissum, which was found in large quantities in Pompeii, and which is spoken of by Pliny (who lists it among the florid colours) and Vitruvius; it was obtained by putting Creta argentaria in the vats containing the shellfish purple dye, then used in the dyeing of the fabrics: the colouring substance of the Murex, the 'ostrum' mentioned by Vitruvius, fixed onto the clay and coloured it; the range of colour tones on the analysed samples is very vast and the different depths of colour depend on the different concentrations of the dyeing solution and on the dilution of the lake with white clay. Purpurissum was made into a paste, cut into cubes the size of a mosaic tessera and left to dry. It was destined, above all, for painting on ceramics and for cosmetic use: in fact, its components, which were completely harmless for the skin, made a perfect powder which, thanks to the addition of white clay, offered all the shades most suitable for the female complexion. The purpurissum produced in Pozzuoli was, according to Pliny, the best, better than the one coming from Tyre; in Pozzuoli, its colour was intensified and revived by the addition of colouring juice extracted from madder. Along with Egyptian blue, purpurissum was the most expensive colour and consequently, there were various imitations and falsifications on the market; among these, the most common were selinusia clay dyed with madder or with the juice of hyacinth flowers.

The second lake, of a beautiful yellow-gold colour, came from violet juice that, as well as supplying a violet lake by the usual method, also supplied a yellow lake with the same juice, which was boiled until the colour veered towards yellow; Vitruvius informs us that this lake was also prepared in imitation of sil Atticum, the most beautiful and precious type of yellow ochre; in fact, many lakes were also used to imitate or falsify the most precious and costly colours. So, indigo was falsified by dyeing selinusia or anularia clay with woad, or by boiling it in the water of dried violets and dyeing it with eteria clay; aerugo, with marble powder or pumice stone dyed with weld (*Reseda luteola*) juice; the same juice was also used for dyeing a clayey substance called "alumina shistum" and for falsifying crysocolla; caeruleum aegyptium was imitated and falsified by producing a caeruleum less pure and of a poorer manufacture. 8

5) THE MEDIEVAL PALETTE

Divine light in colour

In the early centuries following the year 1000 attitude towards colour is characterized by the search for a light radiating from the colour itself; as Lia Luzzatto and Renata Pompas clearly underline, the chromatic taste for strong and saturated colours, already present in Carolingian art, is enriched in brightness and transparency by the encounter with the theological discourse on the mystic aspect of light:

"The medieval dialectic between spirit and matter, between good and evil renewed the symbolic power of the contraposition between light and darkness, attributing to light the divine origin, the quality of the spirit, the subtle and the immaterial, and to darkness the negativity of sin, represented by the material, the opacity and density. This philosophy enlightened the Middle Ages with bright colours, subtending that perfection and beauty of earthly things could be only found in brightness; the more colour had incorporated light in its materiality, the more beautiful it was considered; transparency and gloss were charged with a moral connotation.(...)

"The passion for the clarity, brilliance and translucent stimulated many artistic works, from metal decoration with enamels to the use of transparent paints for the finishing of their works of art, to the stained glass windows, which spread out from the 12th century. Painters made colours shine by using brilliant pigments which were enhanced by being close to the glittering of gold; but nothing seemed to better represent the medieval theological-philosophical orientation than the glass windows, which let the coloured light filter in to the religious buildings (...)

"The purity of the glassy materials allowed one to experience a chromatic range lit up by glows, with combinations of reds and sky-like blues, of greens and purples, blues and yellows, through which the light was permeated with colours, and this way the 'splendor', that is the presence of the supernatural in the matter, became real. (...) So, for the medieval man, what was intense, brilliant and bright was fine; it was a long, kaleidoscopic season crossed by a lively and unique chromatism. Even the clothing resembled the new inclination of the colours, which tried to rival the shine of the light, combining saturated hues in contrasts that exalted each other. (...) An international style was born, in which the thinness of the vertical line and the use of flowing fabrics were the common elements: the light- weighed drapes glowed with their iridescent effects; the soft velvets allowed strong coloristic intensity; embroidery, gold applications, and the tailoring which allowed the viewing of linings with contrasting colours lit up the garments. " [1]

Pastoreau underlines that: *"For the medieval theology light is the only part of the material world that is both visible and intangible. It is <<visibility of the ineffable >> (St. Augustine) and, as such, an emanation of God. (...) If the colour is light, it becomes part of the divine by its own nature. Trying to extend the place of colour in this world - especially into the church -is the equivalent of pushing back the darkness for the benefit of the light, therefore of God. The search for colour and the search for light are inseparable. The debate about the nature of colour is still in full turmoil in the 12th century and causes practical implications in every aspect of life.*

"The answers given in the course of the debate will determine the place of colour in the environment and in the behaviour of a good Christian, in the places he frequents, in the images he contemplates, in the clothes he wears." [2]

"The beauty of a colour, first of all, depended on its brightness and its intensity. The high saturation and the absence of shades and halftones, in addition to giving the colour that expressive power needed to express its symbolic meaning, made the colour tend to share the condition of light, of gold and gems, considered for a long time the symbols of artistic value. This aesthetic of colour proceeded in harmony with the doctrine of the 'metaphysics of light' that, according to the Neoplatonic philosophy, interpreted the world as an irradiation of God – the supreme light, thus giving the light not only a mystical and spiritual value, but also an aesthetic one.

"Many thinkers of the 13th century were taken by the problem of the light from this point of view and, among them, Roberto Grossatesta: < the beauty and perfection of each corporeal thing is light ...>, Witelio: <... the more light everything owns the more it is divine> ... and Saint Bonaventura: <... Light is the most noble thing among corporeal things, everything the more light it has, the more it possesses the divine being ...>

"The preciousness and shine in a work of art, at least as far as painting on wood panel is concerned, first of all is apparent in the gold grounds; on the preparatory layer of red bole, a color that exalted the warm refraction of gold, metallic leaves were laid; they were as thin as a veil, so as to form a surface of abstract purity, luminous to the highest degree, and the effect of which was amplified in the dim light of the candles. " 3

Colour becomes a means of divine exaltation because colour is first of all considered as light, and as the light, in medieval theology, is visibility of the ineffable and, as such, emanation of God, and, as already said, bringing the colour inside places of worship means pushing back the darkness for the benefit of the light, and therefore, of God. 4

Hence the choice of golden backgrounds and large flat fields of pure and bright colour, and of the most beautiful and expensive colours by the richest patrons in order to honour the Divine through the most precious materials. Gold has ancient associations that make its value transcendental. Gold is the substance of royalty, therefore, in religious art, offering it to God was the best way to demonstrate one's devotion. The fact that gold is incorruptible, that it doesn't oxidize and does not lose its luster over time, makes it the true materialization of the eternal divine splendor; whoever wore 'cloths of gold' dressed himself with divine light and became the symbol of the earthly kingship bestowed by a divine will; it was the highest expression of a very high rank in a hierarchy predetermined by God's will.

Initially called 'tartaric cloths', the production of cloths of gold originated in the Mongol empire and later developed in Syrian and Egyptian Khanates.

After 1291, following the papal prohibition of trading with Syria and Egypt, Venice and Genoa turned their business to the Black Sea and the Mongol empire.

In the inventory of the papal treasury of 1295 these cloths, probably diplomatic gifts, are often cited.

The reproduction of cloths of gold texture was a great challenge for painters, but also an incentive to improve the gilding technique; such artists as Simone Martini, Gentile da Fabriano remained unrivalled at working on gold.

Working on gold required a special skill. The gold could be laid in the form of gold leaf on a ground of red bole, previously spread with glue, (*"Bole is a soft, greasy textured, orange or red-brown clay, pigmented by the same iron oxides which constitute the red earth pigments. It serves two main functions: the first is to provide smooth cushioned surface against which the gold leaf can later be burnished, and the second is to impart a warm rich colour to the gold.*"5) then it was smoothed with a burnishing tool, usually an agate stone, or the leaf could be laid under the layer of colour of the dress and then 'sgraffita', that is scraped to highlight the underlying gold decoration. The gold ground could be then worked with different techniques and tools: burin, punch, chisel, so as to produce a wide range of effects of diffusion and golden refraction of light.

Burin was a very thin chisel that allowed one to cut the leaf and remove the exceeding parts; punching-work made use of stamps called punches for engraved or imprinted decorations; punch is a roughly cylindrical metal tool with a decorative motif cut into one end. This motif is imprinted into gilded gesso (gypsum) by punching, that is, placing the punch perpendicular to the gilded surface and striking the other end with a hammer. Raised patterns were obtained with 'pastiglia', a solid compound of glue protein, gypsum and gold powder; it was applied in thick layers so as to be in relief.

In the *Uffizi Annunciation* the angel's greeting words are of golden 'pastiglia'. In the *Maestà*, 1312-15, by Simone Martini, located in the Palazzo Pubblico in Siena, the floral ornamentation is made with 'pastiglia', while the decorations of the halos are obtained by using a punch, the first important example of punching-work applied to painting art.

When one used sgraffito technique, first the area to be represented as the cloth of gold was gilded; next a layer of the predominant colour of the textile was painted in the usual egg tempera medium over the whole area of gold leaf to be patterned. The design of the textile would then have been transferred to the paint surface by dusting powdered pigment through the pricked outlines of a paper or parchment cartoon. On lifting the cartoon the pattern would appear as lines of dots on the paint surface.

The decorative design was scratched into the paint layer with a wooden stylus. It was essential that the paint had not dried completely, so that it could be neatly removed without damaging the delicate gold layer underneath.

The final stage was the tooling of the exposed gold with small stipple punches to make the cloth of gold shimmer and sparkle in flickering candlelight. 6

In the *Annunciation* by Simone Martini and Lippo Memmi, 1333, (Uffizi, Florence), one of the finest gold dresses of all medieval painting is worn by the announcing angel; Gabriel's dalmatic of white and gold Tartar silk is embroidered in gold with small stylised lotus flowers and leaves, a decorative motif typical of the Yuan Dynasty.

"The 'Uffizi Annunciation' is glazed over tooled gold leaf, with the punch-work on the stole.

To reproduce the angel's beautiful cloth of gold, Martini covered it with a layer of gold leaf over an adhesive foundation of red bole, and brought out the decorative motif both with the sgraffito technique and with punching to accentuate the contrast between the fabric ground and the embroidery." 7

Humanistic Renaissance rationalism will sweep away this metaphysical vision of light and colour, and the latter will become the subject of natural light losing all theological ties.

Gold will become the material of luxury and a display of wealth and power without the divine connotation of the previous centuries. Painting abandons the large flat fields of pure and dazzling pigments to switch to the lights and shadows of reality, to shaded colour, to harmonious chromatic combinations, to colour invested by the natural light that softens the combinations between different hues.

Origin of the raw materials

Throughout the Middle Ages, the number of new pigments increased notably; as well as the materials inherited from antique times, techniques were used to create many new colours and pigments that adapted better to the new supports used in painting and in other artistic forms. The great international industry, which became the backbone of the European economy, was largely responsible for the research of new technologies for new colours, and a fundamental contribution in the discovery of new colours came, as we shall see, both from the Arabic alchemy and the Western one. The great artistic blooming, which was already in motion in the 12th century, would reclaim ever larger quantities of raw materials for the creation of colourants and pigments, so considerably influencing the turning point for trade, as well as the agricultural landscape of the late Middle Ages, as some of the colouring extracts most in demand for the dyeing of prestigious fabrics, such as silk, were also widely used in the production of pigment lakes for painting and miniature; for example, the documents of the time certify that, since the first half of the 12th century, the consignments of Italian woad, leaving from Genoa for England, were numerous and heavy; the indigo extracted from woad was, for centuries, not only the most prestigious colouring and the only one for dyeing silk blue, but it was also used a lot in painting, both as a pigment or for colour mixtures, or as a substitute for more costly pigments; its cultivation became particularly widespread and economically important for France and Germany too; so much so that, when they saw it threatened by the introduction into the European market of the less costly and more precious indigo produced by the Indigoferas of the New World, they did not hesitate to defend their product with drastic measures. On Italian territory, the cultivation of madder, weld and saffron as a support for dyeing, painting and miniature, continued to spread.

Many of the natural minerals for the preparation of pigments were obtainable in the Italian caves and mines, even if the national production could not always satisfy the demand completely; azurite, also called "Azuro de la Magna", was also extracted from some mines in Sardinia and Tuscany; in these two regions there were also important caves of yellow ochre and umber; there were silver, copper, lead and graphite mines in Sardinia; the Verona area abounded in green earth and yellow ochre; and in Tuscany, the mines of Mount Amiata, rich in natural cinnabar, are still used today, even if it is exclusively for the extraction of mercury. Pozzuoli has been famous since ancient times for its red earth and sulphur mines; orpiment and realgar were obtainable in the volcanic areas of Vesuvius and Etna.

Nevertheless, many raw materials were imported, some from very faraway lands, like, for example, the lapis lazuli - necessary for the production of ultramarine, which came from the mines of Badakhshan, situated in the present day Afghanistan, which Marco Polo visited in 1271; the limited quantity extracted, the difficulty of extraction due to the hard rock, the long transport and the laborious preparation of the pigment made ultramarine the most expensive colour in painting, more than gold itself. Oriental indigo, brazil wood, Indian lac, turmeric and red jasper also arrived from the Orient; for centuries, these goods, together with many others, were brought to the West by Arab merchants who bought them in India and transported them by sea as far as the port of Hormuz in Persia, and then, travelling overland in a long caravan chain, they reached the commercial ports of the East Mediterranean: from Baghdad to Alexandria, Cyprus or Rhodes, where they were then bought by the Italian merchants, who distributed them in the West and in Northern Europe. The Marine Republics, with their commercial outposts in the East, supplied the Italian market with the most important goods of the best quality, at a very inferior cost compared to other European areas, where many raw materials arrived with infinitely higher prices; it was not by chance that the precious ultramarine was used a lot by Italian painters, especially between the 14th and 16th centuries, but fairly little by the painters of North Europe, where its price often increased tenfold. Venice, with the power exercised along the trading routes for the Orient, became one of the most important European sales centres, for lapis lazuli too, and later on, in the 16th century, it became the production centre of an ultramarine that was considered to be the best in commerce. Then, in certain periods, the prices of goods were subject to a constant fluctuation, owing to the greater or lesser availability of the raw materials; in fact, these did not always arrive regularly from their place of origin, as there were too many uncertainties and dangers that could compromise the successful outcome of the expeditions; nevertheless, in the period of time that goes under the name of "pax mongolica", which lasted from about 1240 to 1360, there was, more than at any other time, the possibility of a safe journey and return, thanks to the political stability of the vast Mongolian Empire and to the constant patrolling of the whole territory; in this way, the commercial exchanges with the Orient and the volume of Italian trade with China and India assumed vast and unexpected proportions; as compensation for the risks, and for the enormous fatigue and absence for many years, there was the possibility of incredible profits. [8]

Interest for the Orient and influx from the Orient are also reflected in art; the Sasanian iconography exercised a notable influence on many architectural decorations of early Italian Gothic; in painting, too, one can notice the interest towards the Orient on the part of some artists, among whom is Giotto and in particular the masters of the Sienese school, who used letters from Arabic calligraphy or from Mongolian script, liberally interpreted, to adorn the borders of the Madonna's or the saints' clothes, or else the haloes or frames; this was obtained thanks to an exceptionally skilful use of gilding techniques; in other cases, some personages in the painting are wearing garments of obvious, Oriental inspiration; for example, some of the young girls who dance in Ambrogio Lorenzetti's *The effects of good government* (Palazzo Pubblico, Siena) are wearing light and transparent dresses, with the dragonfly motif that is typical of Sung painting, or with undulating silkworms; and in the fresco *The martyrdom of the Franciscans at Tana* (Basilica of San Francesco, Siena) also by Lorenzetti, the artist, with a precise symbolic use, inserts three personages who are of evident Mongolian ethnicity. 9

Another sector which, in turn, absorbed a discreet quantity of dyeing plants and minerals, was that of Pharmacopoeia; in line with the indications of Theophrastus and Dioscorides on the medicinal properties of plants and other substances, nearly all the dyeing plants were also used for medicinal purposes; the chemists prepared a lot of so-called "simple" medicaments, also using precious stones such as jasper, emerald, malachite, lapis lazuli; these were reduced to powder and given either alone or mixed with something else, as it was believed (just like in the ancient civilizations), that they possessed mysterious and supernatural virtues. Alum, too, was an object of intense trading; during the Middle Ages, once the mines that had supplied the Romans with the precious material were exhausted, they turned to the ore deposits in the Eastern Mediterranean; after the conquest of Phocaea in 1267, Genoa detained the monopoly of the extraction and the transport of the alum until 1455, when the conquest of the area by the Turks, cut off the supplies; it was a moment of grave crisis for textile manufacture, as alum was fundamental for the mordanting of the fibres to undergo dyeing: but it was just as important for the leather tanning industry and for the preparation of the lakes for painting; nevertheless, the crisis was soon resolved thanks to the discovery of a large ore deposit at Tolfa, near Civitavecchia, then under Papal dominion; the significance and the importance of such a discovery is clearly expressed in the words pronounced on the occasion by Pope Pius II: <we have won the greatest battle against the Turks>. 10

The Contribution of the Alchemists

The term "alchemy" includes all the attempts and speculations which, through the study of the permanent changes in substances, based on the Aristotelian assumption of the sole matter, aimed to transform metals by means of the philosophers' stone, and to perfect human matter so making it incorruptible, by means of the elixir of life. An extraordinary mass of (often refined) techniques, surrounded by mystery, cultivated by learned men and charlatans, always suspected of heresy, spread by texts that were often apocryphal, full of abstruse symbols, and written in esoteric language; alchemy expressed the human aspiration to know the secrets of matter, in order to dominate it. In spite of the erroneousness of its bases, important scientific discoveries are owed to alchemy. 11

The alchemists' ambitions are well exemplified by the words of Roger Bacon who, in his *Opus tertium* of the 13th century, categorically states that <*alchemy is operative and practical: it teaches one how to create noble metals, colours and many other things, better and in greater quantity with artifice than if they had been created by nature*>. 12

Ever since its origins in Hellenistic Egypt, alchemy was strictly related to the technology of colour; "(...) *its origins lie not in the metaphysics but in the practical crafts of ancient times. Alchemy is, at root, an art of transformation. It provided a theoretical framework that enabled experimenters to make some sense of the changes that the agencies of fire, water, air, vapors, and time wrought on materials. Since, as we have seen already, these changes were often accompanied by an alteration in color, it can come as no surprise that practical alchemy would be the means by which artificial colors were provided to artists. (...) Color underpins the alchemical belief in transmutation. A substance's color was deemed an outward manifestation of its inner properties. Lacking much information beyond this superficial characteristic, alchemists had every reason to suppose that a metal with the appearance of gold was none other than gold itself. (...) There is good reason to argue that red is the primary hue of both medieval chemistry and art. Alchemy accords red a special significance. It is the "color" of gold, deemed more beautiful when more ruddy, and it signifies the culmination of the Great Work: the creation of the Philosopher's Stone."* 13

The change of colour in the process of transformation of the material was essential in order to reach the final stage to which the colour red corresponded. It shouldn't surprise us, therefore, that the synthesis of mercury sulphide, or cinnabar, was prepared by alchemists, even if it is thought that it was already being used in China, in the 3rd century; they believed that sulphur and mercury were the basic components of all metals, and that all metals differed from gold only in the relative proportions of sulphur and mercury and that they could therefore transform everything into gold, thanks to a simple change of relations between the two basic components; *artificial cinnabar* or *"vermilion"* is considered to be the most important technological innovation of Medieval painting; it was widely used during the whole of the Renaissance; in oil-painting, the colour was preserved practically unaltered, thanks to the protective action of the oily substances, against the action of the atmospheric agents. The preparation of vermilion came about by direct synthesis of the elements in the so-called dry process. The discovery of *artificial orpiment* - obtained by smelting realgar and sulphur together - was also attributed to the alchemists, as well as *mosaic gold*, so-called because it was used to gild the mosaic tesserae; it is a tin disulphide that goes under the form of yellow scales, soft to the touch, with a golden metallic brightness. The most widespread method of preparation required great skill in the art of using fire, as a low and constant temperature gave a bright yellow, a higher temperature gave a darker yellow but excessive heat gave it a greyish tone. Due to its lack of stability, as well as its poisonousness, it was used very little in painting, while it was largely used in miniature, as an important substitute for authentic gold. [14]

Sulphuric acid, called "oil of vitriol", was synthetized by the alchemists through the distillation of natural sulphurs and the dissolution in water of sulphur tri-sulphide (sulphuric anhydride) so developed. In the 15th century, the method was perfected by using hydrated iron sulphide (green vitriol), distilled with sand, as a raw material. The vitriols, which are iron sulphides, would be used not only in the preparation of some pigments, but also for the black tones on silk, especially in Genoa.

The First Medieval Treatises On Colour

A few treatises dating back to between the 8th and the 9th centuries allow us to know the materials and the techniques that were used in dyeing, painting and miniature in the very early Middle Ages; in that period, the antique terminology of colours and, even more, of the origin of the materials, changes considerably; from here onwards, there is often great difficulty in the correct identification of the substances mentioned, or there is great confusion or misunderstanding about the true nature of certain colours, as, in certain cases, they have been renamed with the name that the classics used for a different type of pigment: this is the case, for example, of the Latin "minium"; as we have seen, in the classical antiquity, this term indicated red mercury sulphide in its natural state, or in other words the natural mineral called Cinnabar; yet, already in that period, some people referred to oxide of red lead with the same terms; red lead was also called "cinnabaris" by some, a term commonly used by the classics to indicate a red that was of vegetable origin; these three colours, very similar in appearance, have got nothing in common as regards their chemical composition and therefore it is extremely difficult, if not impossible, to identify the true nature of some dyestuffs when, in a treatise, one simply finds references and not a recipe that clearly describes the components. Further problems in interpreting the terms used, as well as understanding the recipes, is due to the fact that the technical terminology used in some treatises is not to be found in other Medieval recipe books, and it is also untraceable in the more complete Latin dictionaries.

This is the case of the most antique manuscript of its kind to have come down to us, the so-called "Manuscript of Lucca", which was found in the Library of the Rectory of Lucca and published for the first time by Ludovico Antonio Muratori in 1779.

As can be deduced from its long, original title, *Compositiones ad tingenda musiva, pelles, et alia, ad deaurandum ferrum, ad mineralia, ad chrysografiam, ad glutina, quaedam conficienda, aliquae atrium documenta, ante annos nongentos scripta*, the treatise is a collection of technical procedures; its aim is to reveal a patrimony of "secrets" to the craftsman, which have been handed down for centuries. There is a clear link with the Alexandrian treatises of the 3rd century and in fact, many recipes are already present, formulated in more or less the same way, in the Papyrus of Leyden, which goes back to the 3rd century; the 157 recipes concern teachings on various artisan practices: the colouring of the artificial stones for the production of mosaics, their gilding, silvering and burnishing; the dyeing of skins, wood, bone and horn; the extraction of minerals; the composition of metallic alloys, the lamination and the drawing of gold, silver and tin; a good number of recipes also concerns the production of colours of mineral, vegetable and animal origin for painting and dyeing. The use of purple extracted from murex, and the special technique of the gilding of the parchments denote the strong link of this treatise with the classic, Byzantine tradition.

Among the colours of mineral origin, we find *orpiment*, an arsenic sulphide of a beautiful yellow colour, that changed to orange when it contained particles of *realgar*; in the treatise in question, only the natural mineral is mentioned; yet, we know that it was in the Middle Ages that the production of *artificial orpiment* began, even if the exact moment is unknown; it was made by mixing realgar and sulphur together, a practice that was already more than common at the time of Cennini's *Book of Art*. On the other hand, artificial Cinnabar, afterwards named "vermilion", is spoken of, and the method of preparation is described in detail, that is: by putting sulphur and mercury in a sealed container and cooking it on a low flame; it is thought that it was the Arabian alchemist, known by the latinized name of "Geber", who discovered the chemical procedure towards the middle of the 8th century. The recipe for the preparation of a substitute for cinnabar (one of the most imitated and falsified colours ever since antique times) could not be left out: it is obtained by mixing calcined red ochre and "siricum"; with calcination, the red ochre, - a brownish red colour in its natural state – assumed a bright red colour and it was sometimes used alone as a cinnabar surrogate; the siricum mentioned here corresponds to the classical syricum and it is, in turn, a mixture of red lead and red ochres; during the Middle Ages, "siricum" became synonymous of "minium" in the sense of red lead oxide.

For the preparation of 'litargirio' (lead monoxide), two different processes are given: one with lead and the other with silver, as if dealing with two different substances; in actual fact, lead monoxide, which is a by-product from the extraction of argentiferous silver lead, can turn out more or less reddish or yellowish, depending on the method used to obtain it, and it was called "gold" or "silver", on the basis of the assumed colour.

For the preparation of chrysocolla, a term that, in the Middle Ages, meant different compounds of copper, one starts off with compounds of copper treated with basic lead carbonate and soap; the result ought to be a basic carbonate of green copper, similar to the classical crysocolla. In the following chapter, under the same term, there is, instead, a copper and alum compound, that probably supplied a blue with a base of copper sulphide. Copper salts, or basic carbonate and sulphide, were at the base of a deep blue colour, defined as "lulax, lulacin"; the tone and depth of colour were corrected with the addition of vegetable extracts; in one recipe, verdigris, copper sulphide, alum and "uvatum"- a blue extract of woad - are mixed. Strangely, lapis lazuli (that, in the Middle Ages, became the most prestigious and sought-after mineral for blue and azure shades) is absent in the preparation of the blues.

The basic lead carbonate (lead white), later known as 'biacca' in Italian treatises, is referred to in various terms, some of which are not verifiable in other sources; the method followed is the one already described by Dioscorides, Vitruvius and Pliny.

The term *prasinus* means "dark green", and in the Medieval treatises on colours, it is always used to describe the green earth corresponding to the "creta viridis" of the classics, nowadays called "Verona earth", composed of a clay coloured with green, due to the presence of ferrous silicate; the Latin word "prasinus" derives from the Greek "pràsinos"= green, colour of the well, deriving, in turn, from the Greek "pràson"= well.

The organic dyes present in the treatise are mostly of vegetable origin, flower, root or bark. Some of the flowers mentioned are not recognizable, they remain untranslatable because the terms used to indicate them are not present elsewhere. The vegetable extracts were quite often a component of elaborate recipes in which other substances were present, like for example, lead white, alum, soap, copper salts.

"Uvatum", a woad extract, could be used alone in painting, but in the treatise of Lucca, it is always mentioned only as a component of the various blue colours obtained by mixtures of vegetable and mineral products.

Madder, referred to as "Rubia silvatica", is present in the recipe for the preparation of the lake that is obtained from the reaction of the alizarin, the colourant contained in the root of the plant, with alum. In the era to which the treatise belongs, that is from the 8th century onwards, madder must have been very much in demand; this is testified, for example, by the "Capitulare de Villis" of Charlemagne, which contains an edict that orders the growing of madder in the farm gardens of the whole Empire.

Reseda luteola (weld) is called "luza" and corresponds to the "herba lutea" of the classics; the use of its colourant extract is mentioned both for dyeing and for the preparation of a yellow lake, suitable for painting and for miniature, always obtained by letting the colourant extract precipitate in alum.

"Ficarim" was a compound of a red shade, prepared by cooking a red lake (probably from madder or kermes) together with urine; the powder of calcined crab shells and corn flour was then added; the mixture was then left to dry in the sun.

Another red mentioned in the treatise is Dragon's blood; known as "dracontea sanguineus", this colour is the "cinnabaris indicus" of the classics, and in the Middle Ages it was also to be found under the name of "sanguis draconis".

There are only two organic colours of animal origin: kermes and 'porpora' (purple). Kermes is mentioned here with the terms "coccus", "coccarin", "vermiculum", "bermiculum"; the last two are the terms that were commonly used in the Middle Ages, together with "vermilium"; their meaning, "little worm", reveals that it was only in the Medieval period that they began to understand the animal nature of kermes, which, up till then, was believed to have been of a vegetable origin. Kermes, used for dyeing fabrics and skins, is also mentioned in the red dyeing of parchments, as an imitation of the much more costly murex purple. The latter is cited with the terms "porphira", "conquilium", "jotta decotionis conquilii"= sauce of shell decoction, with clear reference to the method of extraction of the colourant precursors.

In the recipes for the preparation of colours, the term "pandius" – its use, in the Middle Ages, is referred to as various blends of colour of different composition - is repeated several times; it turns up in various recipes for the dyeing of parchments; in the first recipe the skin, treated first with alum and then with "vitriolium", is dyed with "bermiculum" (kermes); in the second, after having mordanted with vitriol, it is dyed with reseda juice (jotta luze); in the third, which is more complex, it is dyed with "melinum" (a white clay, which comes from the Island of Melo, in the Cyclades), then with "concius" (tannin), red coral powder, lake (probably from kermes), "calciatarin" (copper sulphide) and "galla" (oak galls, containing tannic substances), all of which were remixed in urine. In the fourth recipe, madder – cooked in urine and then treated with alum- appears, thus obtaining a madder lake. Dyeing was also done with reseda mixed with "lulacin" (probably indigo). In the *Compositiones*, a "picmentum pandium" is described: known as "pandius porfirus", it is composed of "decotio conquilii" (purple), "cinnabarin" (cinnabar), and "siricum" (probably red lead); all of which is ground, mixed with urine and dried in the sun. From most of these compositions, pigments of colour were obtained which varied from brick red to reddish brown; in the cases where blue colours were prevalent, pigments of blue or green shades were obtained. 15

The treatise *Mappae clavicula* belongs to the end of the 9th century or to the beginning of the X century, and resumes, in part, the recipes of the Lucca manuscript, including those regarding dyeing. The treatise is divided into two parts, the most consistent of which includes 294 rules of chemistry and artistic techniques that were applied, and with about a hundred recipes for the preparation of colours.

The *De coloribus et artibus Romanorum*, written in Italy in the 10th century, is a treatise of considerable interest, because of the knowledge it contains regarding the colours used in painting and miniature; both this treatise and the previous one are not the work of a single author but are probably the fruit of a union of texts, derived from various sources, and they reveal the tendency for the direct and traditional conservation of the procedures, through the resumption (more or less unaltered in most of the recipes) of the materials and procedures that were used in the antique tradition, to which the contribution of new sources, including those of Islamic origin, were added. The "De Coloribus" had great fortune throughout the Middle Ages; in fact, it can be regarded as a perfect and detailed manual, above all for decorators and scribes, whose work was not limited only to the fulfilment of the artistic work, but also included the preparation of all that was necessary for its execution: from the colours to the paintbrushes, to the inks, to the glue. At the time when the treatise was written – at the height of the Carolingian age – there was a renewal of contacts with the Byzantine culture and a consequent, refined production in the environment of miniature, above all among the monks in the great monasteries, who were adept at decorating and illustrating the religious books, side by side with the lay artists who also contributed to the creation of precious codices for the Palatine court. *"The extension of the palette, a more complex mixture of colours, the use of shading and an ever-growing use of vegetable dyeing juices, in order to reach the delicateness and transparency typical of miniature, are the fruits of the great schools of Tours, Chartres, Reichenau, San Gallo, Montecassino, Bologna and others still."* 16

The "De Coloribus" already presents a fairly wide range of recipes for making colours with vegetable juices, and in both the "Mappae clavicula" and the "De coloribus", new mixtures are advised for the background colours: this is how "vergaut" appears – a mixture of various colours that gave a fairly pale green; it was obtained by mixing orpiment and mineral azure, or orpiment and indigo, or yellow ochre and indigo, or even verdigris and indigo; the azure of lapis lazuli, called lazur, appears; dragon's-blood and orpiment were mixed to obtain an orange tone; *folium* appears – a vegetable juice of a colour that varies from red- brown (*folium rubeum*) to red-violet (*folium purpureum*) and to bluish-violet (*folium saphireum*), obtained from the fruit of the *Chrozophora tinctoria* – an euforbiacea of Oriental origin, also known as Eliotropio minor, which would be widely-used both for dyeing and for miniature.

In the "De Coloribus", a red colour – extracted from various types of exotic legumes and used very much in the Middle Ages, makes its appearance: previous to the massive import from the Americas of other species of *Caesalpinia*, 'red wood' arrived in Europe from the Orient, the native area of the *Caesalpinia sappan* tree; its wood was introduced to the West by the Venetians, thanks to their trading with the East; its bright red colour- the colour of embers – earned it a series of names, deriving both from the Arabic "wars"(dyeing plant) and from the French "braise" (ember). 17

In Marco Polo's "Million", it can be found mentioned as "berci", from which "verci" and "verzino" derive; in other texts we can find it as "brexilium", "brasilium", or "brezil" and, more recently, "brazil-wood"; it is from the term "brezil" that the name "Brazil" in its homonymic state, derives, christened thus because in that land there was an incredible amount of other, new species of *Caesalpinia*. The Oriental type was widely used in Europe from the early Middle Ages, not only in dyeing but also in the preparation of the red aluminated lakes for painting and miniature; the wood contains a glucoside that, by decomposing, gives place to the substance today defined as "brazilin"; this, through the action of air or oxidants, changes easily into a red dye that is easily soluble in water; when treated with alum, it precipitates under the form of insoluble red lake.

From another, slightly later treatise – that of the French monk Peter of St. Omer – here is the recipe for the preparation of the lake:

"*Take the filings or shavings of brazil wood and put them on the fire to boil in red wine in a clean pot.*

Then, once the lake has been diluted with urine, put them together to boil and, when this has been done, drain and squeeze it. Then, take the alum and mix it with those substances in a fireproof recipient, and stir it for some time. Next, remove it from the flame and put it into a bowl. Then rub it energetically on a rock, pick it up, and let it dry in the sun. Afterwards, replace it to be conserved in a box or in a vase." 18

The attitude that these treatises share is that of secrecy; they are shown as "keys" to gain access to antique secrets, with clear admonitions not to let this mystery fall into vulgar hands; thus the author of the *Mappae clavicula* swears that he will not reveal his knowledge to anyone, except his own son.

On the other hand, the attitude of the author of the *De diversis artibus* (On divers arts), written towards the end of the 10th century by the monk Theophilus, is very different, as it's pointed out by Ball:

"Theophilus' book stands out because of its unusual directness and clarity. It is no random collection of snippets from ancient books but rather presents systematically the techniques of the practicing artist. Indeed, unlike the authors of the recipe collections, Theophilus was a practicing artist: his formation bears the stamp of experience. And there is no call for secrecy, but instead an entreaty towards openess:

< Let [the artisan] not hide his gifts in the pursue of envy, nor conceal them in the store-room of a selfish heart but . . . let him simply and in a cheerful mind dispense to those who seek.> " 19

Theophilus roamed through various parts of Europe, and his work contains ideas from various German schools of miniature: the Scriptorium of Reichenau, the schools of Regensberg, Cologne and Saltzburg. Even in Theophilus' work some techniques for the preparation of various substances can be found, that have been practically unchanged from the Alexandrian tradition like, for example, the various recipes that teach one how to write in gold, that have been passed, unaltered, from the papyrus of Leiden to the "Compositiones" and, subsequently, to the "Diversis artibus". Obviously, alchemic influences persist in Theophilus as well; in fact, in some recipes for pigments, some of the concepts that are put forward, belong decidedly to the magic sphere; in effect, the alchemists' theories and the manufacture of pigments do not only weave together in the aforementioned treatises, but also in many, later works, lasting until the 17th century and beyond.

Theophilus believed that the value of colours depends on the intrinsic preciousness of the raw materials from which they are obtained, the pigments are appreciated as such, and the materials are regarded as a means to give religious value to the artwork.

" *To Theophilus, art was a devotional activity, the aim of which was to glorify God. To this extent he exemplify the painter of the twelfth century: a monk whose work is exclusively religious and who is accomplished in a variety of arts and crafts included manuscript illumination and metalwork. All of these, including painting, were conducted as anonymous activities – opportunities for pious meditation rather than for self-advancement. Even secular works in the early Middle Ages are usually unsigned. And the largest body from religious art from this time consists of illuminated manuscripts, the painstaking and often gorgeous work of innumerable nameless monks. Little is said in Theophilus' book about design and composition. The emphasis is all on techniques and materials (…) his choice of style and materials reflected a view of the world in which icons and images are not simply symbols of devotions but are invested with the power to intervene in everyday life. (…) a well made icon or picture was considered to possess real religious efficacy. The artist's use of precious materials, such as gold and ultramarine, does not simply imply a wish to show piety by lavishing expense but reveals the hope that the supernatural potency of the work will thereby be enhanced.*" [20]
From this, it can be understood why gold played such an important role in medieval paintings, particularly in the altarpieces:"(…) *gold has ancient associations that makes its value transcendental. Gold is the substance of royalty, so what could be more pious than to offer it up to God in sacred art ? And unlike silver and other metals, it was seemingly immune to the passing years – it did not tarnish or loose its splendor.*
The use of gold in medieval art shows us more clearly than anything else how the nature of materials took precedence over any concern for realism. Until at least the fourteenth century, holy

figures on altar panels are framed not by nature's skies or foliage, not by draperies or masonry, but by a golden field that permits neither depth nor shadows. In later ages this metallic sheen was pushed back onto the gilded frame that held the canvas, but for the medieval artist gold was a color in its own right." 21

The Purple Codices

One particular use of purple dyes was that of dyeing the parchments for the creation of the so-called Purple Codices. The origin of parchment as a bearing for script appears to go back to the III century B.C.; its Italian name 'pergamena' derives from the city of Pergamum, which was one of the most important centres of Hellenistic culture; the custom of writing on parchment then spread through the whole of the Roman Empire and with the spread of Christianity, also in North-west Europe. The shape of the pages was rectangular; afterwards, they were sewed one to the other, so as to form long rolls; in the 2nd century A.D., parchment began to be bound in the form of a book.

Parchment was obtained from the skins of various animals, such as calves, goats and lambs, and it was subjected to various treatments to prepare it for use: it was placed in a bath of limewater for various days to remove the hair, then washed and scraped with a semi-lunar knife, thus removing the last of the hair, and then put back into a new bath of fresh lime. Once rinsed, it was spread on a frame and dried in the open air to increase the tension; it was then re-bathed and dried, and this operation was repeated until its surface appeared smooth, scraping it each time so as to make the surface uniform and to thin it; it was then ground, usually with pumice powder and at the end, it was dampened and left to dry in tension one last time, before being cut into leaves. The finest and most delicate parchment, the so-called vellum (It. velino, from the

French 'velin' = parchment made from calfskin) was obtained from the skin of calves which were no older than six months, while the common parchment was obtained from sheepskin or goatskin. In order to apply inks and colours more easily, the surface of the parchment, which maintained its natural oiliness, was sized with white clay powder mixed with Arabic gum. The parchments destined for the Purple Codices were first purple painted or dyed, and then let dry; one then proceeded to the script, which was carried out with precious gold or silver inks, a procedure called "chrysography" (from the Greek crysòs=gold) or "argirography"(from the Greek argyros=silver); the custom of creating these precious manuscripts spread along with Christianity, which, while considering the use of precious materials for clothes to be improper, considered their use for the sacred texts as a sign of the utmost devotion, where purple symbolized the blood spilt by Christ and the triumphant Church, and gold was the symbol of divine light: the ancient pagan symbolism was taken from the same Christianity, and purple and gold became the expression of celestial sovereignty and authority on earth. 22

"Manuscripts with purple coloured pages exhibit a strong symbolic value in late antique and medieval book culture. Usually biblical texts were written with gold or silver inks on parchment dyed or painted with purple colorants. The symbolic value of the purple colour and the use of noble metals for inks indicate the representative character of the books and their use in a royal or imperial context.

"The use of purple dyes or paints to impart colour to parchment of precious codices is mentioned since Late Antiquity. (…)

"According to the high symbolic value of purple codices, it has been hypothesised on historical basis that parchment had been dyed with Tyrian purple, the famous dye extracted from molluscs. Indeed, few chemical analyses have been carried out on purple

codices, mostly by means of non-invasive measurements, and in no case the evidence of the use of Tyrian purple was given. (...) At present, indeed, we have no single evidence of the use of Tyrian purple in codices, while all analyses carried out on purple codices hypothesised the presence of less valuable alternatives, such as orchil from Roccella, Dendrographa, and Lecanora genera of lichens, folium from Chrozophora tinctoria or anthraquinonic dyes such as kermes or madder, these last possibly in double dyeing with indigo.

"Tyrian purple, if present, is only a minor component. The most important contribution to the purple colour of parchment is in fact inferred by orchil or folium". 23

Indeed, shellfish murex dye imitations have been far more frequent than previously thought, even in some of the oldest and most precious purple codices.

The most antique purple codex which has survived, goes back to the end of the 4th or the beginning of the 5th century A.D., but it seems that purple-dyed parchment was already in use before the 3rd century, and Latin and Greek authors from the 1st and the 2nd century A.D. refer to books embellished by a purple-coloured sheath; we also know that a collection of illustrated odes on purple pages was given to the Emperor Constantine as a present.

Some of the most sacred and sumptuously illustrated texts which have reached us, were produced in oriental areas: the most antique is the *Codex Argenteus*; the colour of this codex is bright red, and until recently, it was thought to be dyed or painted with *Purpura haemastoma*; instead recent analyses have revealed the use of dyes other than shellfish purple.

"Codex argenteus, the "Silver Bible" in Uppsala University Library, is the most comprehensive still existing text in Gothic language. It contains what is left of a luxury book of the four gospels, an evangeliarium, written in the early sixth century in

Northern Italy, probably in Ravenna, and probably for the Ostrogothic king Theoderic the Great. The text is part of Wulfila's translation of the Bible from Greek to Gothic, made in the fourth century. The purple colour does not come from the purple snail but from vegetable dyes. The silver writing is predominant, which explains why the book is called "the Silver Book", or the Codex argenteus. The Codex argenteus is written with gold and silver ink on very thin, purple-coloured parchment of extremely high quality." [24]

Accurate technical investigations has been recently carried out by a team of researchers using the most reliable technology:

"The manuscripts involved are datable from 6th to 8th century: they are known as Vienna Genesis (Vienna, Österreichische Nationalbibliothek), Krönungevangeliar (Vienna, Kunsthistorisches Museum Vienna, Treasury), Evangeliario di Sarezzano (Tortona, Archivio Diocesano) and Codex Brixianus (Brescia, Biblioteca Queriniana)

" These precious parchments have been much studied from the artistic and the symbolic viewpoints, but have received less attention in the matters of materials used and the technique of their application. By considering the great symbolic value of purple codices, dyeing of parchment with Tyrian purple has been possibly taken for granted, even without diagnostic counterchecks. Scientific investigation and analysis, in fact, has rarely been employed and just in two cases robust information was obtained employing an invasive analytical approach. (...)

"Our results clearly show that in all cases Tyrian purple can be excluded from the set of the possible colorants employed on the parchment and other dyes shall instead be considered, with folium and orchil as the most probable candidates. (...) bromine was detected in all manuscripts, but further measurements on standard parchment samples allowed to verify that the precursors of orchil

and folium, respectively the lichen Roccella tinctoria and the plant Chrozophora tinctoria, are both rich in bromine, so that this element cannot anymore be considered as a marker for Tyrian purple. (...)

"The more reasonable hypothesis, which conciliates the results from analysis and the scarcity of information from ancient treatises, is that substitutes of Tyrian purple, such as orchil or folium were always used in place of it." [25]

In the *Codex Sinopensis*, too, purple colour doesn't derive from murex purple but from folium. [26]

" The analysis by Robert Fuchs in 1977 of a leaf from the Petropolitanus Codex in the Morgan Library in New York showed that the dye was made from lichens and not extracted from Murex shells". [27]

In another stunningly beautiful codex, the *Rossanensis*, with purple coloured pages, lichen dye has been used instead of murex dye. (see next paragraph)

It's rather surprising that, among the purple codices recently analysed, the only codex in which shellfish dye has been found was created by the Insular art.

A double-checked trace of bromine, indicating the presence of whelk-dye, has been found on one page of an Anglo-Saxon book known as the *Barberini Gospels*. This manuscript dates to the late 8th or early 9th century AD, and the whelk- dye occurs as a background panel to white lettering at the beginning of St John's gospel.

The Anglo-Saxon scholar known as the Venerable Bede completed his *Ecclesiastical History of the English People* in 731 AD. In reviewing the natural resources of Britain in his introduction, he writes that British whelks produce a beautiful dye which does not fade from sun or rain, and grows even more beautiful with age. [28]

"There is also a great abundance of snails, of which the scarlet dye is made, a most beautiful red, which never fades, with the heat of the sun or exposure to rain, but the older it is, the more beautiful it becomes." 29

The sea snails mentioned by Bede belong to the species *Nucella lapillus*, also referred to as *Thais lapillus* or *Purpura lapillus*.

" This shellfish is called dog-whelk or dogwinkle in English; it lives on rocky shores of the western coasts of France, especially in Brittany (Bretagne), and on the British coasts. The purple from this species had already been described by William Cola in 1685 and more recently Su Grierson has described her tests with shellfish of this species collected on the west coast of Scotland. In 1990 we worked on this species in Brittany (...) Despite its size, this small species produces a relatively large amount of dye, which has the reddish-purple hue of the Phyllonotus (Bolinus, Murex) brandaris purple." 30

In Ireland, on the island of Inishkea North, Co. Mayo, archaeologists have found a whelk-dyeing workshop, dated to the 7th century AD, complete with a small, presumed vat, and a pile of broken-open dog-whelk shells.

The palette of early medieval codices

Marina Bicchieri, director of the Chemistry Lab. at ICPAL, has analysed one of the most beautiful purple codices, the *Rossano Gospels*, a codex composed of 188 pages in violet purple, with script in gold and silver and precious illuminations, which comes from the Syrian-Palestinian area:

"The Codex Rossanensis is a 6th century Byzantine illuminated manuscript written on purple parchment, conserved at the Museo Diocesano in Rossano Calabro (Cosenza, Italy). ... The manuscript

is famous for its prefatory cycle of 13 miniatures of subjects from the Life of Christ, arranged in two tiers on the page, the miniature of the four Evangelists, the golden decoration of the letter to Carpianum, the magnificent illumination of Mark inspired by the Sophia and for the use of the very precious purple dye as background for all the parchments, and gold and silver for the text"
The analysis by Marina Bicchieri show the following palette:

White	*Lead white*
Red	*Red lead*
	Cinnabar
Pink	*Red lead mixed with white lead*
	Pink lake from Sambucus Nigra
Orange	*Red lead + goethite*
Yellow	*Goethite*
	Orpiment, only 2 occurrences on pages 3 and 241
Green	*Goethite+lapis lazuli;*
	Goethite+indigo;
	Orpiment+indigo (only on pp 3 and 241)

Blue	*Lapis lazuli*
Indigo	*Indigo*
Violet	*Inorganic red + lapis lazuli*
	Pink lake + lapis lazuli
Black	*Carbon black*
Gold	*Gold, traces of iron*
Original black inks	*Carbon black*
Black inks added on top of silver inks	*Carbon black*

Posterior inks	*Iron-gall inks*
Silvery inks	*Silver with a high amount of copper*

Golden inks	Pure gold
Purple support	Purple lake from orchil 31

The *Vienna Dioskurides* is an early 6th-century illuminated manuscript of *De Materia Medica* by Dioscorides in Greek. It is an important and rare example of a late antique scientific text. The 491 folios measure 37 by 30 cm and contains more than 400 pictures of animals and plants, most done in a naturalistic style. This is the earliest known manuscript to use a solid gold background.

The palette used in this precious manuscript has been identified by a group of experts in achaeometry:

"Two Byzantine VI century manuscripts known as Vienna Dioskurides and Vienna Genesis, held in the Austrian National Library at Vienna, were analysed with in situ non-invasive techniques. ... The analytical study was performed to have a better knowledge on the colourants used by ancient miniature painters, a subject known more on the basis of traditional sources (i.e. medieval treatises) than of analytical evidences. Indeed these illuminated manuscripts are, to the authors' knowledge, among the oldest ever being analysed, so that the colourants found in them can be considered among the oldest evidences of their use. The main feature of Vienna Dioskurides and Vienna Genesis palettes is their richness, exemplified by the simultaneous presence of gold and ultramarine blue; in Vienna Dioskurides cinnabar is also present. Information regarding ultramarine blue is surprising, being the analytical evidence of the use of this precious pigment at least three centuries before its use in Western manuscripts, a feature justified by the fact that the Byzantine Empire was the dominant culture in early Middle Ages in the Mediterranean World. Other colourants include azurite and indigo, red lead, orpiment, red and yellow ochres, while a mixture of blue and yellow colourants, known as vergaut, was used to render green

hues. Organic colourants were also used, such as madder and Tyrian purple, the latter employed to dye the parchment of Vienna Genesis." 32

Imitations of precious materials

Enriching paintings with precious metals has been a common practice in the Orient since the remotest antiquity; its use was transmitted to the Greeks and Romans, and for the Byzantines it became a constant practice to embellish the parchment leaves, both with wide, golden grounds or else by covering only part of the figures with gold. At times, imitations were used in place of real metals, with a base of gilded litharge or orpiment, diluted in Arabic gum. A formula from the *Papyrus of Leiden* teaches one how to prepare gold script, that is: by grinding a thin, gold scale finely and creating a mixture with mercury, to use like common inks. In later recipe books, Arabic gum was added to the same amalgam of gold dust and mercury, and one is advised to dip one's paintbrush in liquid alum. The Western painters paid greater attention to the use of glues and mordants for fixing the gold; the parchments used in the West were usually rougher than those used by the Byzantines and consequently, they required the application of more tenacious mordants, so that the decorations in gold leaf adhered permanently; on the contrary, in the Byzantine codices, where the parchment was much smoother and strong adhesives were not used, the gilding has, in many cases, ended up by coming off. The adhesive most commonly used in the West was egg white, well-beaten and spread on the parchment, and on which the gold or silver leaves were then laid; once dry, they were polished; more leaves could be added on, to give consistency and to create the effect of a relief. The most important surrogate to gold was mosaic gold (a tin sulphide) in the form of yellow scales of metallic-gold splendour; it was called "mosaic" because it was used to gild the mosaic tesserae; its permanence, nevertheless, was fairly scarce and its use remained somewhat limited. Silver, just like gold, was imitated in this case by using a leaf of tin that was then burnished and varnished with linen oil to protect the metal from rusting; an amalgam of tin, mercury and Arabic gum was also used. 33

Shellfish purple was imitated with other dyestuffs; among these, folium has certainly been the one most used on parchment. Folium or 'turnsole' was obtained from *Chrozophora tinctoria*, an Euforbiacea of Oriental origin imported to North Africa and to some areas of Western Mediterranean Europe; the colour of the juice, extracted from the fruit and other parts of the plant, varied from reddish-brown to red-violet and dark-bluish violet, according to the different grade of acidity or alkalinity of the solution; red folium or rubeum was probably the natural colour of the fruit juice, being its ph around 4/4,5; by increasing the alkalinity a more purplish colour was obtained, until one got folium saphireum which had a blue colour.

" *Thus three cothlets could contain the major shades of folium, which could in turn have been varied slightly with white lead or other additives.*" 34

Folium was extensively used by illuminators with great results, but its use was not confined to manuscripts illumination and watercolours: it was, in fact, used in dyeing and as one of the first food colourants. The plant was of important economic value in Southern France in the commune of Grand-Gallargues, which was probably the center of export for folium elsewhere on the continent and to England during the Middle Ages. Friedman reports the account given by N. Joly who visited Grand-Gallargues to see the industry in August 1839:

" *On the morning that Chrozophora tinctoria is gathered, the plants are placed in a horse-driven press, very like an olive oil*

mill, macerated, and the juice – at this point a dark green, nearly blue, and very viscous – is run off through brush strainers into large wooden tubs. The pressings on the strainers are then mixed with urine, which apparently serves as a solvent, and again milled. Once the juice is obtained, it is drawn into long tubs, and pieces of a sort of heavy clean cheesecloth are dipped in it, removed, and immediately dried in sun and wind. The drying must take place on a good day, for if the weather is stormy, the cloths never turn blue. At this point the cloths undergo an exposure of 'aluminiadou', a layer of horse or mule dung about a half meter thick. The dung must be recent and just beginning to ferment, becoming hot in consequence and releasing ammonia vapor. Over this dung bed are strewn handfuls of fresh straw, and the cheese cloths placed on this are covered over with more straw and a light coating of dung or sometimes a large sheet to concentrate the fumes of the 'aluminiadou'. The dyer checks periodically to see that the two surfaces of the cloths are equally colored and that overlong exposure does not ruin the blue tint, which when it leaves, never comes again (instead, the cloth goes yellow). This process continues for about an hour and a half. .... After the cloths were properly dyed, they were baled and exported to Holland for dying cheese. The rags were steeped in water, the cheese dipped in the water and immediately dried off: the action of the lactic and butyric acids made the outer layer of the cheese go red. This local industry apparently continued until the 1870s, when the coming of aniline dyes rendered it obsolete. Other uses of these cloths were for coloring jams and jellies, sugar-wrapping paper, and wine." 35
Another frequent substitute for purple was the decoction of *Orchil*, which was extracted from a lichen, *Rocella tinctoria*, present in many Mediterranean islands; its colouring matter was extracted by letting the grated lichen ferment, in fermented urine. Both folium and orchil, being vegetable colourants, had scarce resistance to

light and so they turned out to be of poor quality compared to murex purple dye, that was unalterable in time; nevertheless, the colourings in the pages of books could be conserved at length so long as they remained closed and protected in the volume and were not subjected to prolonged exposure to light.

Illuminated manuscripts

"The term 'manuscript' comes from the Latin for 'handwritten': before the invention of printing all books had to be written out by hand. This was a time-consuming and labour-intensive process, and could take months or years. Although paper was available in southern Europe from the twelfth century, its use did not become widespread until the late Middle Ages - there was no paper mill in England until the fifteenth century. Before this the usual support for writing was parchment (also known as vellum), made from stretched, treated animal skins. A large manuscript might require one whole cow- or sheep-skin to make a folded sheet of two to four pages, and a thick book could require the hides of entire herds. Medieval books were therefore expensive items. (...) Some manuscripts were made even more precious by 'illumination'. This term comes from the Latin word for 'lit up' or 'enlightened' and refers to the use of bright colours and gold to embellish initial letters or to portray entire scenes. Sometimes the initials were purely decorative, but often they work with the text to mark important passages, or to enhance or comment on the meaning of the text." 36

In the early Middle Ages, most books were produced in monasteries, whether for their own use, for presentation, or for a commission.

Aside from adding flashy decoration to the text, scribes during the time considered themselves to be praising God with their use of gold.

Many monasteries produced manuscripts for the collection in their own libraries, and wealthy individuals commissioned works as a sign of status within the community.

The so-called Carolingian Renaissance of the late 8th and 9th centuries not only created beautiful illuminated manuscripts, but also saved many ancient works from destruction or oblivion, passing them down to posterity.

Carolingian manuscripts are presumed to have been produced largely or entirely by clerics, in a few workshops around the Carolingian Empire.

The earliest workshop was the Court School of Charlemagne (also known as the Ada School) which produced the earliest manuscripts, including the *Godescalc Evangelistary* (781–783); the *Lorschs* (778–820), the *Ada Gospels*, the *Soissons Gospels*, the *Harley Golden Gospels* (800-820), and the *Vienna Coronation Gospels*.

Another style developed at the monastery of St Martin of Tours, in which large Bibles were illustrated, based on Late Antique bible illustrations.

The last, and best, example was made for Charles the Bald in about 845-846.

Charles the Bald, like his grandfather, also established a Court School which produced several manuscripts, the *Codex Aureus of St. Emmeram* (870) being the last and most spectacular.

Luxury Carolingian manuscripts were intended to have treasure bindings - ornate covers in precious metal set with jewels around central carved ivory panels - sometimes these were donated after the manuscript itself was produced.

Ottonian art reflected the dynasty's desire to establish visually a link to the Christian rulers of Late Antiquity, such as Costantine,

Theoderic, and Justinian as well as to their Carolingian predecessors, particularly Charlemagne; Byzantine art also remained influential, especially after the marriage of the Greek princess Theophanu to Otto II. The Byzantine influence is evident in the gold bases and in the size of the most important figures, which are always portrayed as being much bigger than the surrounding personages, and this characteristic would last for a long time in art, until the end of the fourteenth century.

Ottonian monasteries produced most if not all of the most magnificent medieval illuminated manuscripts. They were a major art form of the time, and monasteries received direct sponsorship from emperors and bishops, having the best in equipment and talent available. The range of heavily illuminated texts was very largely restricted to the main liturgical books, with very few secular works being so treated.

A number of important manuscripts produced from this period onwards in a distinctive group of styles are usually attributed to the scriptorium of the island monastery of Reichenau. The "Reichenau school" specialized in gospel books and other liturgical books, many of them, such as the *Munich Gospels of Otto III* (c. 1000) and the *Periscope of Henry II* (Munich, Bayerische Nationalbibl. clm. 4452, c. 1001–1024), were imperial commissions. 37

Insular art, also known as Hiberno-Saxon art, is the style of art produced in the post-Roman history of the British Isles. Most Insular art originates from the Irish monasticism of Celtic Christianity, and the period begins around 600 AD with the combining of 'Celtic' styles and Anglo-Saxon (English) styles.

The influence of insular art affected all subsequent European medieval art, especially in the decorative elements of Romanesque and Gothic manuscripts.

Carpet pages are a characteristic feature of Insular manuscripts, although historiated initials (an Insular invention), canon tables and

figurative miniatures, especially, Evangelist portraits are also common.
Carpet pages are pages of mainly geometrical ornamentation, which may include repeated animal forms, typically placed at the beginning of each of the four Gospels in Gospel Books. The designation "carpet page" is used to describe those pages in Christian, Islamic, or Jewish illuminated manuscripts that contain little or no text and which are filled entirely with decorative motifs. The insular tendency for the decoration to lunge into the text, and take over more and more of it, was a radical innovation. The earliest surviving Gospel Book with a full programme of decoration (though not all has survived) is the *Book of Durrow*: six extant carpet pages, a full-page miniature of the four evangelist's symbols, four full-page miniatures of the evangelists' symbols, four pages with very large initials, and decorated text on other pages.
The *Lindisfarne Gospels* is one of the greatest masterpieces of Anglo-Saxon and Celtic art. It was probably made between 680 and 720, in the island monastery of Lindisfarne.

"It is the work of a very gifted artist who merged words and images to create a beautiful, enduring symbol of faith.

"This was a time of great change. Britain was a land of many cultures, with an emerging national identity and vigorous new forms of learning, literature and art. The Lindisfarne Gospels was a stunning creation of the new 'insular' culture.

"Writing and painting sacred texts were seen by monks as an act of meditation, during which the scribe might glimpse the divine. It was a high calling but very hard work. When it was finished it was a book to see and be seen. But it was also the maker's personal 'opusdei'- a work for God.

"The Lindisfarne Gospels is a glowing example of a new style of 'insular' art, in which the artist fused different styles.

"There are carpet pages and Insular initials of unprecedented complexity and sophistication, but the evangelists portraits, clearly follow Italian models.

"The carpet-pages are enormously complex, and superbly executed.

"The artist must have been a skilled chemist. Using a handful of local materials he developed an extensive colour palette including: purples, crimsons and blues from plant extracts such as woad, lichens and folium (turnsole); yellow from orpiment; red/orange from toasted lead; green from verdigris or by a blue-yellow mix; white from chalk, crushed seashell or eggshell; black from carbon.

"Pigments were mixed with adhesive beaten egg-white (glair). Ink was made from oak-galls and iron salts. Some fine details were added in gold-leaf or powdered gold ink." **38**

As happened to many precious purple codices, folium or turnsole was also widely used in some of the most beautiful Hiberno-Saxon manuscripts.

"Folium must have been known to the English as early as the Gospel of St. Augustine, Cambridge, Corpus Christi College MS 286, a manuscript that dates from the sixth century. It was ostensibly sent from Rome by Gregory to Augustine of Canterbury and was in England by the end of the seventh century. By about the eighth century, the pigment must have been in general use among Hiberno-Saxon artists, as can be seen from the Book of Kells, the St. Chad Gospels, and particularly the Lindisfarne Gospels. All three types of folium – rubeum, purpureum, and saphireum – are used by the Lindisfarne artist, presumably Eadfrith, bishop of Lindisfarne from 698 to 721; it is generally believed that the Gospels were painted between 687 and 698. The outer frame of an Evangelist portrait at folio 25v is a shade midway between rubeum and purpureum, while the color of the tunic is between purpureum and saphireum. A reddish or acid form appears in the outer frame

of the portrait of Luke on folio 137v, while the plum color in Mark's cloak on 93v is the pure form of the purple color. Luke's pallium is the pure saphireum." 39

The *Book of Kells* dates to around 800, or, for some scholars, up to a century earlier. It is far more comprehensively decorated than any previous manuscript in any tradition, with every page (except two) having many small decorated letters. Although there is only one carpet page, the 'incipit' initials are so densely decorated, with only a few letters on the page, that they rather take over this function. Human figures are more numerous than before, though treated in a thoroughly stylised fashion. Colours are very bright and the decoration has tremendous energy, with spiral forms predominating. Gold and silver are not used.

The results of technical examinations highlight the sophisticated use of a restricted palette of organic and mineral pigments. These have been applied with great creativity, as pure colour, and as simple mixtures. Variety has been achieved though considered juxtaposition and simple layering.

Pigments identified include:

blue (indigo), red-orange (red lead), yellow (orpiment), green (indigo and orpiment; verdigris), black (carbon and iron gall ink), and white (gypsum). 40

The *Benedictional of St. Æthelwold* (London, British Library, Additional MS 49598) is a 10th-century illuminated benedictional, the most important surviving work of the Anglo-Saxon Winchester School of illumination. The manuscript is decorated on an extremely lavish scale, and is generally accepted as the masterpiece of late Anglo-Saxon illumination, and of the Winchester style.

A wide range of colours, many overpainted to achieve a different effect, and much gold and silver are used. The style of the miniatures is characterized by brilliant colour, exuberant acanthus ornament, and figures who often overflow the space within the elaborate border and are shown overlapping it.

The *Stockholm Codex Aureus* (National Library of Sweden, MS A. 35, also known as the "Codex Aureus of Canterbury") is a Gospel Book written in the mid-eighth century in Southumbria, probably in Canterbury; its decoration combines Insular and Italian elements. Other important illuminated manuscripts produced during the eighth and early ninth centuries are the *Vespasian Psalter*, three Mercian prayer books (the *Royal Prayer book*, the *Book of Nunnaminster* and the *Book of Cerne*), the *Tiberius Bede* and the *Royal Bible*.

Around 1200 centres of education shifted from the cathedral schools to universities in European cities such as Paris, Bologna, and Oxford. Although the monastic scriptoria continued, the manufacture of books increasingly took place in the towns. Secular stationers accepted commissions from patrons, increasingly students or other lay people, and sub-contracted work to specialized craftsmen and women on a piece-work basis. New texts began to circulate for the urban and rural secular elite and middle classes, such as romances, chronicles and ancient histories, with a particular preference for the legends of Troy and of Alexander the Great, the Gladiators, the Bestiaries, with descriptions and tales of imaginary animals and creatures, and full of symbolic meanings; the Bestiaries, very popular in the 12th and 13th centuries, were the first texts to be written in vernacular.

The *Aberdeen Bestiary* is one of the best known of over 50 manuscript bestiaries surviving today; it has over 100 animal miniatures

The *Rochester Bestiary* is a parchment manuscript dating from c. 1230-1240. It is illustrated with 55 finished miniatures of various animals, each at the end of the passage describing that animal.

The herbal books, that were reserved at the beginning for doctors and had few illustrations, turned later on to a public that was prevalently layman, and they were enriched by precious illustrations in an astonishing way; precious, not only for their artistic value, but also because they became one of the most important testimonies of the various aspects of everyday life at that time.

The *Tractatus de Herbis* is a treatise of medicinal plants painted in 1440, now in the British Library.

It stands out compared to the other herbals not only for the beautiful and accurate illuminations but also for its author's modern approach to the subject matter: a multilingual list of plant names is linked to the visual representation of the plant, so avoiding confusion and the risk of administering the patient a herb different from the one prescribed by the physician.

The manuscript is a volume with 109 folios of large parchment (365 mm x 265 mm). It is illustrated with nearly 500 polychrome representations of plants, animals and minerals, which were all used as primary materials to produce drugs. 41

In the 12th century, the first copies of romances appear, which were destined to become the most famous profane texts of the Middle Ages and that offered the miniaturist the possibility of expressing his talent in an infinite variety of subjects; towards the end of the 14th century, they began to copy and miniate the masterpieces of contemporary medieval literature: Dante, Petrarch, Boccaccio, Chaucer. *Books of Hours* also emerged as the most popular book, used for private devotions. In addition, vernacular languages became increasingly popular alongside Latin texts.

The most precious illuminated manuscripts became the object of a real and proper collection on the part of the great patrons; in the 13th and 14th centuries, the court of Burgundy and Flanders became the hub of production for the most famous manuscripts of that period; the Duke of Berry (1340-1416), brother of King Charles V of France, possessed a splendid library with more than three hundred manuscripts; Jean de Berry is the great exemplar of late medieval patronage, and one of the greatest patrons of art of all time. In his library there were some of the most beautiful books in the world.

The Duke commissioned fifteen lavish Books of Hours: the most celebrated of all is the *Très Riches Heures du Duc de Berry*. This was begun around 1410 by the Limbourg brothers, whose work exemplifies the courtly style prevalent in various European centers around 1400, which combined elegant, sinuous figures, decorative colour, and selective realism in pictorial details such as animals, insects, or plants. 42

Although left incomplete after their death, the decoration continued over several decades by other artists and owners. The manuscript contains 66 large miniatures and 65 small.

Another outstanding Book of Hours from the Duke's collection is the *Belles Heures:*

"Created between 1405 and 1408 or1409, probably in Paris, the Belles Heures, or Beautiful Hours, a private devotional book, is one of the most sumptuous manuscripts to have come down to us from the Middle Ages. Commissioned by Jean de France, duc de Berry from the Limbourg brothers, the most gifted artists of their time, it is the only manuscript completed by them in its entirety. The richly illustrated text is enhanced by seven unprecedented picture cycles devoted to Christian figures or events that held special significance for the duke. Using a luminous palette, the artists blended an intimate Northern vision of nature with Italianate modes of figural articulation. The keen interest in the natural world and the naturalistic means of representing it, so striking in the 172 illuminations, foreshadow the work of Jan van

Eyck and the ensuing generations of outstanding 15th-century painters in the South Netherlands." **43**
Among many other stunning Books of Hours worth mentioning, we like to cite *The Hours of Jeanne d'Evreux*:
"The 209 folios of The Hours of Jeanne d'Evreux include 25 full-page paintings with paired images from the Infancy and Passion of Christ and scenes of the life of Saint Louis. The figures are rendered in delicate grisaille (shades of gray) that imparts an amazingly sculptural quality, and the images are accented with rich reds and blues and touches of orange, yellow, pink, lilac, and turquoise. In the margins, close to 700 illustrations depict the bishops, beggars, street dancers, maidens, and musicians that peopled the streets of medieval Paris, as well as apes, rabbits, dogs, and creatures of sheer fantasy. All are brought to life by the keen observation, accomplished draftsmanship, and consummate imagination of the artist.
This lavishly illustrated prayer book (Book of Hours) was created between 1324 and 1328 for Jeanne d'Evreux, queen of France, by the celebrated Parisian illuminator Jean Pucelle (active ca. 1320– 34) and was intended for use by the queen during private prayer throughout the course of the day. Upon her death in 1371, Jeanne d'Evreux left the prayer book to King Charles V. At his death, the book entered the collection of another much lauded bibliophile, his brother Jean, Duke of Berry." **44**
In Italy, in the 15th century, Federico of Montefeltro had the biggest and most prestigious collection of books of his time, and between thirty and forty copyists worked at his court; no less prestigious was the Court of Este, where Taddeo Crivelli and other artists illustrated what is considered to be among the most precious illuminated manuscripts of all time, the *Bible of Borso D'Este*. This Bible consists of two folio volumes of more than 1,000 individual

illuminations; the miniatures were executed between 1455 and 1461.

The completion of an important manuscript required a certain number of years; we know, for example, that to copy and miniate the *Bible of Winchester* took fifteen years, without the work being totally completed; it took ten years for the *Bible of Borso D'Este*, and sixty years for the Duke of Berry's most famous Book of Hours, completed in two different times by different artists. 45

The colours in "De Arte Illuminandi"

In the early Middle Ages, art had a character that was predominantly religious, and the artists who worked in anonymity inside the large monasteries were above all religious, though often flanked by lay artists; however, from the 12th century onwards, art began to move gradually from the monasteries to the cities; one of the consequences of the progressive secularization of art was an ever-growing and higher specialization among artists; in this way, the first corporative organizations of arts and crafts were formed, to safeguard the work of the craftsmen from the rivalry and the economic uncertainty, but it also established strict rules and distinctions in the execution of the profession: a painter could not execute the skilled work of the miniaturist and vice-versa; the statute of the corporation also decided which materials could or could not be used, and for what purpose; for example, the use of the most precious materials was only allowed for important subjects; one became a member of a corporation after years of apprenticeship in a workshop, and the qualification of "master" (one authorized to accept commissions) was obtained after having presented an artwork of one's own to the corporation, as evidence of the skill attained; therefore, being a painter meant belonging to a well-defined corporation and exercising a profession for a fee; these changes were well accepted also through the art of writing treatises, which, in turn, became more specialized. The "De Arte Illuminandi" (On the Art of Illumination) is the only medieval treatise to have been passed down to us, which deals only with miniature. The manuscript, compiled by an anonymous author in an Italian workplace, goes back to the end of the 14th century and was discovered in the National Library of Naples, in 1872. This text illustrates exhaustively the various phases of the illuminators' work, the tools used, the materials for the colours and the method of preparing and using them, and the pictorial techniques.

As has already emerged in part from the previous treatises, the number of raw materials from which the colouring substances were extracted, and which were in common with the art of dyeing, shows itself to be even more relevant here; in painting, the colours of vegetable origin had poor resistance to the more direct exposure effects of light and air; on the contrary, in illumination the action of the atmospheric agents is extremely limited and the colours have remained unaltered for centuries, even if they are of an organic nature.

The room where the illuminator carried out his work had to be very similar to an alchemist's laboratory; before the bloom of commerce permitted a more rapid finding and purchase of raw materials, the illuminator had to equip his workroom with a series of products able to do any sort of auxiliary work that was necessary for the fulfilment of the artistic operations, such as the preparation of the glues, the colours, the beating of the metal leaves for silvering and gilding, as well as the construction of the instruments for the drawing, the painting and the polishing: the goose feather for writing and designing the borders, the metal point for the outline of the drawing, the paintbrushes of various sizes, made from the hairs of squirrels' tails; marble pestles and mortars for the grounding of the mineral colours or bronze ones for the harder stones, such as lapis lazuli and jasper, or of gold for precious metals. Then, there was a vast series of containers of every type and material for the conservation and depuration of the various substances, such as phials, alembics and filters, and then oxen horns, leather bags, shells or turtle shells to preserve the colours, burnishers for polishing the gilding and also for smoothing the parchment leaves, a great number of *clothlets* for preparing water colours; illumination is, in fact, a water painting, and the coloured pieces of cloths were the typical water colours of the illuminators; the clothlets were small pieces of clean, linen fabric, that acted as a portable reservoir for the pigment. The clothlet was soaked in alum water and dried, then vegetable juices were squeezed onto the cloth which was then dried again. This procedure was repeated several times until the pigment built up. 46

"Clothlets were a most convenient form of colours for illuminators. It was only necessary to put a bit of clothlet into a dish, and wet it with a little glair of gum of water, and the colour would dissolve out of the cloth into the medium, forming a transparent stain. A good many colours were prepared in this way for late medieval book painting, as transparent colours came to be more and more prized by the painters of miniatures. Almost any coloured vegetable juice could be prepared in this way...." 47

In the index book IX of the "De Arte Illuminandi", the method of preparation of folium clothlets is described: the pieces of linen were bathed once or twice in limewater, obtained by putting out the quicklime in water, then washing them in clear water and letting them dry. Once they were well-dried, they were dipped into the dye extract, well-soaked and left immersed in the dye for a whole day, after which the clothlets were spread out on racks placed on a bed of earth soaked in stale urine, and they were left for three or four days or until they were completely dried out; the ammoniacal vapours that exhaled from the urine that had been exposed to air for a certain time, created an alkaline environment which acted as a fixative on the colour; in the case of folium, the ammoniacal vapours also developed the blue colour. In order to preserve them up until the moment of use, the clothlets were placed between the pages of books or in well-sealed glass vases, and quicklime was then put inside as a protection against dampness.

Arabian gum and egg white were the binders most-used; the use of fish-glue was quite frequent; egg white was also used for the final varnishing of the painted parchments, so giving a delicate, superficial gloss to the colours; for a brilliant mixture of colour, a mixture of Arabic gum, albumen and a bit of honey were used. Other types of glue were used for different purposes, such as the sizing of parchments before executing the pictures, or for the adhesive mixtures for gilding; to preserve the solutions of gums, glues and albumen for a long time, a small dose of antiseptic was added, usually camphor, cloves or realgar (the latter has an effective power to impede the putrefaction of the albuminoids).

Fermented urine and lye were the alkalizing products most used for the extraction of the main organic dyes that were obtained from flowers, woods and roots of native plants, as well as exotic ones.

In order to obtain the yellows, the author of "De Arte" mentions fine gold, yellow earth (yellow ochre), saffron, orpiment, turmeric roots and "dyer's grass", one of the terms by which *Reseda luteola* (Weld) is called in the various treatises. Saffron was intensely cultivated in central Italy and already in the 13th century it was an export product, above all towards Germany, and this is why a mention of it can be found both in the Italian and German recipe books; the colourant was extracted from the inflorescence stigmas which, once immersed in alkalized water, released a brilliant yellow orange colour; it was also used in illumination to revive gilding, but it was not used much in painting because of its poor lightfastness. A beautiful yellow lake was obtained from *Reseda luteola*, making the extracted colourant precipitate with alum and incorporating white powders such as powdered lead white or marble. In order to obtain green, green earth or mixtures of orpiment and indigo were used; a very pure green was obtained from blue lilies (*Iris germanica*): here is the recipe according to D.V. Thompson Jr.'s translation: *"Take these fresh flowers in the springtime when they are blooming, and pound them in a marble or bronze mortar; and squeeze the juice with a cloth into a glazed porringer. And in the juice soak another linen cloth, clean and soaked once or twice in a solution of rock alum and dried. And when the cloths are thoroughly saturated with the juice of the lilies in this way, let them dry in the shade, and keep them between the leaves of books; for a very lovely green, splendid for use on parchment, is made out of this juice preserved in this way by combining it with giallorino. And note that after the cloths are dry, if they are again soaked in this juice and dried, they will be better."* [48]

The author of the treatise also mentions "prugnameroli" - fruits from a plant that could be *Rhamnus catharticus* L., commonly called 'Spincervino' (Persian berries), - which is a shrub that belongs to the Ramnaceae family and grows wild in most of Europe; the fruits, also called "yellow grains" or "Avignon grains" are made up of a black drupe which is strongly purgative; they were used a lot for greenish yellow dyeing; in miniature, an aluminated lake, taken from the juice of such fruits to obtain green tones, was used.

Cinnabar (natural red mercury sulphide) and minium (red lead), clearly distinguished for the first time, were used for reds. A pinkish colour, called rosetta, was obtained from the extract of brazil wood; two types of rosetta were used for illuminating: one was a thick, opaque type, used for ornaments, the bodies of letters, fabrics and for shading the leaves; the other was a fluid and transparent type, used for shading or for glazing. To show what a long and laborious work was necessary for the preparation of colours in that era, here is the recipe for the first type of rosetta, according to D.V.Thompson Jr.'s translation:

' Rose color, otherwise called pink'
The body-color pink is made in this way. Take some of the best brazil wood (and this is the way to test <the best kind>: if you put it in your mouth, it tastes sweet when you chew it, and changes to rose color), and with a knife or a piece of glass scrape off as much of this wood as you want and put it into a lye made from the wood of vines or oaks (and if the lye is older it is better). And put this into a glazed dish which will stand the heat: and have the lye cover this brazil, so that whatever part of it is extractable may be thoroughly extract by this lye. And let it stand in this lye for a night or a day to soften. Then put it on the fire, and heat it to the boiling point, but do not let it boil; and stir it often with a stick. Then take account of how much scraped brazil there was, and take the same quantity of very nice white marble very thoroughly worked up on the porphyry to an impalpable powder, or scraped with a knife, and as much sugar alum or rock alum as there is of the brazil. And grinding them thoroughly, mix them gradually in this dish, always stirring it with a stick, until the froth which it makes subsides, and it is well colored. And then it is strained through a linen or hempen cloth into a glazed or unglazed porringer. And know that some say that the lye, after it is well colored, should be strained through a cloth into a glazed dish; and after getting it fairly hot, they put in the alum and marble. And it will take up the color immediately; and the water will separate almost clear above it, and you pour it off carefully. And this is better. But the lye must be two weeks old, or made with rain water which has been spoiling in a stone jar or, as is most usual, in a hollow wooden vessel, because that water is

much the best and brings out the best color. Know, also, that some people consider it better to have the moisture of the lye soaked up by the porringer; and that others put it into a glazed jar, let it settle, and afterwards gradually and carefully draw off the lye and let the material dry. And still others hollow out a fired earthen brick and put the material into this hollow to dry. And when you want it to keep for a long time, work it up with gum water and let it dry; and put it away in small pieces. And if anyone wants to make it richer, he may, when he puts in the brazil, put into the lye with it some dyer's grain, if obtainable, to the amount of an eighth or a sixth part of the weight of that brazil, more or less, at will, because it makes a more permanent color and will be more beautiful; and proceed as above. However, it is a more beautiful color with the brazil alone than mixed with the grain. Do whichever you like. Likewise, if, into the brazil dissolved in lye as above, you put, for body, eggshells, kept overnight in strong vinegar, with the membranes removed in the morning, and washed with clear water and ground to an impalpable paste on the porphyry, together with rock alum in the weight aforesaid, and put it into a sieve of linen cloth, and pour the filtrate back into the sieve three or four times (and all the good substance will stay in the sieve), and you let it dry in this sieve, in a breeze, so that the sun does not strike it, and put it away, and do as before, it will be very good." **49**

Lampblack and vegetable coals were used to obtain black; lead white or ceruse was used to obtain white.

From the fruits of the *Chrozophora tinctoria* is obtained the juice called "folium" – already described in this chapter – ; it is also mentioned as "torna-ad-solem" herb, (English = turnsole) a term that corresponds to the French "tournesol en drapeau". The illuminators' clothlets soaked in folium juice and exposed to ammoniacal vapours, took on a wine colour and they were also used for the preparation of cosmetics and for the dyeing of textile fibres, including silk. The already-known mixture of indigo and lead white or azurite or "ultramarine" were advised, for obtaining sky-blues. 'Azuro de la Magna' is the term for azurite most commonly used in the 14th century medieval treatises where 'Magna' is a corruption of the medieval Italian name 'Alemania', the European territory which corresponds to present day Germany; even if some deposits of azurite were also found in the Siena region, the greatest quantity came from Germany and this is why, in the Medieval and subsequent treatises, we find it under the name that reminds us of its place of origin. The mineral was ground on stone with dense gum water, then washed with water, filtered to rid it of impurities and left to dry before being used; in the "De Arte", it is advised to dilute it with Arabic gum and a few drops of albumen. "Ultramarine blue" was considered to be "the best of all"; this colour is one of the great conquests of the Middle Ages in the creation of new pigments; the blue mineral from which it was obtained was lapis lazuli, the 'caeruleum shyticum' of the classics; yet, in ancient times, a method of purifying it from those impurities that often gave it a greyish hue, was still unknown; in the Middle Ages, between the 12th and 13th century, a method of extracting the colour and leaving it free from any remaining impurity was discovered, so obtaining a splendid and really pure, deep blue. It has been calculated that about 100 kilos of mineral were needed to obtain between two and three kilos of pigment; after having ground the lapis lazuli, the powder was mixed with waxes, oils and resins, until a malleable paste was formed; the paste was wrapped in a cloth and immersed in a container of very diluted wood ash; it was then worked with the hands until the fine particles of blue mineral, the lazulite, spread throughout the liquid and settled on the bottom; the wood ash was then thrown away and the deposited pigment was collected and left to dry; the impurities – calcite, sodalite and pyrite, remained, on the contrary, incorporated in the waxy mass.

This operation was repeated many times; the colour that was liberated in the first phase of purification was the best, as it was formed of bigger particles, that is those with the deepest and most luminous colour; the subsequent extractions left a pigment of a less intense colour and therefore of an inferior quality; in the final phase, a colour tending towards gray was obtained, which was called "ultramarine ashes", and was used in painting, especially to create glazing with transparent oils, of a pale blue; all qualities of ultramarine were used in painting, with prices that varied considerably from the best to the poorest quality. In spite of the very high cost, the illuminators always made great use of the best ultramarine, also thanks to the fact that very small quantities were necessary; in painting, on the other hand, they tried to reserve its use for works of particular importance, destining the precious colour to the central figure in the painting, or when one wanted to underline the higher rank, compared to the others present in the painting.

The sky-blues in Medieval art

The high cost was indeed the only contraindication that could limit the use of ultramarine in painting; it was, in fact, a colour suitable for all pictorial techniques, endowed with a good covering power, and with an excellent stability to all atmospheric agents and to lime; in fact, the results of the tests carried out on paintings up until now, show that there have been very few cases of colour alteration throughout the centuries. The less costly alternatives gave very different results; indigo, the only alternative with a deep tone that was similar to that of ultramarine, tended easily to change in the light, like all colours of an organic nature; azurite produced a very delicate tone of blue if very finely grounded; to obtain a tone that was close to that of ultramarine, the ground granules had to be left fairly big, and this complicated the application as egg tempera could no longer be used, and an animal glue was needed to be able to mix it in the proper way, and this involved the spreading of many layers of pigment in order to have a dense colour with good covering power; the final result was a beautiful sky-blue, though unusable in the fresco where azurite, on contact with the water left by the plaster, became green and changed into malachite, as it happened, for example, in the frescoes painted by Cimabue on the ceiling of the Superior Church of Assisi and in a great many other Medieval frescoes, where skies and waters have become green; in other cases, the azurite became very dark, almost black; this is the case, for example, of the Virgin's cloak in the *Madonna Rucellai* (Uffizi, Florence), painted by Duccio di Buoninsegna in 1285 and which seemed very dark before being cleaned, and also that of the Virgin of the *Annunciation* by Simone Martini,1333, (Uffizi, Florence); in most cases, the blackening of the azurite is due to the yellowing of the oil or to the resins of the varnishing; parts of the varnish can remain trapped between the large particles of the pigment; in such cases, the attempts made in the past to remove the paint with strong alkaline solutions proved to be inefficient, and even contributed to a further darkening. In any case, azurite remained the raw material that was most used in tempera painting as a substitute for ultramarine; it was often sold as ultramarine and, given the similarity of the colours of the two minerals, whoever manufactured the colours had to verify their true nature every time, with the help of a method already known to the classics: a fragment of the mineral was heated until it became incandescent, then it was left to cool; the azurite became black, while the lapis lazuli did not change colour. Ultramarine was generally used for the more important commissions; one significant example is the *Maestà* by Duccio, painted between 1308 and 1311 for the main altar of the

Cathedral of Siena; tests carried out on the pigments during the restoration have revealed the presence of ultramarine in many parts of the painting, and no other types of blue were found. Ultramarine has also been identified in the Virgin's cloak in the exquisite *Trittico* by Duccio, now in the National Gallery in London. In spite of this, azurite was widely used in many of the altarpieces produced by Duccio and by his workshop, also in the Virgin's cloak, as seen in the *Madonna Rucellai*, commissioned for a chapel of Santa Maria Novella in Florence in 1258; in this case, given the importance of the commission, the use of azurite in place of ultramarine is rather surprising; as in the *Polyptych No. 28,* conserved in the picture-gallery of Siena, the analysis with infra-red rays has shown that the Virgin's cloak and St. Paul's robe are in azurite, while ultramarine was reserved for St. Peter's robe and for the corner rising above St. Peter; in this way, Duccio underlines the greater importance given to St. Peter, even though the reasons are unknown. In Simone Martini's works and in his workshop, there was a considerable use of ultramarine of the best quality, an even greater use compared to his contemporaries in Siena; Ambrogio Lorenzetti uses ultramarine for the most important works and azurite for less prestigious commissions; in some cases, the use of a small quantity of ultramarine on top of a layer of azurite has been identified: a technique, this, adopted successfully also by other artists, which allowed one to obtain a dense and intense blue with a more reduced use of ultramarine. The artists, through the use of ultramarine and probably on the customers' request, underlined and drew attention to favourite saints or to the figure of the patron; it was a purely artistic way of expressing one's devotion and/or of displaying the patron's wealth. 50

Another alternative blue was supplied by the so-called 'smaltino', that is, smalt, which is a potassium glass of a blue colour, owing to the addition of minimum and variable quantities of cobalt oxide during its manufacture; cobalt oxide was smelted together with potassium carbonate and silica; the mixture was poured into cold water where it disintegrated into small particles which were then ground.

Smalt was very resistant to light and lime, but, being a glass pigment it was transparent and consequently had scarce covering power; also, it was not very suitable for oil painting because of its tendency to turn opaque when it came into contact with oily binding media. The production of vitreous smalts began in the ancient Mesopotamian civilization and cobalt oxide is present in the paints and in the vitreous coatings of Ancient Egyptian vases; smalt was widely used in China from the Tang dynasty onwards for glazed ceramics, and powdered smalt used as a pigment has been identified in Chinese murals dating back to between the 11th and the 13th centuries. 51

The principal source of cobalt used in the preparation of blue smalt in Europe since the Middle Ages, is the smaltite mineral, of which mines exist in Saxony and in the Scandinavian peninsula; successively, it is probable that also other cobalt minerals were used, such as erythrite and cobaltite, which is present in mines situated in Norway, in India and in Azerbaigjan. For a long time, the use of smalt as a pigment remained widespread almost exclusively in the Orient; few examples of its use in painting in the Middle Ages have been found in the Italian area; one example are the mural paintings in the *Loggia dei Cavalieri,* in Treviso, that were executed at two different times: the tempera paintings go back to 1200; the fresco ones to 1300 and they depict the assault of Troy. The tests on the pigments that were used have revealed the use of ochre and earth for the yellows, reds, greens and browns, of minium and cinnabar for the more vivid reds, of lampblack for the black and of enamelled blue for the azures. 52

One should not exclude the possibility of an Oriental, or more precisely, a Byzantine influence on the use of enamel in these paintings, that were probably executed by artists coming from the Eastern Empire. However, starting from the fifteenth century, the Italian painters, too, began to use it increasingly and Venice, the "city of colour", became one of the most important centres for the production of smalt.

"The Book of Art" of Cennino Cennini

A document of exceptional importance is the treatise written at the end of the fourteenth century by Cennino Cennini, a painter from the school of Giotto, who worked for twelve years in the workshop of Agnolo Gaddi, son of Taddeo. Cennini's treatise is a precious testimonial not only for the history of art, but also for the history of technique; it fully introduces the reader into the environment that was typical of a Florentine workshop in the late fourteenth century, where one obtained a high qualification in exchange for a long and tedious apprenticeship; one learned everything in the workshop and the figure of the master is no longer that of the medieval craftsman, at the service of the Church and Our Lord, but rather that of an intellectual who achieves glory and prestige, just like the most illustrious citizens; it is the secular attitude of revaluation of the social dignity of art which is gradually strengthened as the middle class of the corporations gains more social power – especially in fourteenth century Florence.

"... the changing social structure moved painting to a new milieu: from a craft concerned with adornment in a religious context to a trade performed by guildsmen for mercantile or noble patrons who drew on a wider range of subject matter. This change reflected a broader transformation of society in which mystery and magic – a world pervaded by spiritual forces, a world in which icons had real

power – gave way to commerce, to the primacy of trade over religion, to a practical outlook. To some degree the same process overtook alchemy itself, which kept the trappings of its mystical roots but which was, to a craftsman like Cennino, simply a means of manufacturing. These trends reached their logical conclusion in the centuries that followed, as the forces of rationality began to challenge the authority of the Church and as painters transformed their practice into a wholly secular discipline: not a holy craft but a scholarly and intellectualized "liberal" art." **53**

For Cennini, painting is distinguished by its capacity to give form to imagination, interpreted as the artist's own capacity to imagine a reality that seems natural, and therefore it is to be put into second place as compared to science, but it is considered to have the same dignity as poetry, and therefore the dignity of liberal art. **54**

Cennini declares himself to be a pupil and follower of Giotto who *"changed the art of painting from Greek to Latin and made it modern: and had the most accomplished art ever seen..."*; Giotto had, in fact, brought a radical change to the conception, methods and aim of painting; he overturned the medieval artistic orthodoxy; Ball explains that for the medieval artists: *" painting was a way of telling a story without words. What mattered was that each of the important characters could be clearly identified in the scene, in positions and at a scale that suited their status, and in colors that encoded symbolic meanings and redounded to the splendor of the Lord."*

(In Giotto)" Real human experience is emphasized in preference to the eternal, transcendent verities of theology. Religious scenes contain people who look lifelike, not cartoon-like, and they appear as they might have been seen in the instant. One can say that Giotto's naturalism makes time a component of painting – the image is no longer an immutable symbol but becomes fixed at a moment in real, passing time." **55**

Therefore, for Cennini, the value of art is no longer to be sought only in the primacy of the perfection of the execution techniques derived from the rituality of Byzantine art, linked to the dogma of orthodoxy. The values of that art now become enriched by the strength and novelty of devising and invention, an introduction and a guide to the successive phases of execution. 56

For Cennini, design is not only a preparatory phase of the opera, but has its own autonomous ideal and theoretic value; it is not the design with a simple outline, characteristic of the Byzantine or Romanesque tradition, but a design of light and shade, typically giottesque, that shapes the figures, so giving them plasticity; the light, coming from an individual source, puts the objects in relief; the drawing, or in other words the light and shade relief, is therefore the initial and central moment of the creation, and the colour, like the drawing, will be continually shaped by light tones and by darker ones. As regards the colours, it is their exploitable ductility that matters and not their material preciousness; a hierarchy of the materials valid in themselves for their intrinsic preciousness, as established by Theophilus no longer exists; Cennini explains how to prepare and dose the colours so as to value exclusively their artistic potentiality, or in other words, their capacity to fully accomplish the artist's requirements. Among the aspects that distinguish this treatise from the preceding ones and also from other, subsequent ones, there is also the language used by the author, who writes in vernacular, in a clear, direct, concise style, aimed at expressing the fundamental of the topic in question. These characteristics of Cennini's work place the Book of Art at the limit of two periods but with a clear projection towards the Renaissance. 57

"This text, unique in its kind, and up until now known only by few specialists in the field, is seriously taken into consideration today,

especially in the field of restoration, where this primary source of information is continually consulted." **58**

In Cennino's workshop

Cennino's treatise *"is not only a code for artists, but also a guide for the skilled workers of those marvellous, medieval laboratories in which every kind of decorative work was undertaken, and where one dedicated the same diligence, the same love, in the painting of an altar-piece or in the decoration of banners, chests or printed fabrics."* **59**

Every type and every phase of work carried out in the workshop is meticulously and clearly described, as are the materials and how to use them for the best, depending on the result that one wishes to attain. The "Book of Art" gives us a clear idea of the various work carried out in the workshop, where all that was prepared required time and dedication; the pupils started off doing the most humble tasks, like for example the grinding of the minerals for the colours or the cooking of the glues, it was a long apprenticeship and only the master's guiding could stimulate the pupil to know his own artistic personality; Cennino expresses himself like this at the close of chapter CIV:*" There are many who say that they have mastered the profession without having served under masters; do not believe it, for I give you the example of this book: even if you study it by day and by night, if you do not see some practice under some master, you will never amount to anything, nor will you ever be able to hold your head up in the company of masters"*. **60**

For Cennini, art is *" a balance between applying a style and relying on direct observation, between profiting from the master and refusing manneristic imitation (...) In this way, by creating on the basis of the teaching received from the master, by gratifying* nature, guided by imagination, the artist fully accomplishes his own personality." **61**

Cennino's colours

As we have already pointed out, colour, for Cennino, is a material like any other, which the artist moulds and uses according to his artistic inclination and therefore it is valued on the basis of its flexibility and yield in the various artistic techniques; the artist creates the colour and bends it to his ideas. The raw materials mentioned for the manufacture of colours do not introduce great novelties in comparison with those mentioned in previous treatises; the black from vine-shoots are indicated for the blacks, obtained by carbonizing vine-shoots and then grinding and drying them.

"Certain kinds of charcoal were regarded as much more satisfactory for ordinary painting purposes. Charcoal made from young shoots of grape vines is repeatedly referred to in medieval recipes as the 'nigrum optimum', the best of blacks. This material is called nowadays blue-black, because of the coolness that it produces in mixtures. Medieval painters took a good deal of troubles to secure a good quality of this vine black. It was important that the vine sprigs be thoroughly burnt and reduced to carbon, because otherwise the colour was brownish and unpleasant in consistency; but they must not be burnt in the air or they might be reduced to ashes instead of to carbon. So the vine sprigs used to be packed tightly in little bundles in casseroles, covered and sealed, and baked in a slow oven. The resulting charcoal was used in sticks for drawing; or for painting it was first powdered and ground up dry, and then mixed with water and ground for a long time between two hard stones". **62**

Lampblack consisted of a very fine powder, very light and velvety, which was simply the deposit of soot obtained by directing a flame onto a cold surface; here is Cennino's recipe according to D.V. Thompson's translation:

"There is another black which is made from burnt almond shells or peach stones, and this is a perfect black, and fine. There is another black which is made in this manner: take a lamp which is full of linseed oil, and fill the lamp with this oil, and light the lamp. Then put it, so lighted, underneath a good clean baking dish, and have the little flame of the lamp come about to the bottom of the dish, two or three fingers away, and the smoke which comes out of the flame will strike on the bottom of the dish, and condense in a mass. Wait a while; take the baking dish, and with some implement sweep this color, that is, this soot, off onto a paper, or into some dish; and it does not have to be worked up or ground for it is a very fine color. Refill the lamp with the oil in this way several times, and put it back under the dish; and make as much of it in this way as you need". 63

Cennini also speaks about a very soft, black stone, particularly suitable for drawing and which many experts have identified with graphite. Among the reds we find: artificial cinnabar, which must have been a normally manufactured product at that time, as the author omits giving the formula since it was to be found very easily, *"especially by asking of the friars"*, which leads one to assume that artificial cinnabar was also prepared in the convents; Cennini advises one to always buy it whole and neither crushed nor ground, because more often than not it is falsified with minium or brick dust, and he says not to forget that *"it is not its nature to be exposed to the air, but it stands up better on panel than on the wall; because, in the course of time, from exposure to the air, it turns black when it is used and laid on the wall"*64; and in fact, some types of cinnabar tend to darken in the light, and this change is more noticeable in the mural paintings which are not protected by varnish; the phenomenon is due to the tendency of the red mercury sulphide to change into the black modification; mercury sulphide is, in fact, dimorphic in nature: two types exist, a red one known as cinnabar and a black one known as half-cinnabar, that differentiate between themselves due to some chemical-physical characteristics such as colour, specific weight, temperature of sublimation, system of crystallization. The mercury sulphide has the propriety to change itself from one form to the other, if submitted to pressures like the combination with alkalis, for example lime; the exposition to atmospheric agents such as light and humidity; or the combination with metals contained in other colours, like for example lead white; in the manufacturing process of artificial cinnabar, obtained in a dry process, one passed from the black form to the red one, for the sublimation of the first and successive condensation. 65

'Sinoper', or in other words red ochre, is cited among the natural reds and is suitable for all pictorial techniques; in fact, all pigments with an iron oxide base, not being affected by alkaline substances - contained, for example, in lime - have been fundamental in the palette for frescoes from the Minoan age until today. The red ochre mixed with very white lime paste gives a colour called "Cinabrese", considered perfect for the flesh colour tones in fresco. Cennini then describes the preparation of a red from "*Amatisto o ver amatito*", and describes it as a "*very strong and solid stone*" that is beaten in a bronze mortar, as a porphyry one would break; on the basis of this characteristic, it must be red jasper, cited elsewhere as "lapis amatito", which is compact and very hard, and not, as some thought, hematite, which on the other hand is a soft and breakable mineral. As regards minium, it is considered good only for panel painting but obviously not in fresco, since " *it soon turns black, on exposure to the air, and loses its colour*"; Cennino refers to the facility with which red lead, on contact with air, changes into lead sulphur, which is black. Few lines are dedicated to Dragon's blood which, having the well-known defects of colours of an organic nature, is valid only for miniature.

The series of red colours closes with the one called "Lacca"; Cennino does not specify which type of lake; he says that there are various types and puts us on our guard against using the one made from cloth clippings as it does not last and loses its colour; this lake was obtained by the same method as that used for obtaining the "purpurissum" of the classics, that is by extracting the colour with wood ash or with human urine, from cloth clippings dyed red with kermes; excluding cochineal lake which was still unknown in Europe at that time, Brunello, as well as D.V.Thompson, note that the characteristics of this lake, as described by Cennino, -"*a lake which is worked with gum, and is dry, lean, granular, and looks almost black, and contains a sanguigne color*"- leads one to suppose that it was lac lake, a lake made from the gum lac, the resinous secretion left on the twigs by the scale insect *Kerria lacca* Kerr, which lives on some plants typical of India; the extraction of the dyeing material, the laccaic acid, is obtained by immersing the resin, broken into granules, in hot water. Precipitated with alums, the pigment (also known as Indian lac) was obtained. Cennini ends by saying that "…. *it is good on panel. And it is also used on the wall with a tempera, but the air is its undoing*". This gum lac was also used for dyeing red the silk that had been mordanted with alum, so obtaining a bright red colour similar to that of kermes and cochineal.

Among the yellow colours we find: yellow ochre which, according to the testimony of the author, was to be found in a considerable quantity, along with many other coloured earths, in some veins in the area of Colle Valdelsa; suitable, like all ochres, for frescoes and in mixtures with any other colour.

In Cennini's treatise, the most ancient mention known appears, of a yellow pigment called *giallorino*, of which it is said that "*it is a manufactured one. It is very solid and heavy as a stone and hard to break up. This color is used in fresco and lasts forever, that is, on the wall, and on panel with temperas. This color has to be ground, like the others aforesaid, with clear water; since it is very troublesome to reduce it to powder, you will do well to pound it in a bronze mortar; with this color, with other mixtures attractive foliage and grass colors are made. And as I understand it, this color is actually a mineral, originating in the neighborhood of great volcanoes; so I tell you that it is a color produced artificially, though not by alchemy."* 66

Brunello thinks that Cennini was referring to an old legend, according to which "giallorino" was to be found among the lava of Vesuvius. However, Cennini's description is not sufficiently clear to enable one to deduce what the real chemical composition of such a pigment was; some experts believe that it is lead-tin yellow, which, as it turns out, was used by Spinello Aretino, one of Cennini's contemporary artists, who used it in the painting of *Madonna and angels*, conserved in the Fogg Art Museum of Cambridge, Boston. The only antique formulas for the preparation of "giallorino" are contained in the so-called "Bolognese Manuscript" of the 15th century, in which the two procedures for obtaining lead-tin yellow are described; the most-used kind is the one obtained by melting lead dioxide with tin dioxide at a temperature of between 650° and 800° C; at 700 degrees one has a warm tone of yellow; at a higher temperature one has a lemon yellow tone. In the second kind, as well as lead and tin, silica is present, too; the components are heated up to 800°/900° degrees and the result could correspond to the pigment called " yellow glass" originally from Venice. Both types are suitable for frescoes, as they do not fear the action of alkalis, they have a good covering power and good lightfastness, but, like all lead compounds, they darken on contact with sulphides. On the contrary, according to other experts, it could be lead antimonate, the so-called Naples yellow or Egyptian yellow, already used in Mesopotamia to varnish ceramics; in fact *"the lead minerals are frequently accompanied by antimony ones in the same ore deposits, and a specific test for antimony has not always been done in the analysis of the samples that are defined as lead-tin yellow. Furthermore, in some cases at least, the pigments classified here as lead-tin yellow and Naples yellow could turn out to be analogous"*. 67

Another yellow pigment described by Cennino is orpiment:

*"A color known as orpiment is yellow. This color is an artificial one; it is made by alchemy and is really poisonous. And in color it is a handsome yellow more closely resembling gold than any other color. It is not for use on a wall, either in fresco or with temperas, because it turns black on exposure to the air...A mixture of some of this color, when mixed with Bagdad indigo gives a green color for grasses and foliage. Its tempera calls for nothing but size... Beware of soiling your mouth with it, lest you suffer personal injury."*68 So, Cennini warns us not to use orpiment in mural painting; it is, in fact, unstable in the presence of lime and dampness, and as well the sulphur freed by it reacts to the copper or lead, so forming copper sulphide and lead sulphide, both of them of a black colour; it can, on the contrary, be mixed with ultramarine and with iron-based pigments; Cennini also recommends mixing it with indigo, known here as "abaccadeo", or originating from Baghdad, because the oriental indigo was considered – and rightly so - to be of better quality; from this mixture, a lovely green, suitable for the colour of meadows and trees, could be obtained; orpiment was very poisonous due to the presence of arsenic sulphide and all of the treatises put one on guard against the danger to be run in blending it. The same warning is repeated for realgar, called "risalgallo" here, according to the medieval terminology, while in other texts it can be found as "risigallo"; in the Middle

ages, they also knew the way to prepare it artificially, by blending a mixture of sulphur and arsenic; it was not used much in painting because of its high toxicity and its easy alteration on contact with other colours; Cennini names realgar among the yellow colours; in actual fact, its colour is a lovely orange red; in natural mineral, however, it is mostly to be found associated with orpiment, which contributes to confusing its colour tone with the yellow of orpiment; in spite of numerous contradictions, orpiment and realgar were widely used, as we shall see, by the15th and 16th centuries Venetian painters.

As for saffron, one was warned not to expose it to the air, as it would lose its colour; Cennini advises it for miniature and for obtaining a perfect grass colour, by mixing saffron and verdigris: *"..take a little verdigris and some saffron; that is, of three parts let one be saffron; and it comes out the most perfect grass-green imaginable, tempered with a little size..."* The last yellow mentioned by Cennini is àrzica, " *This color is made alchemically, and is but little used. Working with this color is chiefly a matter for illuminators, and it is used more in the neighbourhood of Florence than anywhere else. This is a very thin colour. It fades in the open; it is not good on the wall; it is all right on panel. It makes a lovely green if you mix in a little azurite and giallorino."*69 In the Middle Ages, the term "àrzica" was used for various shades of yellow, but the one for which it was most commonly used was the yellow lake that was obtained by precipitating in alum the juice of Weld (or Dyers' Weld) blossom, and this is probably what it was, as Cennini says that it has no resistance to air, but he considers it suitable for miniatures.

After the yellows, Cennini inspects the greens; the "terre-verte" is obtained from green earth, it does not have a vivid tone, but it is very solid and is *"good for use in faces, draperies, buildings, in fresco, in secco, on wall, on panel, and wherever you wish...And if*

you temper it, as I will show you <for> the bole for gilding, you may gild with this terre-verte in the same way. And I know that the ancients never used to gild on panel except with this green."[70]
In fact, green earth was used a lot in the Middle Ages not only as a colour in painting, but also to prepare the bases for gilding or silvering, in place of the Armenian bole, a clay of a reddish-brown colour, used above all in the composition of mordants for gilding.
A colour called "verde azzurro"(Thompson translates it as 'malachite') and which Cennini considers good for secco painting and on wood panel should correspond to the chrysocolla of the classics; he says, in fact, that it makes azurite and therefore it must be a compound of copper, probably a mixture of powdered minerals of malachite and azurite. Another green was obtained by mixing orpiment and tempered indigo with glue. Good for wall and panel painting, it was a green resulting from a mixture of yellow and azurite and tempered with egg yolk; the addition of a little àrzica made it even more beautiful.
Always starting off with azurite, another attractive green was created, even though it was unstable in light: some drops of acid juice, obtained from wild plums, were added, which Brunello identified with Hawthorn fruit; in this way, the basicity of the azurite - made from basic copper carbonate - was lowered, so making the colour change from blue to green.
A green that was good on panel but not on wall was obtained by adding to the orpiment a greater or lesser quantity of ultramarine, depending on whether one wanted a darker or lighter shade of green. As regards verdigris, Cennini considered it good on panel, tempered with size, but warns us against putting it into contact with lead white as they are "mortal enemies", in fact, the basic lead carbonate (lead white) and the basic copper acetate (verdigris) react between themselves by dissociating. The last green is a mixture of lead white and green earth and Saint John's white for the frescoes.

Saint John's white and lead white were the two fundamental whites in painting, the first, perfect for fresco because of its excellent resistance to light, dampness and lime, was obtained from lime paste that was repeatedly washed in water, and then dried in the sun; the effect of the carbon dioxide contained in the air transformed the calcium hydrate into lime carbonate; the lead white or ceruse was also prepared in the Middle Ages according to the procedure of the classics: splinters of lead were suspended above a vase containing very strong vinegar; the lead, attacked by the acid vapours, was transformed into basic lead acetate, which fell bit by bit into the vinegar; the residue at the bottom was then collected, dried, ground, and mixed with vinegar, so forming small balls which, at the end, were dried in the sun where the basic lead carbonate was formed, due to the action of the carbon dioxide in the air. 71

Cennini says that it is good on board, but points out that, in fresco, it tends to blacken, and in fact, exposure to air and dampness cause the lead white carbonate to change into lead black sulphide; this phenomenon is particularly evident in the *"Crucifixion"* frescoed by Cimabue in the Superior Church (Chiesa Superiore) of St. Francis of Assisi; in the tempered paintings protected by varnishing, this phenomenon happens more rarely and anyhow, it is possible to intervene with special treatments in order to restore the blackened lead white. 72

In spite of its defects, lead white has always been used in all pictorial techniques and it is the only pigment used without interruption, from the classic age up to the end of the 19th century; in oil painting it is practically perfect, it becomes a soft paste that is easy to spread and does not crack.

Lastly, Cennini speaks about the characteristics and the preparation of the blues; the information is that which has already been described in this chapter; his judgment on ultramarine is a confirmation of the prestige in which this colour was held: "*Ultramarine blue is a color, illustrious, beautiful and most perfect beyond all other colors; one could not say anything about it, or do anything with it, that its quality would not still surpass. And, because of its excellence, I want to discuss it at length and to show you in detail how it is made. And pay close attention to this, for you will gain great honour and service from it. And let some of that color, combined with gold, which adorns all the works of our profession, whether on wall or on panel, shine forth in every object.*" 73

As for Cennini's formula for the preparation of ultramarine, it generally follows the methods already described and shows how laborious the process is, to obtain such a precious pigment: "*To begin with, get some lapis lazuli. And if you want to recognize the good stone, choose that which you see is richest in blue color, because it is all mixed like ashes. That which contains least of this ash color is the best. But see that it is not the azurite stone, which looks very lovely to the eye, and resembles an enamel. Pound it in a bronze mortar, covered up, so that it may not go off in dust; then you put it on your porphyry slab and work it up without water. Then take a covered sieve such as the druggists use for sifting drugs; and sift it, and pound it over again as you find necessary. And bear in mind that the more finely you work it up, the finer the blue will come out, but not so beautifully violet in color. It is true that the fine kind is more useful to illuminators, and for making draperies with lights on them. When you have this powder all ready, get six ounces of pine rosin from the druggists, three ounces of gum mastic, and three ounces of new wax, for each pound of lapis lazuli; put all these things into a new pipkin, and melt them up together. Then take a white linen cloth, and strain these things into a glazed washbasin. Then take a pound of this lapis lazuli powder, and mix it all up thoroughly, and make a plastic of it, all*

117

incorporated together. And have some linseed oil, and always keep your hands well greased with this oil, so as to be able to handle the plastic. You must keep this plastic for at least three days and three nights, working it over a little every day; and bear in mind that you may keep it in the plastic for two weeks or a month, or as long as you like. When you want to extract the blue from it, adopt this method. Make two sticks out of a stout rod, neither too thick or too thin; and let them each be a foot long; and have them well rounded at the top and bottom, and nicely smoothed. And then have your plastic in the glazed washbasin where you have been keeping it; and put into it about a porringerful of lye, fairly warm; and with these two sticks, one in each hand, turn over and squeeze and knead this plastic, this way and that, just as you work over bread dough with your hand, in just the same way. When you have done this until you see that the lye is saturated with blue, draw it off into a glazed porringer. Then take as much lye again, and put it onto the plastic, and work it over with these sticks as before. When the lye has turned quite blue, put it into another glazed porringer, and put as much lye again on to the plastic, and press it out again in the usual way. And when the lye is quite blue, put it into another glazed porringer. And go on doing this for several days in the same way, until the plastic will no longer color the lye; and then throw it away, for it is no longer any good. Then arrange all these porringers in front of you on a table, in series: that is, the yields, first, second, third, fourth, arranged in succession; and with your hand stir up in each one the lye with the blue which, on account of the heaviness of this blue, will have gone to the bottom; and then you will learn the yields of the blue. Weigh the question of how many grades of blue you want: whether three or four, or six, or however many you want; bearing in mind that the first yields are the best, just as the first porringer is better than the second. And so, if you have eighteen porringers of the yields, and you wish to

make three grades of blue, you take six of the porringers and mix them together , and reduce it to one porringer; and that will be one grade. And in the same way with the others. But bear in mind that if you have good lapis lazuli, the blue from the first two yields will be worth eight ducats an ounce. The last two yields are worse than ashes: therefore be prudent in your observation, so as not to spoil the fine blues for the poor ones. And every day drain off the lye from the porringers, until the blues are dry. When they are perfectly dry, do them up in leather, or in bladders, or in purses..."
74

Cennini then suggests a way of improving the tone of the ultramarine, in the case of the colour has not turned out to be perfect, that is, without that almost-purple shade that is typical of the highest quality; he advises one to mix a little kermes and sappan (one of the denominations of brazil wood) that has been previously boiled in wood ash and rock alum.

After the explanations on how to manufacture paintbrushes, Cennino dedicates the successive chapters to good fresco; this part is, even now, the most exhaustive explanation of the technique used in Florence and which then became widespread everywhere in the course of the XIV century. Once again, he warns us to use or avoid certain pigments according to the pictorial technique used, founded on the characteristics and on the reaction that every pigment has with the support materials and with the other pigments: *"You may use any of those colors that you used in fresco, in secco as well; but there are colors which cannot be used in fresco, such as orpiment, vermilion, azurite, red lead, white lead, verdigris and lac. Those which can be used in fresco are giallorino, lime white, black, ochre, cinnabrese, sinoper, terreverte, hematite. The ones which are used in fresco call for lime white as an adjunct, to make them lighter: and the greens, when you want to keep them as greens, call for giallorino; when you want to leave them as sage greens, use white. Those colors that cannot be used in fresco require white lead and giallorino as adjuncts, to make them lighter, and sometimes orpiment; but orpiment very seldom."* 75

In order to spread the colours and make them stick to the support (panel, cloth, wall) they need to be 'tempered' or in other words, diluted in a binding medium; the pigments do not melt in the binding media, but remain englobed, so remaining unaltered through time; the binding media used in Cennini's time stayed in use for centuries; in the so called tempera painting, the binding medium was composed of proteinous materials such as egg white, animal glues, or else of gums or resins; several binding media could be used in the same painting, depending on the pigment-binding combination that was considered to be best; in watercolour, the pigments are diluted in a watery solution of Arabic gum, with the possible addition of honey; in fresco, the colour is spread on a plaster of fine sand and lime; here, the binding medium is the lime paste; once dry, the fresco could be completed with finishing in temper, oil, with gilding and glazes. In oil painting, the binding medium is made up of siccative oils, such as linseed oil, walnut oil and poppy oil; these oils have the property of drying in the air, as they are able to absorb oxygen and, applied on the surface, they are transformed into a fine, solid and elastic film; the pigments dilute easily and the resulting mixture can be spread with a paintbrush on various supports, like wall, board and cloth. Linseed oil, despite the fact that it tends to yellow through time more than walnut or poppy oil, was the oil most used; oil painting is a very ancient technique; already in the classic age they knew the properties of the various oils that were used in mural paintings; linseed, as a binding medium, was mentioned by Theophilus and Cennino dedicates several chapters to oil painting on various supports and to the preparation of the oil itself; therefore, this technique was well-known and it would be inexact to continue to attribute its invention, based on the testimony of Vasari, to Van Eyck; it is true that, in Cennini's time, as he himself says, oil painting was much more practiced by the painters beyond the Alps, while the Italian painters preferred tempera painting; it is, therefore, much more likely that Van Eyck deserves the credit for having led the oil technique to perfection, and Antonello da Messina for having more widely diffused such a technique in Italy.

6) THE TRADITIONAL PALETTE OF THE LATE FOURTEENTH CENTURY FLORENCE

Ghirlandaio's workshop

The cleaning and restoration by the National Gallery of London of six panels all painted by Florentine artists in the last quarter of the fifteenth century have provided paint samples for the identification of the materials used; technical investigations made it apparent that most of the materials used are common in all the paintings and that the differences in their use are generally slight. The panels in question are two works by Botticelli (*Four scenes from the early life of Saint Zenobius* and *Three miracles of Saint Zenobius*, about 1500), one by an imitator of Filippo Lippi (*The Virgin and Child with an Angel* ca. 1480), one by Filippino Lippi (*The Virgin and Child with Saint John*, 1470s), one by Domenico Ghirlandaio (*The Virgin and Child* ca.1480) and one attributed to his brother David (*The Virgin and Child with Saint John*, 1480s). These similarities are of no surprise because all the above mentioned artists are linked to their city and to the tradition of Ghirlandaio's workshop which, in the late fifteenth century, becomes the training ground and the school for a significant part of future generations of artists, including the young Michelangelo. All painters mentioned herein remain faithful to a relatively conservative technical tradition; although some oil was used for specific colours, these panels have been executed with the egg tempera technique, often making use of gilded decoration.

It was probably a conscious rejection of the more experimental and innovative properties of the oil medium, contrary to what Pollaiolo, Leonardo da Vinci and the more conservative Perugino were already doing.

The continuation of this highly traditional technique until the last years of the fifteenth century is associated in particular to Ghirlandaio's workshop; Filippino Lippi, for example, as a pupil of Botticelli follows the technique of the tradition in the early years of his career, but he will abandon it around 1480 when he finds a style of his own and an entirely personal technique.

What is more striking is the consistent occurrence of the same materials in all the paintings and how limited their range was. Apart from the unavoidable use of lead white and carbon black, the same few pigments are used, both on their own and as components of very similar mixtures.

The two blue pigments, natural ultramarine and azurite are used interchangeably on both sky and draperies; among red pigments there are only the red, opaque vermilion and red lakes, mainly derived from lac; the lead-tin yellow was a standard material, but by this period only the 'type I' was used, in contrast to the regular appearance of the 'type II', based on glass manufacture, widely found in Florentine altarpieces of the fourteenth century. The only green pigment that occurs is malachite which becomes a standard presence in Italian fifteenth century palette and is widely used for fabrics, landscape and foliage, replacing the mixtures used in the fourteenth century to obtain green. It is assumed that the lack of alternatives to make satisfactory greens in egg tempera has encouraged the use of malachite which functions fairly well in egg unlike verdigris which works rather poorly in egg and the type of green earth, available by this time, which was too weak in colour and was only useful for underpainting flesh.

In the panels there is both natural and artificial malachite, prepared by precipitating soluble copper salts into an aqueous solution of calcium carbonate. The use of artificial malachite is not confined to Florentine paintings, but was also detected in panel paintings of the fifteenth century by Sienese, Venetian and Ferrarese artists, for example in the works of Sassetta, Bellini, Cosimo Tura and Cossa. In the sixteenth century, with the domain of oil painting, verdigris will be preferred to malachite.

The similarity in the choice of the binding medium is also consistent; in all the paintings lighter colours are pure egg tempera; all artists have employed some drying oil for darker and transparent shades of red, green and blue.

In several paintings copper resinate-type glazes prepared containing oil have also been detected; this tempera enriched with oil is called 'tempera grassa' which has also been used for red lakes. The technique of mordant gilding was equally traditional.

On the lines of the decoration an adhesive paste was spread, on which a gold leaf was laid; the exceeding parts were then removed and used for other works. Only in the two panels by Botticelli some gildings are made with shell-gold, a gold powder which was traditionally stored in a conch shell; treated as a pigment, gold dust was mixed in egg and applied by passing it with a quill or a quill pen; in manuscripts, instead, the binder was Arabic gum.

In conclusion, given the importance of the artists who executed the examined panels as well as that of the workshop in which they had been trained themselves, it can be assumed that the traditional Florentine palette of the late fifteenth century mainly consisted of the following pigments:

Lead white
Lead-tin yellow 'type I'
Yellow ochre
Vermilion
Red lake
Malachite, natural and artificial
Copper resinate for glazing
Green earth, used for painting the background
Natural ultramarine

Azurite
Carbon black 1

Purchasing pigments in 15th century Florence

The preparation of pigments was a time-consuming and labour-intensive work; the first task of a medieval apprentice in a painter's workshop was grinding raw materials and mixing paints.

Artist could purchase raw materials and, sometimes, ready-made pigments from apothecaries or from travelling merchants from Venice, Italy's most important trade centre.

We also know from Cennino that in 14th century Florence painters could purchase a wide range of refined pigments from the friars; in fact, in many convents and monasteries the monks had specialised in preparing pigments not only for their own use, but also for painters. Towards the end of the 14th century, a good number of monasteries had spread in central-northern Italy; they shared an alchemic-type work because of the need to prepare medicaments, and, in addition, many convents became specialised in a particular technical-artistic discipline: in Florence the Gesuati confraternity became famous for the manufacturing of stained glass; the Gesuati also played a role of primary importance in preparing high quality ready-made pigments for painters. Numerous documents testify the purchasing of pigments by famous artists, and this enables us to identify some of the pigments prepared in the friars' workshop. The oldest document tells us that in 1454 they were paid for providing Fra Filippo Lippi with blue pigments of the best quality; it is supposed that the preparation of a superior quality of natural ultramarine had become one of the main activities of the Florentine Gesuati: this pigment, in fact, as well as in the description by Vasari, is also mentioned in 8 different documents; among the purchasers we find Neri di Bicci, Botticelli, Leonardo da Vinci,

Domenico Ghirlandaio, Michelangelo Buonarroti, Filippino Lippi, Benozzo Gozzoli, who purchased ultramarine for the chapel of the Medici-Riccardi Palace in Florence, Pietro Perugino, who also drew the cartoons for many stained glass windows executed by the friars. (In Renaissance art, the term cartoon refers to a full-size preparatory design for an artwork in another medium. They were used in the creation of frescoes, other large-scale wall paintings, and for tapestries. The word cartoon derives from the Italian 'cartone', which simply means a large piece of paper. 2)

Azurite is mentioned in three documents and in other two its presence can be deduced because of its price, too low to be the expensive ultramarine blue.

We find mentioned 'verde azuro', usually intended as malachite.

Arzicha appears three times in Neri di Bicci's note book.

Giallorino, that is, lead-tin yellow, most probably of type I, was among the pigments requested by Leonardo da Vinci. It is also found in Neri's list under the name of 'German yellow'.

We find, then, orders of 'Lacca di cimatura' and 'Lacca' : the former is the already mentioned kermes or madder shearing lake, the latter is usually referred to as (Indian) Lac.

The surviving documents are incomplete, so we don't find vermilion or smalt, but we know that Cennino advises to buy ready-made vermilion from the friars; we also know that in the Sistina chapel Michelangelo used both ultramarine and smalt, and since the Gesuati ran a very active stained glass workshop, it is more than probable that they were also familiar with smalt manufacturing.

For almost one hundred years the Gesuati had provided artists with the finest pigments; one day, in October 1528, during the siege of Florence by the imperial troops, their convent was totally destroyed, thus putting an end to the Gesuati's production of pigments as well. 3

A very important artists' material, especially in medieval painting, was gold. Sienese and Florentine painters, being more tied to tradition, made large use of gold until the late 15th century. In Florence a good number of highly specialised craftsmen, called 'battilori' (gold beaters) provided painters with gold leaf. The gold beaters who worked for artists were members of the guild of Doctors and Herbalist. In the first half of the 15th century, in Florence, there were at least fifteen officially recognised gold beaters. The gold they used had to be pure, so it was established that the source of the gold leaf could only be the official gold mint, the florin in Florence, the 'ducato' in Venice, both of which were made of 24-carat gold. Compared to a gold alloy, pure gold offered many advantages:

".... it is not only brilliant and incorruptible, but it's also malleable and ductile. It is therefore ideal for making the thin sheets required for gilding painted surfaces. Its malleability and ductility enable extremely thin sheets (or leaf) to be produced, thereby reducing the cost, which was nevertheless always high. Cennino Cennini refers that <The gold to be worked should be produced at no more than one hundred sheets from one ducat coin, where they make up to145 sheets ....>

Several other types of gilding were commonly used and the lower quality gilding was applied following an established hierarchy based on the importance of the figures.

From a pure gold coin of fixed weight it was easy to establish the cost, and to indicate the quality of the gold leaf on the basis of the number of gold leaf sheets from one florin or from one ducat; hence the importance of the thickness and the fixed dimension of the sheets.

It seems that- perhaps even before the 14th century-it was possible to obtain 100 sheets from one florin or ducat; in Cennini's time this figure had already reached 145, and by the time Vasari was *writing, even more. The thickness of the gold leaf made from ducats or florins might be greater or lesser, but the sheet measure was standard .... the maximum size of a pure gold sheet was about 7,3 square centimetres. The availability of pure gold coins of fixed weight from the mid-13th century on, was an advantage not only for the world of trade, but also for the world of art, for painters, and for gold beaters".* 4

7) THE CITY OF COLOUR

Colour in Renaissance Venice

Venice became the theater of the great Renaissance season of colour; in Venice, more than in any other city, colour had for some time been assumed as a dominant means of expression, in social relationships and politics, as in art. According to the historians, the particular physical environment in which the city was immersed, contributed to this special attention and sensibility towards colour and towards the Venetian artistic style; the lagoon, which reflects the buildings of the city and changes the colours and nuances continually, with every variation of light; the same waters of the lagoon, which change from the deep blue of the sky to a brilliant green or a dark blue; the often-veiled atmosphere which softens the colours into a multitude of tones.

The houses of the Venetians, in their variety of colours, appear not to rise from the land, as neither their bricks nor their ceramic tiles share the same colour with that of the visible land on which they have been built, nor can the colour of the stones and marbles be compared with the tones and the characteristic aspect of the surrounding rocks or mountains; in the lagoon setting, the buildings and decorating materials acquire a different and distinct aspect and characteristics. By building on unstable land of a muddy foundation, the Venetians needed to keep the supporting structure of their buildings as light as possible; the walls were thinner than anywhere else and vaulted building in stone was almost unknown. On the grand Canal, which was the area most desired for the dwellings of the patricians, the palaces support one another like books on a shelf. There is no solution of continuity between the buildings and the colours. On a lagoon, the borders are not rigid, the tides rise and fall, the demarcation between the water and the buildings is never clear-cut; in no other city is the base line from which the architecture emerges so variable; the physical environment – its consistency and its colours – is extremely sensitive to the variations of time. After a storm, the waters of the canal and the lagoon lose their transparency, they take on a jade green colour, opaque and rippling. On limpid days, the waters are transparent, reflecting both the blue of the sky and the ochre, peach, and rusty red colours of the plasters; on the waters, a trembling mosaic is formed; its tesserae shade from deep orange to blue, to golden sand, in a continual passage of colour and movement of the water. 1

Real colours and reflected colours create an atmosphere of particular fascination and a special sensitivity to the vibration of light and colour; therefore, it is not surprising that in Venice rather than anywhere else, artists have made colour the most important means of expression.

But the tradition and habit of colour also came from the secular relations with the Orient, and from the inevitable flux that Byzantine art exercised on the 'Serenissima'; an art that was rich in masterpieces of goldsmith's art, of splendid mosaics and which favoured vivid colours and gold. Lazzarini remarks that:

"It is noted how, from Vasari onwards, all the treatisers identify Florence with design and Venice with colour. Even if it is partly to discredit, this simplification has an inkling of truth. In fact, it is easy to note how great and constant was the Venetians' love for colour. Not only were the external plasters of their houses frescoed or painted with vivid colours, as we can admire in the large canvases of Gentile Bellini and Carpaccio, and brilliant and contrasting were the tones of the paintings with which they decorated the interiors, but their appreciation and taste for coloured stones and marbles – in the Roman and Byzantine tradition – was enormous. There were so many, that not only were

the white ones often gilded and multi-coloured painted, but even marbles that were already coloured in themselves were gilded and painted, as it happened, for example, in the Ca' d'Oro, which the artist, Giovanni di Francia, decorated "in gold and colour" in 1431(...) If the Venetian school is characterized by colour, this is also owing to the great variety, quality and quantity of pigments and dyestuffs, to be found on the market in the late Middle Ages and in the Renaissance in Venice.

"This city, a very important crossroad for traffic and trade between East and West, has always been a privileged point of provision of those semi-precious minerals that arrived from the near and far East, and they were worked and refined, to then be exported and used as pigments in the whole of the West. Not only coloured "stones" arrived from far away, but also many colouring substances, which for centuries were used by the skillful Venetian dyers, and in the Eighteenth Century, for the varnishing of furniture. A by-product of these arts were those red and violet lakes which have contributed in a fundamental way to the chromatic success of the paintings of the Venetian school, so rich in enamels....The years that go from 1480 to 1580 cover an arc of time that is distinctive for Venetian painting. They take in, in fact, the sphere of activity in the workshops of the Vivarini and of Bellini, the affirmation of the strong personalities of Carpaccio and of Cima, and of the innovative ones of Giorgione, of Tiziano, of Lotto and of Pordenone, of Sebastiano del Piombo and of Paolo Veronese..." 2

The analysis carried out by Lorenzo Lazzarini in the preliminaries of restoration, have allowed us to know the wide range of pigments used by the Venetian painters in the century which he has taken into account, and to highlight the preferences of the various artists in the field of pigments, and their different techniques in the use of colour. One needs to remember that Venice was not only the biggest and most important emporium for imported raw materials: already from the end of the 15th century, Venice refined and produced a wide range of pigments and auxiliary substances of the best quality; at the beginning of the 16th century, plants for the production of vermilion or artificial cinnabar, and for the purification of orpiment, were active; smalt, a by-product of the glassworks of Murano – which was used in painting from the beginning of the sixteenth century, and which had already been used in precedence, to colour the glass blue and to glaze the ceramics - was produced as well; its invention is generally thought to go back to the Italian glassmakers of the fourteenth century, but the idea could also have arrived from the Near East, where the cobalt materials were used by the Egyptians to colour glass, and by the peoples of ancient Mesopotamia, to obtain enamels and blue pigments; if pulverized too finely, smalt loses its lovely dark blue colour but on the other hand, if the powder is too grainy, its use in painting becomes difficult; if mixed with oil, smalt loses considerably its best tones; this in spite of the fact that the Venetian painters used it a lot also in oil painting.

In Venice, beautiful greens (copper based resinates) were prepared, combining them with Venetian turpentine resin which, spread like enamel, formed the colour of dresses and cloaks in many Venetian paintings; in some islands of the lagoon, the famous Venetian lead white – considered to be the best on the European market - was produced along with lead-tin yellow, verdigris, and in particular lake-pigments, a by-product of the dyeing industry: brazil wood, kermes, grain and madder were the raw materials used for preparing the very beautiful reds and purples of the cloaks and dresses in the paintings of Veronese, Titian and Tintoretto; lakes were sold in little balls of various sizes, while the other pigments were sold in blocks or in powder, conserved in jars with the inside in glazed ceramic. [3]

Venice was, without doubt, the most important European centre for procuring pigments that were otherwise not to be found in other cities, like for example the red lakes, of which the production was still a novelty during the 15th century and until the end of the following century, and Venice had practically the exclusivity.

The Renaissance palette had only a few new pigments compared to the Medieval one, yet in this period a range of colours and shades that had never been seen before, appears; what puts such a vast choice at the artist's disposition derives, in reality, from an attitude that was very different from the preceding one regarding the conception of colour, and from the different way of using it which is subsequently made; as well, from the different function that colour assumes for the Renaissance artist, for whom the theological worries of the Middle Ages no longer exist, and the materials have definitely lost all of their symbolic meaning as now, the aim of the artist is to portray the world in a naturalistic way.

"….the strident vermilion, gold or ultramarine color fields of the Middle Ages were unacceptable to an artist whose audience no longer prized the pigments for their own sake, and whose objective was color harmony rather than an ostentatious show of wealth…..One of the clearest indicators of the decline in the Medieval role of pigments as a display of conspicuous consumption is the use of gold. Gilding is clearly nonnaturalistic: gold leaf laid on a flat surface does not look like a three-dimensional golden object…..The artist's skill derived not from rote learning of stylized conventions in a workshop apprenticeship, but from rational apprehension of nature's laws and principles. (…) style, not technical skill, was becoming the painter's most marketable attribute." 4

The introduction of the techniques of oil-painting contributed, in turn, to overcome the old taboo of mixtures; the Venetian painters are the first to widely experiment the possibilities offered by the new technique, using them to create luminous and bold colours.

In oil-painting, the colours are mixed with the so-called siccative oils, which dry slowly, forming an elastic skin that is water-resistant; we are dealing mainly with linseed, walnut and poppy oil, already known and used in ancient times and in the Middle Ages; nevertheless, it was only in the 15th century that, thanks to the Flemish artist, Van Eyck, this technique was brought to the utmost perfection. Ball says:

"... van Eyck realized that the glazing process was of tremendous value for the artist, who, by judicious technique and patience, can obtain deep, rich and stable colors that egg tempera alone can never match. He developed glazing from a craftsman's decorative technique into a method suitable for the finest of paintings. Van Eyck's technique was to glaze oils on a tempera ground, combining the quick drying of the latter with the rich luster and blending possibilities of the former. Thus it would be wrong to imagine painters abruptly ditching their tempera methods for the new approach:the two coexisted for a long time and are well suited to such a marriage. A mixture of tempera and oils is very common in fifteenth-century art; one of the earliest examples is Cosimo Tura's gorgeous 'Allegorical Figure' (c. 1459-1463).

"The glaze acts as a kind of color filter: a red lake glaze over a blue ground, transforms it to rich purple. By carefully building up layers of oil glazes, van Eyck produced saturated, jewel-like colors that look as sensuous today as they must have seemed at that time. It is hard to imagine his 'Virgin of the canon Van der Paele' (1436) ever being any richer than it is now, and the fabulous chromaticity of his Arnolfini Marriage (1434) makes it one of the most admired works in the Western canon. ...

"The Italians were already experimenting with oils in the early fifteenth century; by the century's end, it had become their

predominant medium. Oil paints have other advantages that enhanced their popularity. In oil, each pigment particle is "insulated" by a layer of fluid. So pigments that react chemically with one another in tempera might be stably combined in oil. The painter could then be less fearful about making up complex pigment mixtures on the palette. And the slow-drying nature of the paint is a benefit to the naturalistic painter, offering the opportunity for blending tones and blurring outlines on the canvas. (...) The sharp contours characteristic of tempera work gave way to new styles as oils encouraged painters to engage physically with their materials. Towards the end of his life, Titian was described by one contemporary commentator as painting <more with his fingers than with his brushes> (…) But *changing the medium invariably changes the paint box. Oils, like any binding medium, do not carry raw pigment without modifying its appearance.*

"As the refractive index of the oils differs from that of egg yolk, pigments are not necessarily the same color in both. Ultramarine in oil is blacker than in egg tempera; the rich blueness is recaptured by mixing it with a little lead white. In the face of this insult to its purity, ultramarine could scarcely retain its medieval mystique. Similarly, vermilion – the red jewel of the Middle Ages – appears less vibrant in oil, and red lakes were awarded greater favor. The low refractive index of green malachite leaves it fairly transparent in oil, and its use declined. Verdigris suffers similarly in oils and was commonly mixed with lead white or lid-tin yellow to restore opacity.

"An alternative green called copper resinate, a copper salt of organic acids found in wood resins, became popular around the middle of the fifteenth century. (…) The pigment was made from verdigris, typically by combining it with turpentine resin extracted from pine trees. (…) This new green was used enthusiastically throughout the late fifteenth and sixteenth centuries, notably by

Giovanni Bellini, Raphael, Gérard David, Tintoretto and Paolo Veronese. But its disappearance soon thereafter, may indicate that its Achille's heel had already become apparent: copper resinate, at least in some formulations, darkens rapidly to brown.

"One can imagine that the humanistic concern to match colors to nature placed a greater demand on green than on any other color. Artists overcame their habitual reluctance about mixing to create a wide range of greens from blues and yellows; even precious ultramarine was deployed to this end." 5

Hills clearly explains Bellini's capability at adapting himself to oil technique and to the change of painters' attitude towards blue colour.

"The shift from tempera to oil in Venetian painting was a symptom as much as a cause of changing attitudes to luminosity and colour. (...) By the1470s, when Giovanni Bellini painted the Coronation of the Virgin for San Francesco in Pesaro, he had moved from a largely tempera-based medium to one that was predominantly oil.

"His choice of pigments remained much as before: lead white, natural ultramarine, azurite, vermilion, lake, verdigris and so-called copper resinate, lead-tin yellow, yellow ochre and other earth pigments. A change of medium, however, altered the relative transparency of pigments.

Giovanni was alert to this. Over the smooth gesso of the 'Coronation' he has applied a thin layer of animal glue to prevent the oil medium sinking into the absorbent chalk. Lead-white underpainting was applied seductively to add luminosity to particular zones of colour. The blues were sometimes laid in with an underlayer of azurite, with the final layer mostly derived from lapis lazuli, and almost always mixed with lead white. Occasionally Bellini also mixed the lapis with little smalt, a pigment that consist of finely ground potassium glass in which the colorant is cobalt. Given that smalt is a product of the glass industry, and it was very rarely used in painting before the 16th century, its employment by Bellini -albeit limited – may be indicative of his interest in the technology of Murano glass and its painting with enamel. Intense blue was source of admiration in the early fifteenth century. (…) Adding white to blue – a seemingly small change – is a telling sign of the turn from medieval to early modern colour. Giovanni Bellini, ever aware of luminosity, was quick to register a distinction between the behaviour of blue in oil as opposed to tempera: in egg tempera, as in fresco, addition of white to ground lapis reduced its saturation, therefore, given the expense of the pigment and esteem for its depth of violet-tinged blue, this was to be avoided; in oil, by contrast, a little addition of lead white actually increased the intensity of the blue. Blue pigments, whether azurite or ultramarine and, in the sixteenth century, smalt, lost their colour if finely ground, while large particles required a bigger proportion of oil, yet bonded poorly with the medium and dried erratically; the addition of lead white, particularly in the case of lapis, helped to remedy this problems. Of course pale blue are to be found in painting before 1470s, but often with a jump between the pale and the dark. Only once the long-standing reluctance to mix ultramarine with white was overcome were painters free to discover the value of a whole range of blues in gradation of lightness; only then were painters equipped to rediscover the pale blues and whites that had given a plein-air freshness to some of the thirteenth-century mosaics in the atrium of San Marco. Blue by the fifteenth century was moving away from its association with starry night, the vault of the heavens, to the changeful sky of day." 6

The Venetians were also the first to use canvas as the principal support both for their portraits and for easel-painting, as well as for large scale works. In the 16th century, painting on vast canvases was the Venetian equivalent of internal mural paintings. What originally pushed them towards the search of an alternative to fresco was, in all probability, the salinity of the air, which made fresco particularly vulnerable because of the strong presence of salt in the walls.

Each artist created and used colour according to the different, and extremely personal, techniques; Bellini obtained the final shade with a series of few thin layers of colour in a predictable sequence; Titian spread up to twenty glazes, in order to obtain the exact optical effect of the texture of the fibre and of the flesh-colour; as Lazzarini explains: *"The giorgionesque pictorial matter is composed of the matching of very transparent smalts and pigments with other, opaque ones, to obtain chromatic effects with very varied nuances: one only has to think of the shade of green that is present in the "Tempest"(...)Titian is certainly one of the first who understood and applied the innovative giorgionesque technique, which he perfected and brought to the extreme limit of complexity. His method of working on canvas, superimposing colour upon colour in a continual search of the right chromatic tone, brought forward without any saving of material, even of the most costly pigments, is an almost constant feature of his painting. Titian always paints with a considerable number of brush-strokes that are characterized by complicated mixtures of pigments, both in his young works as well as in those of his maturity and old age.... The palette used by Titian is always very rich, and the chromatic matching seems masterly. His technical particularities are numerous. For example, the light blues and pinks that are obtained by grinding ultramarine and cinnabar very finely, or the red lakes; the really unusual mixtures like cinnabar-asphaltum in order to obtain the reddish-brown tones appear to be constant."* [7]

In the *Assumption*, the analyses before restoration have revealed the presence of white lead, burnt sienna and cobalt in the red cloak of Our Lady of the Assumption and in that of St. John; of white lead, burnt sienna and cinnabar in the red garment of the apostle on the right; of white lead, lead-tin yellow, burnt sienna and cobalt in the green clothes of the two apostles and of some of the angels; of burnt sienna and cobalt in the blue cloak of the Madonna; burnt sienna and cobalt were also used for the lower part of the sky and for other clothes. [8]

The Venetian painters dedicated particular attention not only to colour but also to the texture and structure of the fabrics, and they knew how to reproduce the magnificent silk garments that were produced and worn in Venice, with incredible realism and perfection. Titian dedicated particular care and study to the yield of black; he discovered early on that oil colour could offer results that were able to compete with the chromatic game of velvet itself; in this way, Titian became the master of black. In the *Averoldi polyptych*, signed by Titian in 1522, the analyses carried out by Lazzarini on the black garment worn by the Archbishop Averoldi in the painting, have revealed the following stratification: on a wooden support and on a background in chalk and glue, a first layer of lead white, shaded in gray with little lampblack, has been spread; this is followed by a layer of burnt sienna with lead white and a bit of vermilion; a film of siccative oil; a reddish-brown layer of burnt sienna with vermilion and a bit of lead white; a thick dark brown layer of lamp black, vermilion and a bit of dark violet lake; a layer of lamp black with a bit of lead white and few grains of azurite; a thin layer of lamp black with a little vermilion and little lead white; a dark blue layer of azurite mixed with dark violet-blue lake; glaze of dark violet lake; final varnishing. Titian passed from mixtures of warm colour including vermilion and ochre in the lower layers to mixtures of cold colours including azurite and violet lake in the final layers. [9]

"Titian used colour as a constructive means: not for decorative or symbolic purposes but as a real means of artistic expression. His

pictures are composed and unified with color. (...) Titian's most famous work, Bacchus and Ariadne (1523), includes almost every pigment known to the early sixteenth century. The greens are malachite, green earth, verdigris, and "copper resinate". Ultramarine is used profligately- not only in Ariadne's robe, but also in the remarkable sky, the distant hills, and even the shadows of some of the flesh tones. Ariadne's scarf is vermilion, its strong opacity here needed to contrast with the blue robe; and Titian has given it added brilliance by glazing a thin layer of coarse-ground darker pigment over a thick layer that is more finely ground. Such touches make it clear that the painter knew how to extract the best from his materials. The orange robe of the cymbal player in Bacchus' entourage is unusually vivid, for Titian has here taken advantage of Venice's access to realgar." 10

The use of realgar, almost always associated with orpiment, is typical of the Venetian painting of the Renaissance; in the altar-pieces, most of the orange and yellow tones in the cloaks and garments of the saints are obtained with realgar and orpiment, often mixed; orpiment is certainly the yellow that is used with most frequency. Vivarini uses it a lot, even for the saints' garments, Bellini often mixes it with other yellow pigments, so strengthening the effect and obtaining his own personal shade of yellow, known for this reason as 'Bellini yellow'; in the *Crowning of the Virgin*, he uses four types of yellow pigment: orpiment, lead-tin yellow, yellow ochre and yellow lake, almost certainly prepared with Reseda. Towards the end of the 15th century, orpiment, shaded by the orange tone of realgar, is utilized to confer on garments and furnishing fabrics, strong colours made brilliant by the copper highlights. In the *Madonna of the orange tree* (1496-1498, Gallerie dell'Accademia, Venice) painted by Cima da Conegliano, the interior of the Madonna's cloak is one of the first examples of orpiment shaded with realgar, in order to give a yellow-orange tone to the fabric, identical to that of the fruits of the tree. It is in this period that orange acquires value as a colour in itself, well-defined, and no longer only a gradation of yellow; its emergence as a colour that is clearly distinguished from yellow is particularly evident in the majolica from about 1470 onwards; in majolica, the yellow is obtained from antimony, the orange from antimony and iron; after the sixteenth century, one notices the tendency to increase the quantity of iron, to create deep and vivid orange tones. An exemplary proof of the chromatic strength and of the contrasting capacity that orange and auburn can have in fresco, is offered by Michelangelo in the *Tondo Doni* (Uffizi, Florence) and in the vault of the Sistine Chapel.

The emergence of orange, auburn, brown, as distinct colours, takes place at the same moment in which violet, aubergine violet and purple begin to assume their own character, quite distinct from blue and from red. 11

Lazzarini notes that *"Bellini uses violet more than any of his contemporaries, which he obtained by mixing ultramarine and red lake, or using violet lakes directly ."* 12

The fascination exercised by these colours is well noted in Titian when, in 1510, he paints the *Holy Family and The Shepherd* (London National Gallery): Joseph's clothes, instead of being painted in the usual shade of yellow, are painted in vivid auburn and violet. The attraction felt by the Venetian painters for colours that were generally disregarded or avoided elsewhere, doubtlessly felt the effects of the influence that was exercised by Greek art and mosaic; in the late 15th century, Venice imported a considerable number of icons from Crete; in these paintings, the range of colours – cinnamon violet, dark red, blue and ochre – are closer to the deep harmony of the fourteenth-century painting of Paolo Veneziano than to the pink and blue of Jacopo Bellini and Antonio Vivarini, one century later. The Italian Madonnas of the fifteenth-century, whether they are Florentine or Venetian, generally wear a red dress and a blue cloak; the Cretan icons offer an alternative model: in them, the Madonnas mostly wear a blue dress and a violet-brown cloak. The Venetian painters are neither the first nor the only ones to use brown tones, but they have a leading position in demonstrating the potential richness of brown as a colour; without doubt, the mosaics of Saint Mark's constitute a wonderful example, with their vast range of brown, sand and beige and the continual play of light that is created by the contrast between a luminous, brilliant colour and a dark one. Inspired by the mosaicists, the Venetian painters, from Paolo Veneziano onwards, used less green and more brown and red for the flesh tones than the Tuscan painters. As well as this, the influence of Greek icons in the late 15th century, with their solemn violet brown for the Madonna's cloak, may have contributed to reawaken interest on the part of the Venetians for the brown tones, by virtue of their similarity to the most imperial and indefinable of colours, purple. 13 The Venetian painters also made wide use of a vast range of dyeing substances; unfortunately, these are easily perishable in time; Cennini had already warned people about using them, because of their lack of stability when exposed to fresh air and light; but the short-term result was excellent and the flourishing Venetian dyeing industry could offer any type; even though they are difficult to single out in laboratory analysis, their presence, nevertheless, is certain in the paintings of the most renowned artists of that time. Lakes, which, as we already know, were obtained by letting the dyeing substances precipitate in alum, when they were not mixed with other pigments, were spread in a fine layer to change a colour; in this way, yellow lake, which was very much used by Giovanni Bellini, for example, was spread on azurite in order to obtain a shade of green; on the other hand, a shade of violet was obtained with a thin layer of red lake, generally kermes lake. 14

The technique of glazing is used by painters along with the invention of oil painting. It was applied as an oily film of transparent colour on a layer of opaque colour already dry; this creates an optical mixture between the two layers of paint and an effect of light similar to that of a coloured glass that would not be obtainable by mixing colours directly. With glazing one can vary the saturation, brightness, tint and texture of a surface; its use would fulfil two main purposes: the painters of this time did not have the brilliant pigments that will be available a few centuries later; furthermore the glaze created that extraordinary brightness which was impossible to obtain otherwise. Only few transparent dyestuffs were suitable for glazing; the main pigments traditionally used for glazing were madder, kermes and cochineal lakes, natural ultramarine, verdigris, indigo and various organic yellow lakes. The bright and saturated colours of silk cloth and dresses were almost always glazed. One more advantage offered by glazing is that one can get many more shades of the same colour because by superimposing glazes one can gradually reach the preferred tone, while by superimposing glazes of different colour one can create a wide range of intermediate colours which cannot be directly obtained from the original pigments.

Titian remains the unsurpassed master in the use of glazing to get the effects of colour, light and texture that he wanted.

Many great painters who followed, including Rubens and Van Dyck, studied in depth his paintings and tried to understand the technique that allowed him to reproduce so perfectly and amazingly all the characteristics of silk dresses, from the thick crimson velvets to the flowing satin robes.

Titian often applies thin layers of translucent colour on others of opaque and already dry colour, thus the two colours take on an intensity and vividness very different from the effects produced by a simple mixture of the two, because the light filters through the transparent glaze and is reflected on to the underlying colour, thus giving the painted object an almost three-dimensional look. Veronese (1528-1588) is also famous for his intense and brilliant greens; a well-known example is the green silk dress worn by the butler in the painting *Feast in the House of Levi*, 1573 (Gallerie dell'Accademia, Venice). Pigments analysis of some of his paintings reveals that the strongest and brightest greens were obtained with glazes of copper resinate on solid substrates of verdigris mixed with lead-tin yellow and lead white or of verdigris mixed with malachite as in the case of the deep green shawl of the man in *Respect, Allegory of Love*, 1575, now in the London National Gallery. In other cases, the glaze is made of verdigris on a substrate of malachite, verdigris and lead white. 15

The 'vendecolori' of Venice

The palette of the Venetian masters could also take advantage of the innovative materials which were available in the shops of the 'vendecolori' (literally 'color sellers'); these workshops, where craftsmen and artists of every sector flocked, became a place of curiosity and exchange of interdisciplinary knowledge.

Archival research conducted by Barbara Berry and Louisa Matthew have brought to light the presence in Venice, from the end of the fifteenth century, of numerous 'vendecolori' specialized in the preparation of colours for the Arts: they were true professionals of colour manufacture who had nothing to do with the apothecaries or the colour traders of other cities.

From the list of goods found in their workshops it is clear that the 'vendecolori' supplied a wide variety of artists: painters, dyers, glassmakers, potters; their shops had definitely become a place of encounter and exchange of ideas between artists of different artworks, inevitably giving impulse to innovative ideas and experiments in the choices and the techniques of using the many available materials. These professional colour-makers were able to prepare any pigment in a wide range of shades or to prepare a specific colour shade according to an artist's request.

This concern led the experts of the National Gallery in Washington, in collaboration with those in London, to review a series of samples already detected and belonging to the great Venetian masters. The hypothesis of a Venetian palette, highly innovative and enlarged if compared with conventional materials, has proved to be right. 16

The new technical investigations have revealed an extensive use of materials that until that time had been only used by artisans and artists from other sectors. In Lorenzo Lotto's book of accounts there is the record for the purchase of 'zalolin from Vazari' (yellow for potters): its name suggests a frit or a glaze partially melted, of the type used by the artisans who painted glass and ceramic.

To achieve special effects of brightness and brilliance, the Venetian painters were using materials not specifically designated for oil painting; it was apparent they made a greater use than previously thought, of vitreous substances, among which appear frits and colours for painting on glass and earthenware, as well as powdered glass, blue enamel and one yellow vitreous enamel obtained from oxide particles of lead and tin suspended in a transparent and vitreous mass; this last pigment is widely used in the painting by Jacopo Tintoretto *Christ at the Sea of Galilee* (1575-80) (National Gallery, Washington); the green enamel in the painting is probably a mixture of blue glass and yellow glass; the latter is, according to the modern terminology, lead-tin yellow type II, produced by heating lead and tin with the addition of silica at 900-950°C; the result of the fusion was a glassy yellow pigment that was then pulverized and sieved through a dense net. The lead-tin yellow type I is obtained by heating a mixture of lead oxide and tin dioxide at temperatures of 650-800 ° C. 17

The type II, despite the misleading terminology, has a more ancient history than type I; used in Europe as early as the twelfth century, it was gradually replaced by type I in the second quarter of the fifteenth century, with the exception of Venice where the use of both types is attested throughout the sixteenth century; tied to the production of yellow glass, we find it widely testified in Bohemia and Florence throughout the course of the fourteenth century, a period during which a production of glasses and glass bottles, mainly yellow and green,was taking place in the Tuscan capital.

We find ample evidence of the use of type II in the paintings on wood-panel by Nardo and Jacopo di Cione who give us a beautiful example in Saint Peter's bright yellow cloth represented in one of the 12 main panels - now in the National Gallery in London - which form the front altarpiece painted for San Pier Maggiore church in Florence (1370-71). During the fifteenth century instead, the type II disappears from the palette of the Florentine school in which only the type I is used, probably introduced into Italy from northern Europe in the XV century- one of its first names is 'German yellow'- and linked to the technology for the production of yellow and white glazes for ceramics. 18

As already said, the professional colour-makers of Venice were able to prepare any pigment in a wide range of shades, and according to artists' personal need.

"Painters and agents went to Venice to obtain pigments and painting supplies from major urban centres: Florence and Ferrara are the most frequently found in documents (..) A partial list of painters who travelled to Venice or purchased through an agent includes: Gentile da Fabriano, Lorenzo Monaco, Domenico Veneziano, Benozzo Gozzoli, Cosmé Tura, Ercole de' Roberti, Andrea Mantegna, Filippino Lippi, Alessio Baldovinetti, Fra Bartolomeo, Dosso e Battista Dossi, Garofalo, Raphael and Gerolamo Genga. Venetian painters in the sixteenth century also

procured pigments for out-of-town patrons. The most well-known cases are Titian, his son Orazio, and Tintoretto, all doing business with the Spanish court ....
" When Titian and Orazio Vecellio and others acted as agents for the Spanish court, procuring pigments in Venice for export to Spain in the 1570s and 1580s, they were acting as guarantors of quality for pigments purchased from 'vendecolori' ." 19

In 1548 Titian was at the imperial court of Ausburg to paint the famous Equestrian portrait of Charles V (Prado Museum), which was to celebrate the emperor's victory against the Protestant armies. The red is around Charles' helmet, horse sash and on the horses' trim; to capture such vivid reds Titian requested a half pound of red lake to be brought from Venice to Ausburg; his instructions reveal that he regarded that pigment *"so burning and so splendid .... that in comparison the crimson on velvet and silk will become less beautiful."* 20

8) ANTWERP'S GOLDEN AGE

The great art market of Northern Europe

During the sixteenth century Antwerp became one of the most important and avant-garde art markets in Europe: Jan Gossaert, Bruegel the Elder, Frans Floris, Marten de Vos are some of the most famous representatives of the painters community. In 1515 there were already 100 workshops operating in the city, a number that would have steadily grown in subsequent decades, a situation unparalleled in any other European city with the exception of Rome. This explosion of the arts market, as well as other activities related to the industry of luxury goods, is to be connected to the position gained by Antwerp as the leading commercial hub north of the Alps: British merchants began to use Antwerp as a passage to the East to facilitate their wool export, the Portuguese landed their goods there from the colonies to be redistributed in the rest of Europe, and from southern Germany merchants with loads of silver came to buy spices and fabrics; by this period, the port of Antwerp was in a very advantageous position for the development of luxury industries such as tapestry weaving, diamond cutting, silk weaving, processing of fine glasses, which attracted an increasing number of artisans and artists from other cities. An exclusive innovation in Antwerp was then the commercial infrastructure available in the city, whereby artists could exhibit their artworks at one of the many sales-rooms designed to market luxury goods. Special galleries for the marketing of painting were already available in the mid-15th century.
In the mid-sixteenth century no less than one hundred stalls had been converted into large shops where artworks were put on display and sold, mostly to international customers. It was an art

market for which most of the painters, unlike elsewhere, did not produce on commission, but on their own initiative, trying to anticipate the demand. It was a fertile environment for the rapid development of pigment manufactures and highly specialized retailers' shops. Among the various pigments produced - white lead, smalt, lead-tin yellow - vermilion, sent especially to France, was the most highly valued and was the true pride of Antwerp, to the point that in a seventeenth century treatise the author, Théodore de Turquet Mayerne, declares that "*a man in Antwerp makes vermilion three times more red than the ordinary*". 1

Antwerp's greatest adoptive son

And it is in Antwerp where Rubens, the great Baroque heir of Titian, opened his studio; in that same studio a very young van Dyck will work as assistant and will complete his artistic education; as Rubens had done, he will assimilate the lesson from Titian but he will abandon the colourist accents of the Venetian master. Rubens during his long stay in Italy remains fascinated by the technique and by the colour of the great Venetian masters, but, above all, it is the lesson from Titian that will leave an indelible imprint on his painting. He makes copies of many of his paintings, studies his use of colour in depth and his extraordinary ability to transfer the light, the softness and the iridescent effect of silk drapes onto canvas.

During their stay in Genoa, both Rubens and, a few years later, van Dyck, are called to portray many persons belonging to the city's most prominent families and to hand down their image: faces from which a regal austerity always exudes deriving from their consciousness of the prestige conferred by power.

In Italy, the two artists study in depth the greatest Italian painters of the sixteenth century, especially Titian, Veronese, Tintoretto, sublime masters in transferring onto the canvas and making lifelike the consistency of the silk fabrics worn by the sitters.

Rubens leaves for Italy in 1600 and will stay there for eight years; in Genoa he is struck by the magnificence and grandeur of its palaces, with their immense rooms where only life-size portraits may cut a fine figure.

By this period the portrait is the only way to leave a visual memory of oneself and therefore it assumes a celebratory role of primary importance: the type of composition, the inclusion of the sitter in a courtly context and the clothes of the characters convey the idea of wealth and power with immediacy; dresses are the most immediate and powerful means to convey in life as in portraits one's social status; aware of the message transmitted by the clothes, the men of noble Genoese families are always portrayed in their official robes peculiar to the office they held; and noblewomen are always portrayed in their richest garments.

In 1606 Rubens painted the portrait of the Marchesa Brigida Spinola Doria (National Gallery, Washington) a year after her wedding, and the dress she wears could have been her own wedding dress; *"The marchesa's silvery satin dress is built up of layers of translucent glazes and highlighted with thick, freely painted strokes. Rubens combined this bold, painterly style—which he learned from his study of Venetian artists like Veronese, Tintoretto, and Titian—with the tradition for detailed, carefully observed surfaces from his native Flanders."* 2

"Both of Rubens's versions of The Judgment of Paris (c.1600 and 1635-37) (Prado Museum) show a Venetian influence in their use of primaries: bright yellow in the heavenly light and draperies, strong blue in the sky, brilliant reds in the flesh tints and garments.

"Rubens achieved his pure, glowing colors by applying the pigment onto white grounds, rather than using the muted red- browns or grays, typical of the time. Nowhere is this more apparent than in

150

Samson and Delilah, (c.1609), where raw color fills the canvas. Delilah's red dress, which overheats the sexual charge of the scene, is almost unadulterated crimson lake, brightened with touches of vermilion and highlighted with lead white. " 3

The palette used by Rubens for this painting is composed of:
Lead white
Carbon black of two types:
1) wood-charcoal in the deepest shadows of the purple drape
2) bone or ivory black in the grounds of the carpet in black
Ochres, often mixed with other pigments, in shades of red, brown and yellow
Yellow ocher in the middle tones of Delilah's dress
Umber glaze in the brownish suits of the elderly woman; manganese reveals the presence of umber that is used not only for its colouring properties but also as a drying agent to speed the oil drying process.
Among the most colourful pigments, the most conspicuous presence is the crimson colour of pure lake pigment of Delilah's satin dress, whereas it is mixed with vermilion in the underlying layer of opaque colour. For Delilah's dress Rubens has probably used kermes lake, while for the cloth it's more likely the use of a lake of vegetable origin, most probably madder lake. Lakes are mixed in other areas of the painting, especially in the translucent reddish brown of the background architecture.
Vermilion, mixed with red lake, for carpet
Lead-tin yellow in brighter parts of Delilah's dress, mixed with lead white in the candle flame
The purple cloth hanging from the ceiling was not obtained, as one would expect, by a combination of red and blue, but by a combination of a crimson lake pigment, lead white and coarse black soot of coal. In fact, the soot of coal mixed with white clearly gives a bluish color. 4

Ruben's ability to render on the canvas the reflections of light on the soft silk texture will be perpetrated in his portraits by van Dyck. In 1623 Van Dyck painted the portrait of the Marchesa Elena Grimaldi Cattaneo.

The painting closely echoes Peter Paul Rubens' Portrait of the Marchesa Brigida Spinola Doria

"Throughout his career Van Dyck competed with his immensely famous peer (and teacher) Peter Paul Rubens (outliving him only by a year). Yet Van Dyck's style and approach were distinctive. Note, for example, the way he made the Marchesa Cattaneo appear to float, her dress swaying, as if she has been captured in a passing moment, in contrast to the greater formality of Rubens' portrait. Van Dyck aspired to what he called an "airy style," interpreted to mean qualities of grace, ease, and effortlessness. In this work, even the clouds seem to carry that message as they drift over the distant landscape". 5

To masterfully reproduce Genoese silk, velvets and satins worn at the court of Charles I of England, where he is called as official painter, van Dyck uses Titian's techniques, learned during his period of study in Italy; Van Dyck's palette however differs quite a lot from that of his great masters, Rubens and Titian; it's a sign of an era with different tastes and a new aesthetic.

9)   THE BAROQUE PALETTE

"The Baroque period represents a strange episode in the story of color creation and use in art. The painters of the late sixteenth and seventeenth centuries did not value novelty as much as sobriety and control in their color choices. By the dawn of the seventeenth century, the advocacy of Giorgio Vasari and the scholars of the Italian academies had largely secured the superiority of disegno over colore. The influence of this idea soon spread to France, and a muted palette and dark chiaroscuro became the predominant style of European art." 1

But it was not only the influence of the academic dictates to make the artists flee from the use of vivid effects and from the chromatic brilliance of the Renaissance; the painters of the late 16th and early 17th century, worked in a context that was dominated by the intolerance and the authoritarianism of the Counter-Reformation.

"The Church, seeing its authority undetermined by humanistic rationalism, rallied and imposed a theological set of values akin to that of the Middle Ages.(...) The ecclesiastical reactionaries were sophisticated enough to recognize that art is a powerful tool for the propagandist. Pictures – the potential text for a "Bible of the illiterate" – speak to the uneducated, when words cannot. At the Council of Trent, which began its deliberations on church policy in 1545, it was decreed that religious art should depict things in a transparent manner, with laborious codifications. All angels must have wings, all saints halos. If their identity is not obvious, they must bear labels, and never mind the demands of realism or aesthetics. (…) Artists who continued to uphold the humanism of the Renaissance, *risked censure and worse.*

"In 1573, Paolo Veronese (c.1528-1588) was forced to defend his Feast in the Home of Levi before the Inquisition, who demanded to know why the work contained figures not mentioned in the Bible;

he confessed, ingenuously, that they were there to fill up space (there was a lot of it to fill). But still he was commanded to rework the picture."

"The shrewd propagandistic strategy of the Jesuits knew how to stimulate the hearts of men through ecstatic emotion.

"Painters of the late sixteenth and seventeenth centuries worked in a context constrained by a new religious intolerance yet overheated by pious passion." 2

Reformation and Counter-Reformation induce them to work from a palette that is composed of austere colours and of the contrast between light and shadow which, in the hands of the great artists, leads to highly dramatic effects on canvas.

Pastoreau singles out some of the dominant and recurrent characteristics that the Protestant painters give the palette ".. an authentic chromatic specificity: general sobriety, dislike of a medley of colours, dark hues, effects of grisaille, play of monochromy (above all in the range of grays and blues), search for local colour, escape from all that attacks the eye, infringing the chromatic economy of the picture with the breaking of shades. In the work of several of the Calvinistic painters, one can even speak of a real Puritanism of colour, in that these principles are applied in a radical way. It is, for example, the case of Rembrandt, who often practices a sort of asceticism of colour, based on dark tones, not numerous (up to the point that he is, at times, accused of monochromy), restrained, so as to leave space for the powerful effects of light and vibration. From this palette, that is so particular, a strong musicality and an undeniable spiritual intensity leaps out." 3

And concerning Rembrandt (1606-69), Ball writes: "Rembrandt's restricted palette excludes several of the brightest pigments available in the seventeenth century. His blacks (charcoal and bone black) and browns (including Cologne earth, as it would have *been called) are supplemented by most of the earth colors: ochers, siennas and umbers. His red lakes were mainly madder and cochineal. Blues, too, he used with restraint – mainly smalt but sometimes azurite .... His principal yellow was lead-tin yellow, which was never the brightest of colors. (…) But this limited palette had advantages, for it consisted largely of reliable, stable colors that have aged well. This was no mere good fortune: Rembrandt knew which materials would last and how to combine them safely.(...)The late Renaissance and the ensuing Baroque period, became an era of deep shadows, of brooding blacks placed in dramatic counterpoint to fulvous highlights. Correggio, Caravaggio and Rembrandt were the thaumaturgists of black and brown. Can it be coincidental that amid this golden glow and heavy gloom emerged several new yellow, ocher and brown pigments? Never before the seventeenth century was the artist so well-equipped to cover the canvas with lustrous highlights, modulating through ruddy shades to a pitchy murk."* 4

In the Baroque palette burnt Sienna, with its warm reddish-brown hue, gradually passing from reddish brown, umber and Cologne earth are always present; burnt Sienna is obtained by calcining the natural one; calcination is carried out in furnaces of a moderate temperature, or else on a red-hot plate; the earth is exposed to the heat until the required tone has been obtained; during the calcination process, the water - due to the effect of the heat – is removed from the hydrated iron oxide; the burnt type is darker and more transparent than the natural one, and of a beautiful brown colour, tending towards orange.

Umber appears in artistic literature at the end of the 16th century; its name indicates the type of use that was made of it; it was, in fact, used above all for the shadows of yellow and red draperies, for those of complexion and hair.

Cologne earth, the name of which derives from the great findings in the area of the homonymous German city, is a pigment with a high content of organic substances, such as peat, earthy brown coal, pitch coal; iron oxide, aluminium oxide and silica are present as well; it was used mainly by the Dutch and Flemish painters, among whom was Van Dyck; he made also use of a very solid pigment which was extracted from iron sulphide or "green vitriol" through calcination; in this way, one obtains an iron oxide; its colour varies from dark red to dark brown with nuances of violet. 5

"Van Dyck and the English school that succeeded him, also took his browns from an unappealing tarry substance, called asfalto or bitumen. It is hard to credit that this unpromising stuff, that was not at all promising, a residue from the distillation of crude oil, would ever have been accorded much value except in an age obsessed with brown. Rembrandt was a skilful enough craftsman to use it without mishap in his reddish-brown glazes, but in the hands of an immoderate experimenter like Reynolds it was disastrous. It does not properly dry at all, and thick films tend to run. Moreover, as the surface layer congeals, it shrinks and wrinkles, causing any material painted over the top to crack and curl. The French painters of the early nineteenth century, in thrall to a version of chiaroscuro that demanded deep, translucent shadows, seized on bitumen's seductive warmth of tone, only to discover its insidious effects too late. (…) Van Dyck was fond of glazing his shadows with a similar dark, tarry pigment called bistre (…) made from the soot of burnt beechwood or birch bark. It was not a new material, having been used in manuscript illuminations since at least the fourteenth century, but one needed skill and knowledge to make much of it in oils. (…) At least these murky materials were relatively cheap. The same can be said of red ochers and earths that colonize much of Van Dyck's canvases. Yet color manufacturers of the Baroque period discovered how to make their

own versions of these natural pigments and thereby gain control over their hues.

Iron, the martial metal of the alchemists, gave birth the Mars pigments: synthetic iron oxides that ranged in color from yellow through red to brown and even a kind of chocolate purple ("Mars violet"). (…). Later methods of manufacturing Mars red allowed the color of the product to be tailored to order. The real impetus for the production of Mars compounds came, however, in the eighteenth century, when sulfuric acid became an important commercial item, especially as a bleach for the textile industry." 6

The painters of the 17th century used to mix several different lakes to obtain the various shades of red; the arrival from the New World of a series of new dyestuffs, amplified the range of reds; it was Mexican cochineal, above all, that supplied particularly brilliant red lakes.

"When Spaniards arrived in Mexico, Aztecs have been bred cochineal for centuries. Among various wild species they had selected the easiest to be domesticated and which produced the best quality and quantity of colorant, which is composed of carminic acid. Within few decades from its discovery, this scale insect would become, after gold and silver, the third most important voice of the Spanish exports to Europe". 7

New products also arrived from the East, along with the great kaleidoscope of goods that the Dutch and the English transported to Europe; among these there were gommagutta and "puri" or Indian yellow.

The name gommagutta (gamboge) derives from the fact that it is a resinous substance that comes out in drops (Latin = "gutta") from the incisions made on the wood of some plants of the Garciniae family, originally from the East Indies and from Cambodia; its colour is a very intense golden yellow, transparent, delicate but with scarce resistance to light; used in ancient Egypt and in the ancient Orient, it was introduced to Europe by Dutch merchants at the beginning of the 17th century, and it was used and appreciated above all by the first Flemish oil painters.

Indian yellow is an organic dyestuff, obtained from the urine of cows that are fed exclusively with mango leaves. It is made up of euxantate of magnesium.

"The mango leaves, in the metabolic process of the cows, cause an increase of the secretion of the bile; the excess of bile passes into the urine, which is of a strong yellow colour; this is boiled and the sediment is collected and dried....Used in India both for painting (for miniature in particular) and for dyeing, it also found use in the Western countries, in which it turns out that it was already used in the 17th century.

"It is a stable colour in its pure state, it is not poisonous, it has a strong colouring power; because of its transparency and light, it was very suitable for dyeing, and used a lot by painters of water colours...In the course of the 19th century, Indian yellow was exported to England, where the colour underwent a further process; it was rinsed and purified, separating the yellow from the greenish part, and, made up into small blocks, dried again. Prepared in this way, like a pigment for artists, it was, in turn, exported in the whole of Europe as an English specialty. In commerce today, substitutes with a lake base are designated under the name of Indian yellow....Very few written identifications of the pigment in the Western works of art, have appeared. An interesting discovery is that of Kuhn, regarding the painting of Jan Vermeer " Woman weighing gold", going back to 1662-1663. His analysis reveals a transparent, yellow colour; its main, inorganic component is magnesium. Microscopic observation also shows a weak birefringence of crystals of the pigment, similar to those noticed, always by Kuhn, in other paintings of the 19th century, in which the use of Indian yellow has been proven." [8]

A yellow which reappears on the scene is antimony yellow or Egyptian yellow or Naples yellow, as it was called ever since its introduction into Europe; as we have already said, it is composed essentially of lead antimonate, it has a high covering power and good chemical stability, it alters only if it comes into contact with sulphur or iron based pigments, and it is suitable for all pictorial techniques.

10) THE EIGHTEENTH CENTURY PALETTE

"Many important historical and cultural reasons regard France as the leading nation in eighteenth-century Europe. The political centrality of eighteenth-century France corresponds with its equally barycentric position in the evolution of the arts.

"Eighteenth-century France opens with a great novelty, the abandonment of the severe and noble classicist forms, for a freer and fresher tone (..) For a large part of the eighteenth century, French painting favours a light style with pretty subjects, scenes full of grace, portrayed "in fashion" in which good taste, refinement and nonchalance are displayed.

"The passage of style coincides with the political change of the Regency period (1715-1723), before the enthronement of Louis XV and the affirmation of the gallant and subtly erotic taste favoured by Madame de Pompadour. This period marks the return to the painterly colorism of Rubens and to the 16th century Venetian 'tocco' painting. It takes the form of a true "fashion" which rapidly spreads through Europe." 1

The first great interpreter of the attitudes and propensities of the French society by this time, is Jean-Antoine Watteau (1684-1721). His paintings feature figures in aristocratic and theatrical dress in lush imaginary landscapes. Their amorous and wistful encounters create a mood but do not employ narrative in the traditional sense. During Watteau's lifetime, a new term, fête galante, was coined to describe them.

The sweetness of his palette is an homage to Rubens and the colorism of sixteenth-century Venetian painting recast in delicate pastels to suit the scale and aesthetic of Rococo décor will decisively affect the other two great interpreters of Rococo tastes, Francois Boucher and Jean-Honoré Fragonard (1732-1806). 2

The principal interpreter of the Louis XV style is François Boucher (1703-1770), author of numerous portraits of Madame de Pompadour in various poses and types of dress.

An extremely eclectic artist, in the portraits of the Pompadour he uses pastel colours, warm and bright, those preferred by the Pompadour herself for her clothes and furnishing fabrics. His palette, around 1760, includes: lead white, Naples yellow, yellow ocher, vermilion, madder and cochineal lakes, brown ocher, burnt sienna, blue enamel, Prussian blue.

Jean-Honoré Fragonard's (1732-1806) palette is a tribute to Rubens and the Venetian colourists of the sixteenth century; Fragonard's quick, elusive touch, which, at first glance, makes many of his works look unfinished, as if they were sketches, was greatly appreciated by the Impressionists, in particular by Morisot, Cassatt, Monet and Renoir: in fact, the freshness and the speed touch in *The Reader*, ca.1770, (National Gallery, Washington) look like a conscious anticipation of Impressionism.

Not for nothing in 1874 the Goncourt brothers quoted Fragonard's style: "*More than any of his contemporaries, Fragonard cultivated this rapid manner of painting which grasps the general impression of things and flings it on to the canvas like an instantaneous image.*" 3

In the Rococò period, colour enjoys a moment of renewed protagonism. Newton's studies on the origin of colour deprive it of that aura of mystery and divine, magic origin: " *in a painting or in a work of art, colour can now accomplish functions that were previously barred, or in other words it can classify, distinguish, hierarchize, direct one's look, and above all it manages to show that which the drawing alone is not able to show.*" 4

Gianbattista Tiepolo (1696-1770) dictates the taste for elegant decoration in the courts; his frescoes that decorate the Italian and Spanish courts are full of sunny scenes, vividly coloured, clearly inspired to the recovery of the great Venetian Renaissance tradition.

The Rococò is an explosion of imagination, gracefulness, light and colour, - colour that will be once again tamed, recomposed and subordinate to design by the Enlightenment and neoclassic taste in the second half of the century.

On the eighteenth-century palette, the whole range of colours reappears, and many of them are a novelty in the field of pigments, in the course of the century.

The "martial" colours, discovered at the end of the previous century and so-called because they were obtained from the "martial" metal (iron), enter production during the eighteenth century. They are prepared from oxide of hydrate iron, co-precipitated with alum and an alkaline substance, lime or potassium. The proportion of the mixture determines the tone of colour; the precipitate is collected, rinsed carefully and left to dry. Once *Mars yellow* is obtained, the other colours are then obtained for successive calcinations: orange is obtained first of all, then red, black, brown, violet. The chemical and physical properties of the martial colours are the same as those of the natural iron oxides; Mars yellow has the same chemical composition as that of the yellow ochres, but it can be distinguished from them as it is soluble in hydrochloridic acid, it contains a high proportion of alumina and it does not contain silica. They are pigments that have an excellent stability; they are, in fact, unalterable to light, humidity and lime and they have a high colouring power. Suitable for all pictorial techniques, they also have a good siccative capacity in oil painting. One of the discoveries that was received most enthusiastically by the artists was that of the blue pigment, known as *Prussian blue*.

As far as the choice of blue was concerned, the palette of that era was still quite limited: the brilliant splendour of ultramarine and the luminous light blue of azurite tending towards green, are well noted. Smalt, in its best formula and freshly spread, could have a surprising intensity of colour; nevertheless, in practice, there was not a blue among these pigments that could meet the various demands of the painter. Ultramarine was rarely to be found, extremely costly and, partly due to its evident purple nuance, it was, in many cases, unsuitable for mixing with other colours.

In the second half of the seventeenth century, azurite, too, became more and more rare, and it appears that, in the course of the 18th century, it was hardly used any more; its synthetic equivalent, verditer, seems to have always enjoyed a good reputation as a colour for decoration, but a certain grainy consistence and a greenish aspect, which tended to become more evident with the passing of time, made it much less popular among the painters of oils and water colours.

Smalt assumed a very pale tone when it was ground very finely, and it tended to sink in the oil; as well as this, in an oily binding, it gradually lost its original colour. All these blues were transparent; their depth of colour was maintained only if ground into coarse powder. Indigo, the only blue pigment of organic origin used at that time in oil painting, had a deep shade of colour and, mixed with yellow, gave lovely greens; but, as its tendency to fade was well-known, it was untrustworthy. Therefore, the choice of blue pigments at the start of the 18th century was really very scarce. In 1710, the discovery of a new blue pigment, *Prussian blue*, is announced; the pigment is described as being very long-lasting, both in oil painting and water colours, resistant to acids, unalterable when exposed to atmospheric agents, easily grindable into a very fine powder, with an excellent covering power, perfect for mixing with other colours and able to resist quicklime; finally, another virtue that was certainly not to be ignored was the fact that it cost a tenth of ultramarine; it was the perfect blue for artists, who obviously welcomed it with euphoric enthusiasm, and for a certain length of time, they were able to appreciate exclusively its qualities before also discovering its defects. 5

Its discovery, as in many other cases in the field of applied chemistry, was purely casual; between 1704 and 1705, a grocer and colour-maker from Berlin, a certain Diesbach, sold a beautiful red lake that was obtained by making cochineal precipitate with potassium, charged with iron sulphate; one day, while he was preparing the lake, he realized that he had no more potassium, and so he procured a certain quantity from a spicemaker by the name of Dippel; this fellow sold him adulterated carbonate of potassium, which he had already used personally, to rectify an animal oil of his invention. Instead of the usual brilliant red lake, Diesbach obtained a beautiful, blue precipitate. 6

Diesbach, having no idea of what had really happened, turned to Dippel in order to find an explanation; Dippel maintained that the blue colour was due to a reaction between the iron sulphate and the contaminated alkali. In fact, *"the alkali had reacted with Dippel's oil, prepared from blood, to make potassium ferrocyanide. (..) This then combined with iron sulphate, to form the compound that chemists call iron ferrocyanide, known more familiarly (even to them) by its pigment name, Prussian blue. (..) Of the synthetic procedure, French chemist Jean Hellot remarked in 1762 that <nothing is perhaps more peculiar than the process by which one obtains Prussian blue, and it must be owned that, if chance had not had a hand, a profound theory would be necessary to invent it>."* 7

Dippel, after many experiments, improved the formula and put the product onto the market with the name of Berlin blue, maintaining the secret of the procedure for more than ten years. Then the pigment began to be manufactured in Paris, and in the arc of a few years, it was manufactured in the whole of Europe; its quality and its price made it the ideal blue; nevertheless, already in the 18th century, the unconditional enthusiasm scaled down quite a bit when even Prussian blue showed itself not to be without its defects; by mid-century, it was already clear that the pigment could not be used in fresco, as in fact the lime destroyed it; as well as this, its poor stability on exposure to light and its tendency to change tone if mixed with white pigments - possibly because of the action of the lead contained in it - was evident. The unstable character of the pigment and its changeable reactions on exposure to light were described later on, in 1834, by Franz Fernbach, author of an essay on oil painting. He, after having decorated a board with pigments bound with copal and made smooth with turpentine essence, left it to dry in the sun; he went away for a certain period and on his return, he noticed with horror that the areas that had been painted with Prussian Blue, were almost completely discoloured. He waited until the following morning to repaint them and when he got ready to work, he was even more astonished on seeing that the colour had restored itself in all its intensity. After such an experience, Fernbach recovered the parts painted with Prussian blue with thick sheets of paper, and again put the board in the sun: no change took place. This unstable behaviour of Prussian Blue on exposure to light, was demonstrated almost regularly by George Field (1777–1854) in the first half of the following century, when he led a series of experiments on the stability of pigments, using them both on water-painting and on oil-painting; Field exposed identical samples to the effect of sunlight and of the spoiled air of a ....toilet; he allowed five weeks to pass, until the coating of Brazil wood or the cochineal lake had lost their colour; he then repeated the experiment with identical samples carefully wrapped in paper, to be able to compare the actions; the pigment samples had been used with three different depths: a thin glazing on white; a coat of medium depth, a thick layer. In oil, samples that had been mixed with lead white were always included. The pigments were considered stable depending on the loss of colour that they showed, as compared to the ordinary lake pigment taken as a comparative element. His samples of Prussian blue had veered towards violet, due to the effect of the humid and unhealthy air, and they had discoloured in different measures in the sunlight, regaining, however, full colour if removed from the conditions which they had undergone for the test. [8]

Different types of Prussian blue existed on the market, like, for example, China blue, Antwerp blue, Brunswick blue, Paris blue, Monthiers blue; in fact, there were different methods of preparation and in each one, along with the ferrocyanide of potassium, various components came into play and in different doses; these gave place to different types of the pigment and determined a greater or lesser stability.

In spite of the unusual and changeable behaviour of Prussian blue, it had in any case great success, because of its enormous covering power, and its capacity to produce beautiful and transparent tones if mixed with other colours; a vast use was made of it in the various decorative arts and in the 19th century, it played an important part in the palettes of David, Ingres and the Impressionists and of Picasso during his Blue Period.

Two greens were also obtained, then, from Prussian Blue, in which it was mixed with gamboge and which we can find in the paintings of Hogarth and Constable. Nowadays, the colours in ferrocyanide are still produced on a large scale, but with processes that are considerably different and much more rapid.

The basic palette used by Canaletto (Giovanni Antonio Canal, 1697-1768) for *San Simeone Piccolo* is formed of Prussian blue, green earth, Naples yellow, yellow ochre, vermilion and often a mixture of natural cinnabar and artificial cinnabar, umber, lead white; Canaletto, like other Venetian painters of the 18th century on canvas, used very stable pigments and their works have been relatively damaged by the action of the light; nevertheless, in San Simeone, the sky has suffered a loss of colour due to the fading of Prussian blue, caused by the action of the light; also, it has been demonstrated that the paintings of this period that contain Prussian blue, are much more sensitive to the action of the light, especially when the pigment is strongly diluted with white for the painting of the skies. 9

Canaletto's basic palette is reconfirmed in his painting *Venice: The Feastday of St. Roch*, 1735, (London National Gallery):

" *Prussian blue is in mixture with lead white for the sky;*

Naples yellow is used for the Doge's golden robe, the brightest touches on the tasselled swags over the windows of the Scuola, and the highlights of the frames of the pictures displayed along the walls of the buildings;

Naples yellow combined with reddish brown earth pigment where the paint has a warmer orange tinge;

vermilion for the scarlet robe of the Cancelliere Grande;

red lake pigments are used, not so much as glazes, but in tint with opaque pigments to produce the delicate mauves and pinks of the draperies. For example the paint of the rose-pink textile which hangs from the sill of the second storey window is a mixture of red lake pigment and white, whereas the lilac robes of the three secretaries of the Savio Grande contain the same pigment, but in addition makes use of the bluish cast of charcoal black to produce the required shade of mauve.

In the green areas, only one very intense green pigment has been detected: it is a green earth (terre-verte) very rich in glauconite; it is also used to produce the various shades of green in mixture with Naples yellow, white, black, and Prussian blue.

All the architectures are painted with ochers and earth pigments." 10

167

One colour for which a safe alternative had been sought for a long time, to safeguard the health of its manufacturers, was white; white pigment was, for centuries and above all others, lead white or ceruse, perfect for nuances, because of its great covering power and the scarce quantity of oil that was necessary to spread it on the surface to paint; yet, in fresco, the lead white tended to blacken, owing to the dampness; but the real problem was caused by its high toxicity, which, above all, hit whoever was most in direct contact with the lead in the phases of pigment preparation; after the industrial production of lead white began, the cases of poisoning increased; there are existing reports from the 17th and 18th century, which warn of the grave consequences to the workers' health, especially of those whose job is the scraping of the lead and the grinding and drying of the pigment; different palliatives were experimented to render the work less dangerous and in the end, new white pigments were created, which were harmless to the health of whoever manufactured them.

The one possessing the best qualities was doubtlessly *Zinc white*; the artists used it very little, however, as its covering power was rather scarce, and in oil painting it dried very slowly; in the second decade of the 20th century, shortly before the product that would definitely resolve any problem came on the market, lead white continued to be the most sought-after pigment in the market. The new pigment was composed of titanium dioxide, it was inert and it possessed a hiding power greater than that of lead white and a notable stability: in a few decades, it conquered the market and became the dominant white of the 20th century and beyond.

The last decades of the eighteenth century and the first of the nineteenth century mark the immense progress in chemical research and in practical experimentation; it is not by chance that in this period, a large quantity of new pigments for art appears on the market, and the artists find themselves facing unexpected new potential for their palettes; yet it is not an easy choice, as it entails trusting materials that have not been experimented sufficiently and of which the result, in time, is unknown; some artists distrust the new pigments, preferring to use the traditional ones, others, instead, throw themselves with enthusiasm into the experimentation of the new colours.

"It is not surprising that those who chose the second road tended to be innovators in artistic style too: in the end, it was precisely the colour on canvas that would become the discriminating factor between the conservatives and the radicals." 11

11)   BETWEEN TWO CENTURIES

A wave of new pigments

One of the methods used, to try to reconstruct the palettes of the painters from the eighteenth and nineteenth century, was the analysis carried out on the paintings and pictorial materials belonging to the artists of that time and preserved up until the present day. One of the most interesting is undoubtedly that of the works and materials of the English painter, J.M. William Turner (1775-1851). As well as using traditional materials, Turner experimented all the new pigments of his time, in the search for colours that were able to change into visual effect the impression that natural light, caught in different moments, left on his mind. Turner's works amazed the contemporaries and caused criticism from the conservatives, not only because of the presence of brilliant and dazzling tones on his canvasses, but also and above all because his technique and his colours expressed an interpretation of reality and of light that was totally new, something which disconcerted the Victorian public.

"Such a vivid colour was unfamiliar and disconcerting. The Victorians preferred, in the words of the art historian Eric Shane, < verisimilitude to painterliness, saccharine colouring to the brilliant hues [of] Turner> - Reynolds and Gainsborough, in other words, who created no doubts about what you were supposed to be seeing. And yet truth of a kind was precisely what Turner and the Impressionists sought rather than shunned: not the "truth" of academic convention, but the truth of the impression that it leaves in the observer's mind. As for the "brilliant hues", there can be no doubt where this came from and why they shocked, for until the early nineteenth century, no one had seen such greens, yellows, and violets as now radiated from the works of the innovators. ...

The atmosphere dominates Turner's works, in which pale suns struggle to penetrate all manner of mists, fogs, clouds, and tempests. 'Sun rising through vapour' (1807) was said by one critic to be a potentially generic title for most of Turner's paintings. (..) These atmospheric confections needed rich, vibrant color, not the subdued earth colors preferred by Constable. .... Turner seized on the new pigments almost as fast as the chemists could dispense them. Cobalt blue, emerald green, orange vermilion, barium chromate, chrome yellow, orange, and scarlet, as well as new yellow and red lakes – he put novel material to use, within a few years of its introduction. To do so was certainly risking disaster: a contemporary engraver, J. Burnet, remarked that Turner dare to use these new pigments when other artists did not.

"One unfortunate consequence is that by the end of the nineteenth century, the poor stability of the new pigments left several of Turner's works in sorry repair." 1

On the occasion of the centenary of his death, the Tate gallery of London exhibited the pictorial materials used by Turner and then carried out an analysis; among the new yellow pigments one appeared: *Mineral yellow*, which was invented and patented by Turner himself; it is oxychloride basic lead that is obtained by mixing two parts litharge and one part ammonia salts in water, until a fluid paste is obtained, which is left to rest for a whole day; the paste is then rinsed, dried and calcinated; once it is cool, the material obtained is ready for use; depending on the temperature and on the length of the calcinations, different shades are obtained, from a light yellow that is quite luminous to a yellowish orange. It is a pigment with a good covering power, suitable for oil painting and tempera painting, but it is not very permanent as it tends to fade on contact with sulphurs and if it is exposed to light. When it was put on the market in the first half of the 19th century, the artists made wide use of it, as it offered a great richness of nuances and tones; then it was gradually abandoned when new chrome yellows came on to the market. 2

In 1797, the French chemist Vauquelin, had discovered a new metal inside a mineral coming from Siberia; Vauquelin baptized it "chrome", which in Greek means "colour", as the metal was able to form compounds of varied and vivid colours, and he understood that the new metal could be used to obtain a pigment: in the very first years of the 19th century, *chrome yellow* (lead (II)-chromate) was already on the market. Its colour varies from lemon yellow to orange, depending on the method of preparation.

"The exact hue of lead chromate can be adjusted by coprecipitating it from solution with lead sulphate: half and half of each salt gives a primrose yellow, a mixture with 65 percent of lead chromate gives a lemon yellow, and an increasing proportion of the chromate progressively deepens to color. Vauquelin found that the color could also be varied by altering the temperature of the synthesis, which affects the size of the grains. The chemist reports that adding an acid to the solution yields a deep lemon yellow, which, he tells us is the most highly prized by painters. And if the pigment is precipitated from an alkaline solution, it take on an orange hue: a yellowish red, or sometimes a beautiful deep red. Predating cadmium orange, chrome orange was the first pure, strong orange pigment that artists had ever encountered (realgar tends towards yellow), and it was soon being deployed to dramatic effect.

"But for all their dazzling attractions, chrome pigments had to be affordable if they were ever going to find widespread use. That was never likely when the only source of chromium was in remote Siberia. In 1918 a French dictionary of "natural history applied to the arts" comments that even Russian artists "pay quite dearly" for lead chromate. Yet in that same year, deposits of the mineral

chromite (iron chromate) were discovered in the Var region of France. Chromite was also found in the Shetland Islands off Scotland in 1820. Such was the avidity with which the new pigments were consumed that the Var mines were all but exausted by 1829. But sources were also discovered in America from 1808, and by 1816 chromium ore was being imported across the Atlantic to England for pigment manufacture.

"Pure chrome yellows and oranges remained rather expensive during the first half of the nineteenth century. But because the tinting strength of the pigment is so strong, it can be mixed with appreciable quantities of extenders such as barium sulfate. This encouraged the use of the yellow in commercial paints. It was used on the coaches of Europe before it appeared on the canary-yellow taxicabs of the United States." 3

Chrome yellow is the base for all the chrome-based pigments in commerce; when it is chemically pure, it is sufficiently persistent to light exposure; compared to cadmium yellow, it is less persistent and very poisonous, but it has a lower cost; as well, it has a strong covering power and the brilliance of its hue cannot easily be matched by using other substances.

In 1809, Vauquelin managed to produce, from the element that had been isolated twelve years previously, pigments of various colours, yellow, red, green. In the arc of about ten years, the chrome pigments were produced industrially; as well as the yellow chrome that has already been described, orange, red and green chrome were also available.

Orange chrome is basic lead chrome, and it is obtained by making yellow chrome react with a strong base; it possesses all the merits of the yellow but without having the defects; it has a colour of extreme depth and purity and a high covering strength, it is very resistant to light and thanks to its basic character, it can also be used in fresco. Despite these qualities, its use is diminishing more and more nowadays, as *cadmium orange* is preferred because it possesses greater stability. 4

A noteworthy contribution to the knowledge of pigments used by the 19th century artists, comes not only through the exam of the survived pictorial materials of the age, but also from the notes left by the same manufacturers of colours and chemicals which, after having pointed out the formula for a new pigment, - differently from what happened in the eighteenth century – publish official relations on the nature, the properties and the procedure used to obtain it. A particularly interesting figure concerning this is that of the previously-mentioned George Field (1777-1854) who was the main supplier of colours to Turner and to the most important painters of that time, and also the most important English manufacturer of colours in the 19th century. Field carried out rigorous experiments on the stability of the new pigments, uncovering qualities and defects, and in this way making the artists aware of the risks that they could run. In 1835, he publishes a text entitled *Chromatography*, a treatise on the colours and pigments and their potential in painting; from the experiments carried out by him, detailed descriptions exist in almanacs that were completed in the period 1804-1825, and preserved at the Courtauld Institute of Art in London; the almanacs contain samples of pigments, notes on experiments, and comments on the colours of that time, with references to contemporary painters, who often supplied him with samples of colour; among the pigments that were perfected by him is the excellent *orange vermilion*, a version of synthetic mercuric sulphide, exalted for its colour tone that is perfect for flesh tones, its covering power and its colour fastness. 5

The term *lemon yellow* refers to both the pigment based on barium chromate and to that based on strontium chromate; the mixing of the two types was very common during the nineteenth century; a beautiful example of lemon yellow is seen in the dress of the

Young Christian Girl, painted by Paul Gauguin in 1894, now in the S. and F. Clark Institute, Williamstown, MA, USA.

In the course of the nineteenth century, nearly all the pigments still used by the artists are synthetized and then put on the market; the methods of preparation have been perfected and speeded up, but the basic components of the pigments have remained the same.

A lovely, inorganic yellow obtained by synthesis at the beginning of the nineteenth century is the *Cadmium yellow* (cadmium sulphide), on the market since 1846; it is obtained artificially from a cadmium salt, the mineral that was discovered by Stromeyer in 1817; depending on the different methods of preparation, yellow pigments with different colour depths are obtained; today, it is undoubtedly one of the most important colours in the artists' palettes, because of its meritable qualities that make it suitable for all pictorial techniques: good covering power, unalterability on exposure to light, to dampness and to the presence of sulphur fumes, resistant to lime, it is not poisonous; only two defects: it does not want to be mixed with lead-based pigments and it is rather expensive.

Cadmium red is a permanent pigment, very opaque, with a tone of deep red: Matisse (1869-1954) loved it very much and made it the protagonist of several of his paintings, such as the famous *The Red Room*, 1908 (Hermitage, St. Petersburg) and *The Red Studio*, 1911, (MoMA, New York), where the artist spreads the pigment flat, with no shaping, to preserve its charm and purity.

It is a compound of cadmium sulfoselenide, patented in Germany in 1892. By varying the proportions of cadmium and selenium one gets a range of colours from orange to dark brown.

Zinc yellow (basic zinc chromate), discovered by Vauquelin in 1809, was developed as an artist's pigment in 1847.

It is a shiny pigment, of a lemon yellow colour; its covering power is inferior to that of chrome yellow, but it resists much better to the action of sulphuric acid; it is used by artists in oil painting and watercolour. 6

In the 18th century, the green tones were still obtained by mixtures of other colours or by copper compounds; the new green pigments discovered at the end of the century, like for example *Sheele's green* (copper arsenite), *Schweinfurt green* or *emerald green* (copper acetoarsenite) a compound of arsenic and verdigris, almost the same as *Paris green* (copper (II) acetate triarsenite) – all of which would be lethal to many people, as we'll see a little further on - and *Brunswick green* (basic copper chloride) still derive from copper and consequently, as with all colours of this type, they had various negative characteristics, such as poor covering power, instability of colour, and high toxicity.

Emerald green, so much loved by Monet and Cézanne for its thickness and its bright colour, fascinated many other artists, interior decorators, designers and dyers who used the instant-soluble version to dye clothes in a colour which had become very fashionable by this time; but a dangerous killer, silent and elusive was hiding behind such beauty. The deadly composition, arsenic and verdigris, has been responsible for many deaths among the children who slept in rooms with walls painted or coated with emerald green-dyed papers because of the fumes of arsenic emanated during the night, and even many adults, in particular those who wore silk underwear dyed with emerald green-based colourant, passed away after long sufferings. In the Victorian houses the presence of such a killer was massive: used in wallpapers, artificial floral ornaments, candles, to colour confectionery and cake decorations! At a banquet held by the Irish Regiment in London in the 1850s, the table decorations were sugar leaves coloured by them (with arsenic green); many of the diners took these home for their children to eat as sweets, thus killing many of them. 7

Although doctors and chemists had understood the danger of such materials as the arsenic-based greens, their appeals went unheeded and in 1870 the UK had become the world's largest producer of arsenic. In the 1870s new green synthetic dyes began to replace the arsenic-based ones; yet, despite the scientific evidence of its toxicity, it was not until the 1960s that the production of emerald green was banned.

(Today the green pigments on the market, even if labeled as 'Emerald Green', are totally free from the deadly arsenic)

In 1780, the Swedish chemist, Sven Rinman, invented the *cobalt green*, calcining cobalt and zinc oxide together; the new green became available for sale in 1835, when zinc oxide was produced on a large scale. Cobalt green, still in use, was defined as being chemically and artistically perfect; it is, in fact, suitable for all pictorial techniques, with an excellent resistance to light and lime, cannot be attacked by alkalis, with a beautiful, brilliant green blue colour; yet it does not have a high covering power, a defect which prevents it from receiving the favour it deserves, from artists. In the early nineteenth century, the chrome colours begin to be manufactured, endowed with lovely deep and luminous shades, and with great chemical stability and permanence; in 1838, in Paris, the most stable of all the green pigments is manufactured, which is *viridian* (hydrated chromium oxide), obtained by various methods, most commonly by the calcinations of a mixture of potassium with boric acid and sulphur. The pigment is a beautiful deep green, with an excellent lightfastness, resistant to dampness, to lime and to all types of binding media. Due to its stability, it is also used nowadays in inks and as car paint.

Cobalt pigments are created during the first half of the nineteenth century; these pigments are endowed with great stability, resistance to light and are unalterable with most of the auxiliary chemical products. The most ancient pigment with a cobalt content was smalt which, at the start of the 19th century, was replaced by a new cobalt pigment synthetized in 1802, *cobalt blue*, (cobalt (II) oxide-aluminium oxide), which was made by combining cobalt oxide and aluminium; cobalt oxide is present in nature in the form of black powder; it was used in the Middle East to apply blue glaze on pottery, from at least the 8th century onwards, and it became very popular in the 14th century when it was used for the ceramics of the Ming dynasty. Cobalt blue is a pigment that possesses many qualities; it is stable, resistant to light and dampness, unalterable by acids and alkalis; therefore excellent in fresco as well; it has a lovely, brilliant colour that varies from light blue to blue green, depending on the proportions of the components. The process for obtaining cobalt blue is published for the first time in France, in 1802, by L.J. Thénard; the procedure used by the French chemist consists of a calcinated mixture of alumina and cobalt-phosphate in variable proportions, depending on the shade that one wishes to obtain; the quantity of alumina present in the mixture determines the depth and the tone of the pigment. Considering its qualities, cobalt blue soon became, and still is today, the object of imitations and falsifications.

Another cobalt pigment is *cerulean blue*, composed of potassium stannate. The process for obtaining it was developed in Germany in 1805; in 1860, it was put on the market by the English company Rowney and Co.

It is obtained by precipitating cobalt chloride with potassium stannate and successively mixing it with silica and calcium sulphate. It is highly stable, inert on exposure to natural and artificial light, unalterable by acids and alkalis, and is a lovely, light blue colour [8]; at this point, it is not difficult to imagine that its high cost constitutes its defect; a defect that, as we have already seen in the case of green, also weighed on the other cobalt colours, including the beautiful *cobalt yellow* (potassium cobalt nitrite), that was for sale as a pigment in mid-18th century, and which the artists baptized "aureolin"; it was widely-used only in watercolour.

In spite of the favour that Prussian blue enjoyed from the artists, the discovery of its defects made it necessary to find a blue with characteristics that were completely satisfactory. The chemists aimed at the synthesis of ultramarine, but it was not so easy to understand its composition as the unity of elements present in lazulite - the mineral that gives the typical colour to the lapis lazuli – is complex and variable; in fact, the samples show different quantities of sodium and sulphur, in some, ions of chloride or sulphur are present. In 1806, the analysis of the composition of ultramarine, carried out by the French chemists J.B. Désormes and F. Clement, is published: it is a compound of soda, silica, alumina and sulphur. On the basis of this indication, the light blue compounds are identified as by-products of some industrial works, particularly that of soda; as well, in 1787, Goethe, during one of his journeys to Italy, had already noticed the presence of light blue deposits in the lime ovens in the area of Palermo; these deposits were removed and cut and used in that area for decorative purposes in place of lapis lazuli. Several years later, the French chemist M. Tassaert, notices the same thing in France, in the glass industry at St. Gobin, where the blue deposits had formed in the soda furnaces. Tassaert asks Vauquelin to analyse that blue material and the result is a composition very similar to the one that Désormes and Clèment had given for Ultramarine.

In 1824, the National Industry Development Company offers a prize of 6,000 francs to whoever is able to find a worthwhile method of industrial production of the pigment, at a selling price of less than three hundred francs a kilo.

In 1826, Jean Baptiste Guimet, a colour manufacturer from Toulouse, synthesizes ultramarine in his laboratory in Paris, and he begins selling it for a tenth of the price of natural ultramarine; the Company awards the prize to Guimet and, two years later, *synthetic ultramarine* is already being produced on an industrial scale.

The artificial ultramarine, also known as "Guimet blue", "French ultramarine", "permanent blue", has, therefore, a chemical composition that is similar to that of lapis lazuli; in the synthesis process, sodium carbonate or sulphate, aluminium, sulphur, wood carbonate, and silica are ground and mixed, then placed in an airless oven to heat up slowly. The substance that is obtained after the cooling is a vitreous mass, of a green colour, that must be ground again, washed in order to eliminate the soluble impurities and dried; after which it is heated to a temperature of 750°C, at which it assumes a blue coloration; the colour tone can be varied by changing the proportion of the components of the mixture. The blue substance, once it has been washed and ground finely, becomes the artificial ultramarine pigment.

"Artificial Ultramarine has regular granules, small and round, different to those of natural Ultramarine, which are of irregular sizes. This diversity between the two pigments makes the artificial Ultramarine appear, under light, more deaden and less alive than the natural Ultramarine, because in the modern pigment, the regular grain makes the light spread equally in all directions, while in the pigment obtained from lapis lazuli, the bigger and smaller particles produce a livelier and more brilliant effect." 9

The properties of artificial ultramarine are similar to those of the natural pigment; it is stable, it has a good covering power, it is suited to all pictorial techniques; even so, when it was available on the market, it did not have the success that it deserved initially, and for a certain period, the artists continued to be distrustful of an artificial product that was able to rival the much-esteemed, natural ultramarine. Towards the end of the century, when the true qualities of the new pigment had been ascertained, including a price that was decidedly ridiculous compared to that of lapis lazuli blue, the artificial ultramarine becomes, together with cobalt blue, the fundamental blue in the painters' palettes.

In his famous painting *Umbrellas*, (National Gallery, London) performed in two different stages, between 1881 and 1885, Renoir initially makes use of cobalt blue and later on of the less expensive artificial ultramarine, blending both of them with red lake to give the blues a slight, iridescent purplish reflection.

The new colours, which present completely new characteristics and possibilities compared to preceding materials, are widely used by the Impressionists who wish to capture on canvas the vibrancy of the colour and the tricks of light in the surrounding reality and in the various moments of the day; but it is not only the availability of the pigments suited to their artistic tensions that permits them to create works with such bright, bold, striking colours; it is also and above all, the way in which the Impressionists use colour that makes their works so special, because of those effects of intense luminosity that are totally innovative compared to the traditional academic painting. Their paintwork is thick and vigorous; in many cases the colours are mixed directly onto the canvas or else the paintbrush is passed with a light touch on the adjoining hues, and it is left to the eye of the beholder to create the mixture, according to the process that is called optical blending of colour. They very often use pure, unmixed colours that are in contrast to each other, to make them stand out as much as possible, using a pale background or even leaving the canvas without any background. In the Impressionist technique, the new theories on colours play an extremely important role in the use of colour. The work of the French chemist, Eugene Chevreul, (1786-1889), *On the law of the simultaneous contrast of colours*, appears in 1839 and immediately becomes a fundamental text for painters; in 1824, Chevreul is named director of the dye-works in Gobelin's tapestry factory; his experience inside the prestigious factory leads him to study and elaborate a rigorous method in the classification of colours and to publish his theories on colour and on its practical application. He notes that the weaving of the yarns is often executed with the matching of complementary tones, or almost, and the result is that, looked at from afar, the colours cannot be distinguished, but blend on the screen.

He discovers that colours change in relation to the other colours which are found nearby, that the complementary colours, or those that are directly opposite each other on the colour wheel, create the deepest effects if placed close to each other; the combinations of red-green or blue-orange cause a real vibration in the eye of the beholder and the colour seems to almost jump out of the canvas.

Brunello summarizes Chevreul's experience like this:

"He had noticed the strange, faded effect of the black yarns used to produce shadings in certain blue and violet drapes. By then comparing the black yarns produced in Gobelin's dye-works with those dyed in other, famous establishments, he did not notice that there was an effective difference of intensity between the various samples; he guessed at once that the apparently faded effect of the blacks on the blue and violet must be due to an optical effect because of the colour contrast, and from that moment on, he devoted himself diligently to search for the law that governed such a phenomenon. In this way, he established that:

1) When two coloured objects are placed next to each other, each one loses its specific colour and it assumes a new one, because of the influence of the complementary one that is near it.

2) Putting two colours of a different tone close to each other, the tone of the stronger one stands out and it increases the tone of the weaker one.

3) If two adjacent colours are complementary, the tones of each are exalted.

"In 1864, another work is published, with the title 'Of colours and their application à l'aide of the chromatic circles'. In this work, Chevreul points out the importance of the fundamental colours, on the base of which he could establish the composition of any coloured mixture. He made use of circles with dyes that were gradually shaded, to fix and define all the compositions perceivable to the practiced eye of the dyer, so obtaining a good 14,000 different tones. In this way, he created that chromatic construction that was perfectioned later on by Ostwald, which is at the base of most of the systems of colour definition, still in use even today." 10

The text of the American physicist, Ogden Rood, would become just as fundamental, *The Modern Science of Colours* (1879), which links the theory of colours to materials, so supplying the artists with a clear and precious guideline. An eloquent example of the application of the contrast of colour is offered by Renoir, in one of his most famous paintings on which we report Ball's comment: *"Boating on the Seine (1879-1880) has a strident orange skiff set against the deep blue water, while the red shadows of the prow complement a patch of green foliage in the foreground and pale buildings cast yellow highlights amid the purples of their shadowy reflections. The pigments in this picture (in addition to lead white) are limited to just seven, with all but the reds being modern synthetics: cobalt blue, viridian, chrome yellow, lemon yellow (strontium chromate), chrome orange (basic lead chromate), vermilion, and red lake. They are applied almost unmixed, and the impact of the new, pure orange is never more apparent, used in thick, pure strokes for the boat's outline. The river is portrayed in pure cobalt blue, with only white added in places and with a glaze of red lake to produce the purple shadows."* 11

Van Gogh, too, had understood well just how effective the combination of complementaries and primaries was; in his two paintings *Café Terrasse on the Place du Forum*, 1888, (Kroller-Muller, Otterlo, Netherlands) and *Night Café*, 1888, (Art Gallery, Yale University), the simultaneous contrast creates two completely different atmospheres. In the first, the artist recreates the quiet, peaceful atmosphere of a 'café' in a small square of Arles in a clear and starry night; the artist to make the eye move around the painting, doesn't rely on composition, but on the use of complementaries; the field depth is created by the fact that the cold colour recedes toward the background while the warm colours advance to the foreground; for the night sky and the door in the foreground he uses Prussian blue and viridian with a touch of red lake; for the yellows he uses lemon chrome yellow and for the oranges a mixture of lemon chrome yellow and geranium lake.

As for *Night Café*, Van Gogh writes in a letter to his brother Theo:

" *I've tried to express the terrible human passions with the red and the green.*

"The room is blood-red and dull yellow, a green billiard table in the centre, four lemon yellow lamps with an orange and green glow. Everywhere it's a battle and an antithesis of the most different greens and reds; in the characters of the sleeping ruffians, small in the empty, high room, some purple and blue. The blood-red and the yellow-green of the billiard table, for example, contrast with the little bit of delicate Louis XV green of the counter, where there's a pink bouquet.

"The white clothes of the owner, watching over things from a corner in this furnace, become lemon yellow, pale luminous green." 12

In fact, the whole painting is a clashing and a striking contrast between reds and greens. The artist depicts it by superimposing thick layers of colour, without saving the amount of pigment used, and he explains why in another letter to his brother Theo in April 1888: "*All the colors that the Impressionists brought into fashion are unstable, so there is all the more reason not to be afraid to lay them on too crudely - time will tone them down only too much*"

Van Gogh, like other painters of his time, welcomes the new bright colours with great enthusiasm, experiences them avidly, but like everyone else he does not know their actual quality or their possible defects; he could not therefore expect that many of his paintings would undergo a total discoloration or a strong darkening where he used geranium lake, which is red eosin, invented in Paris in 1871, and chrome yellow, also used by the artist in his many versions of *Sunflowers*. At least twenty works among those in the Amsterdam Museum on which Van Gogh used geranium lake, a shade that the artist loved, show a significant deterioration compared to the original shades: one that he painted in pink has become white, flowers of purple shades are now light blue with purple blotches. Nor the famous *Iris* in the Metropolitan Museum in New York was spared: the background, now white, was originally a vibrant pink. Light might be the cause of these changes; in fact, comparing the copies of the paintings he made in watercolour, it is clearly apparent that the geranium lake, protected from the exposure to light, has kept all its vibrant hue. Other illustrious victims are some versions of *Sunflowers* in which the chrome yellow tends now to brown, which also happened to the version in the Amsterdam Museum; instead, the version in the National Gallery in London, which is also considered the most beautiful ever, has remained unchanged. Also in this case, light exposure seems among the most probable causes, considering that Amsterdam *Sunflowers* has extensively travelled, while the painting in London has never moved. However it is not yet clear what all the real factors are that have led to the deterioration of the yellow chromate in both this and in other works.

Van Gogh had therefore good reason not to save the new colours because only time would reveal their real characteristics.

And in fact, some industrially manufactured pigments unfortunately contained impurities which, through time, would cause colour changes or discoloration in many paintings by other famous artists.

The work of the painters, especially of those who painted outdoors, was greatly facilitated when, in 1841, the English company Winsor & Newton began to market the new modern colours in tubes of soft material, an invention by the American painter John Rand; it was a real revolution in the palette and in the technique of the painters who worked *en plein air* and who, prior to this invention, had to keep the oil colours in packets of pig bladder to avoid them drying too quickly. So Renoir commented: "*The colours in tubes, easily transportable, have allowed us to paint from life to the full. Without colours in tubes, there would have been no Cézanne, no Monet, no Sisley or Pissarro, nothing of what journalists were to call Impressionism*". 13

Monet's and Cézanne's Palette

After examining the palette used by Monet in 1869 for the painting *Bathers at La Grenouillère* (National Gallery, London), what is significant is not so much the fact that the pigments used for this work represent the entire set of colours which Monet (1840-1926) continued to use in the course of his long career; what is remarkable is the fact that almost all the pigments used in 1869 are products of the same Monet's era, the only exceptions being vermilion and Prussian blue. In fact, Monet uses cobalt blue as the main pigment for water, used pure or mixed with lead white, small amounts of Prussian blue and purple cobalt for the tonal variations of water; chrome yellow and lemon yellow (barium chromate) mixed together to form the bright yellow of the trees in the background; emerald green and viridian, both in various mixtures, to form the different shades of green; chrome green - an homogenous mixture of chrome yellow and Prussian blue – for the vivid yellow–green hue of the foliage on the left side of the painting; cobalt violet, in various mixtures, for example in the blue mid-tones of the blue water and in the violet flowers on the left side. 14

Towards the end of the nineteenth century chrome yellow will be replaced by cadmium yellow; according to the testimony of Moisse, his colour supplier in the last years, Monet requested to supply him: white lead, cobalt violet light, emerald green, synthetic extra fine ultramarine, vermilion -some rare times-, three shades of cadmium yellow: light, dark, lemon; 'ultramarine lemon yellow' (probably zinc yellow). In the years of the Twentieth century, Monet tends to make less use of mixtures and to use purer colors. The palette for *Water Lilies*, painted after 1916, now in the National Gallery in London, consists of:

lead white
cobalt violet light
viridian
cobalt blue
synthetic ultramarine
vermilion
cadmium yellow
zinc / barium yellow

The palette for *Irises*, ca.1914 (London Nat. Gallery) consists of:
lead white
cobalt violet light
viridian
cobalt blue
synthetic ultramarine

cadmium yellow
orange cadmium
zinc / barium yellow
red lake pigment, most likely derived from madder
The pigments in these two palettes are in full accordance with the suggestions given by contemporary scholars such as Vibert who, in the appendix to a cycle of lectures at the School of Fine Arts, gives a list of the 'good' and 'bad' pigments; omitting many as unstable or because they are incompatible in the mixtures, he saves only a dozen: lead white, zinc white, cadmium yellow, vermilion, cobalt blue, synthetic ultramarine, cobalt green, viridian and purple cobalt, a list which largely corresponds to Monet's choice in the twentieth century.[15]

In the 1870s Cézanne (1839-1906) makes friends with Pissarro (1830-1903) and begins to paint with him; his palette changes and takes on a new personality; and from the 1880s, the pigments he uses will remain the same until his death. From the technical analysis of some of his paintings in the London National Gallery it emerges that the list of pigments reported by his friend and artist Emile Bernard during his last visit to Cézanne in 1905 corresponds almost entirely to the following palette:

lead white
chrome yellow, yellow ocher, yellow lake
vermilion, red earth, madder and cochineal lake
viridian, emerald green, green earth
cobalt blue, synthetic ultramarine, Prussian blue.
Cézanne, in perpetual debt to his supplier, initially uses only Prussian blue to which through time he adds ultramarine; when its economic position begins to consolidate, after 1896, we see an increased use of cobalt blue (for example in The Bathers in London)

188

In his paintings in the National Gallery emerald green, vermilion and yellow ocher are often used; lead white and carbon black are in all the works examined; viridian is often used; chrome yellow has been detected in three paintings, including *The Bathers*, dating from 1880; red earth is not prominent; cochineal lake on a substrate of tin is used in *The Bathers*. As for the 'brilliant yellow' and 'peach black' of Bernard's list, it is believed that the former is a variety of Naples yellow prepared by chrome yellow and white lead while the second is probably black of charcoal 16. No trace could be found of 'rose madder', a lake made from madder, very popular as a pigment for artists after the plant was introduced in the Netherlands in the sixteenth century; the dye was extracted with an acid; the precipitate, mainly (pseudo) purpurin, was again dissolved in alum, and once again precipitated with calcium carbonate to obtain a nice pink lake. 17

The new colours were so beautiful, dense and bright that many artists regarded them as a work of art in themselves.

A new vision of color

Cézanne's statement that colour on its own is the fundamental element to create a work of art was to deeply mark the twentieth century.

Cézanne perceived colour as a living entity, he said that "*colour is living, all alone it breathes life into things*" and he made colour the vehicle for the most profound meanings.

In the new perspective, colour is fully freed from tradition, it is colour that gives shape, which is itself the form, which is the face and the voice of the emotions, passions, joys, tragedies or dreamlike visions of the artist.

For the Symbolist and Gauguin the symbolic value or meaning of a work of art stems from the recreation of emotional experiences in the viewer.

Gauguin revealed the mysterious and metaphysical values of colour.

Matisse felt colours as 'forces' working in concert; he said that *"with colour one obtains an energy that seems to stem from witchcraft"*

Matisse rejected the traditional three-dimensional space and sought instead a new picture space defined by the movement of colour planes.

"In Summer 1906, during his brief Fauvist period, he created brilliantly colored canvases structured by color applied in a variety of brushwork, ranging from thick impasto to flat areas of pure pigments, sometimes accompanied by a sinuous, arabesque-like line". **18**

The Fauve arbitrary combine bright colours and energetic brushwork to structure the composition; they use colour instinctively as a way to give and to release emotions; by eliminating every nuance, every effect of volume and depth, they use intense brushstrokes of exuberant, bright colours, mostly primary and in stark contrast; unnatural and vibrant colours, symbol of the complete independence of the work with respect to the subject; the tendency to use colours like notes, to get the same emotional effects of music through colour, is already evident in the Fauves; and the link between music and painting is even more evident in Kandinsky (1866-1944) and in the painters of the Blaue Reiter who often use the term 'vibration' to indicate the visual effect caused by the colours that try to imitate the sounds and translate into images the same emotions; abstract images that can express the same state of mind that one feels when one listens to music; a spiritual colour that can give voice to the artist's inner subjectivity, a colour that produces strong emotions, a colour able to reveal the inner world because what does matter is not the sensory effect but the spiritual resonance; unreal and often delicate colours in the dreamlike and idealized world of Franz Marc (1880-1916); he shared with Kandinsky colours that give a spiritual dimension to the matter and communicate the values of interiority; his famous horses are often blue, the colour of the deepest spirituality, and there is a whole world of animals represented with unnatural colours to emphasize that you are not facing a naturalistic representation, but rather the evocation of a dream or the visual representation of an emotion the artist was feeling at the moment he was painting. [19]

The beautiful color harmonies of Marc are based on a mostly 'modern' palette in which, in addition to red earth, vermilion, Prussian blue and black ivory, are all the best pigments of the latest production: white zinc, lemon yellow, alizarin lake, emerald green, viridian, cerulean blue, synthetic ultramarine, cobalt violet.

In the years of the 'blue period', from 1901 to 1904, Picasso makes use of blue, in its various gradations, as the only colour able to express his personal pain and depression but also the suffering of the entire humanity; he makes use of cobalt blue and Prussian blue, sometimes adding merely small quantities of cadmium yellow to create different shades. Once he got through that sad period, his palette began to grow more and more until it became the forerunner of innovative experimentation.

With *Les Demoiselles d'Avignon*, 1907, (MoMA, New York) we face a turning point not only for the development of Picasso's artistic personality but also of all art to come. The palette used for this painting includes: lead white, vermilion, cobalt blue, ocher, bone black, emerald green and cadmium yellow. [20]

A few years later the palette of the eclectic and eccentric genius of the incipient century will include something totally new in painting. An early champion of industrial materials in the field of fine arts, Picasso begins to experiment paints for interiors from 1912 onwards, well before the introduction of PVA, alkyds and acrylics, later made popular by artists such as Jackson Pollock, David Alfaro Siqueiros and Morris Louis.

The choice of the artist for such non-traditional materials seems to be dictated by their consistency and by the availability of a wide range of colours as well as by a radical avant-garde interest in introducing these products for the home- paints and paints for walls and boats- in his artistic production. The glazes produced by the French firm Ripolin were soon discovered by other artists; the paintings by Picasso, Picabia and his contemporaries believed to contain these new materials would become known as 'Ripolin paintings'. In fact, Ripolin colours were bright, they formed a flat, shiny surface, on which no sign of the brush remained, and they dried quickly. A splendid example of the result can be seen in The Art Institute of Chicago: *The Red Armchair*, 1931, is an oil on canvas painted by Picasso with Ripolin colours. [21]

However, there are still many supposed 'Ripolin paintings' by Picasso to be analysed; to carry on this task new groups of researchers have been recently formed both at the AIC and at the Museum of Antibes, which has an extraordinary collection of works by the Catalan artist.

With Picasso and his daring innovations we are already in the full twentieth century, a period which brings many other innovations both for the birth of the most diverse artistic movements and for the use of new materials.

12) A PALETTE WITHOUT LIMITS

Revolutionary new materials

In 1920, more than one hundred years after the discovery of the metal in 1796, a new white is available on the market, the *Titanium white* which consists of titanium dioxide. This new white will entirely replace both lead white, highly toxic, and zinc white whose covering power was not satisfactory. It is the only important inorganic pigment of the 20th century; it is a very durable material, with great covering power and which can be used for many applications in addition to its use as pictorial material.
The beginning of the 20th century sees the emergence of three groups of synthetic organic pigments.
In Germany, where most of the European chemical industries were concentrated, thanks to the advances in structural organic chemistry, it turns out that insoluble salts of azo dyes could be synthesized without having to turn them into lakes. The first azo pigment is yellow tartrazine patented in 1884; the year 1911 sees the birth of another group of *azo pigments,* known as Hansa, including Hansa yellow G, very bright and of great commercial success. The colour of these pigments ranges from lemon yellow to red burgundy and they started being widely used in paints and inks. Discovered by chance in the first half of the 20th century, the group of blue and green pigments called *Phtalocyanine*, revealed remarkable properties such as colour intensity, fastness to light and chemical reagents; very popular among the artists they became the bestselling pigments ever.
At the beginning of the mid-twentieth century *quinacridone colours* make their appearance on the market; they have excellent stability to light, remarkable covering and colouring power, and are particularly used as car paint; their colours range from orange-red

to violet; they gained the favour of the Abstract Expressionists in New York who welcomed them because of their strong shades.

In the 1930s there is a new output on the market, that is the colours based on *synthetic resins*, the new synthetic binders that revolutionize the way of using colour; the novelty is therefore not in the pigment or in the dye, but in the dispersion medium, which consists of a series of organic polymers of various types, including acrylic resins, polyvinyl acetate resins or PVA, and alkyd resins.

The American industry offers for sale a good number of new synthetic paints for cars and enamel paints for interiors, which prove to possess considerable new qualities and advantages; they have bright colours, fastness to light, they can be spread with great ease; the new binders, synthetic resins, also allow a quick drying. Initially, most of the manufacturers of such coatings remain completely unaware of the fact that most of these products end up on the canvas of great artists like Pollock (1912-1956), Siqueiros (1896-1974), Stella (born in 1936), Warhol (1928-1987).

Industrial paints " *were cheaper and more readily available, especially during World War II, when natural raw materials were difficult to obtain. They also appealed to artists who wanted to experiment with nontraditional materials to create nontraditional art. David Alfaro Siqueiros, Franz Kline, and Willem de Kooning were some of the artists who turned to industrial paints in the creation of their works. In Jackson Pollock's ink and enamel drawing of ca. 1948–49 the red synthetic paint has a raised body and shiny appearance. The physical characteristics of this synthetic paint, which allow it to flow and drip, are integral to Pollock's unconventional methods. This paint can capture movement and gesture, from the finest line to the largest blobs, reflecting the speed and angle of application. ...*

"The development of acrylic paints specifically for artists by Bocour Colors in the late 1940s and early '50s was one of the most

significant innovations in artists' materials. These first paints were acrylic resin solutions. Marketed as Magna, these highly pigmented paints, which could be thinned with turpentine and used with oils, made them immediately attractive to modern artists such as Morris Louis, Kenneth Noland, Jules Olitski, and Roy Lichtenstein. Louis, a close collaborator in the development of Magna color, used it to create the strong colored stripes of his painting Alpha-Pi. The complete saturation of the unprimed canvas with the pure, high-tone color in thin transparent washes was only achievable with the new synthetic paint, an acrylic resin solution. Mark Rothko also used these paints. Like Louis, he experimented with this medium and was able to achieve matte, near-powdery surfaces with very strong saturated color. (..) In the mid-1950s, acrylic emulsion paints, often referred to as "acrylics," were also being developed and marketed to contemporary artists. Andy Warhol and Helen Frankenthaler were among the first artists to use this new medium. Like other successful synthetic media, acrylics are highly versatile in terms of texture, gloss, and thickness. They can be diluted in water instead of turpentine or paint thinner, they dry very quickly, and, unlike Magna color, they do not resolublize with the addition of other layers of acrylic. This allows the artist to paint layer upon layer without disturbing the previously applied paint. Acrylics also cause less change to paper and textiles, giving the artist more freedom in choosing supports for the work of art". 1

American Expressionism

In the late 1930s and early 1940s, New York replaces Paris as the centre of the artistic world, becoming the world's new capital of modern art; American artists active in New York in the 1940s, including, among others, Jackson Pollock and Mark Rothko, are considered the first generation of Abstract Expressionism of the New York school.

They *"advanced audacious formal inventions in a search for significant content. Breaking away from accepted conventions in both technique and subject matter, the artists made monumentally scaled works that stood as reflections of their individual psyches— and in doing so, attempted to tap into universal inner sources. These artists valued spontaneity and improvisation, and they accorded the highest importance to process"*. 2

Abstract Expressionism, *"encompasses two very different sensibilities. One, exemplified by the work of Jackson Pollock and Willem de Kooning, is characterized by energetic brushwork and rhythmic, dynamic compositions; the other, contemplative in tone and made up of subtle color harmonies, relatively static compositions, and simple forms, is embodied by the paintings of Mark Rothko."* 3

For these artists painting is a demonstration of creative freedom, an energic, individualistic and signs-gestural expression free from any compositive, formal, figurative influence.

In 1936, in New York, Jackson Pollock and David Alfaro Siqueiros share their own laboratory, often frequented by artists who will be greatly affected by the new techniques and new pigments that the two artists are experiencing in those years and by their relationship with colour.

Siqueiros starts using resins, varnishes and paints for cars and is the first of the great Mexican muralists, to make use of the airbrush for artistic purposes. He slowly pours, sprays, dripping colours to achieve the effects they create unpredictably; many of his works are also characterized by large decisive and vigorous outlines.

"Early on, the Abstract Expressionists, in seeking a timeless and powerful subject matter, turned to primitive myth and archaic art for inspiration. Rothko, Pollock, Motherwell, Gottlieb, Newman,

and Baziotes all looked to ancient or primitive cultures for expression. Their early works feature pictographic and biomorphic elements transformed into personal code. ... Jungian psychology was compelling too, in its assertion of the collective unconscious. Directness of expression was paramount, best achieved through lack of premeditation. ... In 1947, Pollock developed a radical new technique, pouring and dripping thinned paint onto raw canvas laid on the ground (instead of traditional methods of painting in which pigment is applied by brush to primed, stretched canvas positioned on an easel). The paintings were entirely nonobjective. In their subject matter (or seeming lack of one), scale (huge), and technique (no brush, no stretcher bars, no easel), the works were shocking to many viewers. ... For Abstract Expressionists, the authenticity or value of a work lay in its directness and immediacy of expression. A painting is meant to be a revelation of the artist's authentic identity. The gesture, the artist's "signature," is evidence of the actual process of the work's creation. It is in reference to this aspect of the work that critic Harold Rosenberg coined the term "action painting" in 1952: "At a certain moment the canvas began to appear to one American painter after another as an arena in which to act—rather than as a space in which to reproduce, re-design, analyze, or 'express' an object, actual or imagined. What was to go on the canvas was not a picture but an event." 4

In all his 'drip' paintings, Pollock works from above with the canvas lying on the floor.

*"On the floor I am more at ease," he said "I feel nearer more a part of the painting since this way I can walk around it, work from the four sides, and literally be in the painting."*5

In such works as N.28 (1950, MET Museum), " *using various techniques - pouring enamel paint from a hole in the can, dropping from a stick, flingling, and dizzling - he applied paint from a* distance above the surface, using gravity and motion to form linear skeins". 6

In the 'Action Painting' the artist, through the action, that is the act of painting, directly expresses his inner drives of that moment, "*an immediate, free, spontaneous painting in which the whole body of the artist is involved in the making of the artwork the execution of which is entrusted to the gesture of the arm (..) The action painting is the expression of a mood, the explosion of a charge of energy, the explosion of an inner impulse that are not expressed according to a predetermined plan, but follows almost automatically an uncontrollable impulse from the depth ... "* 7

" *Pollock believed his free and yet controlled application of paint had a connection to his inner being—his unconscious—which was in turn connected to larger forces outside the self. One Number 31, 1950 (MOMA, New York) exemplifies this relationship between the self and the universal. When asked to describe the relationship between his work and nature, Pollock stated emphatically, "I am nature."* 8

American Abstract Expressionism is also the domain of colour to which Rothko approaches with a very different interpretation; Mark Rothko (1903-1970) embodies the abstract lyricism: a recall to the contemplation of the harmony of colour fields, intense or delicate, with light and transparent glazes. Rothko uses oil colours, together with the new acrylic paints and often powders the painted surface with powdered pigments, thus giving colour a satin and ethereal look.

To apply the colour he often makes use of sponges rather than brushes, "*and of a chromatic material diluted at most, almost impalpable, in order to create a visual effect of immateriality, and a sense of mystery and transcendence.* " 9

"*Color should provoke in viewers a quasi-religious experience, even eliciting tears*". 10

When the great art collector Duncan Phillips, the founder of the Phillips Collection in Washington, saw the paintings by Rothko, he felt an immediate empathy, revealing a deep understanding of the emotional impact of colour. Phillips bought three paintings, *Green and Maroon* 1953, *Green and Tangerine on Red* 1956 and *Orange and Red on Red* 1957.

In looking at the paintings by Rothko, Phillips wrote:

"What we recall are not memories but old emotions disturbed or resolved -some sense of well being suddenly shadowed by a cloud- yellow ochres strangely soffused with a drift of gray prevailing over an ambience of rose or the fire diminishing into a glow of embers, or the light when the night descends."

In 1960 Phillips designated a specific room for Rothko's paintings: "a small, cosy room with one painting on each wall (in 1964 he had purchased 'Ochre and Red on Red' 1954) with dim and soft lights to enhance the resonance of the colours, and with chairs for prolonged viewing. From the outset, the room was intended as a meditative space, even referred to by Phillips as a type of 'chapel'. (..) Rothko visited the room and treasured the atmosphere." 11

In most of the paintings of pure colour executed in 1968 Rothko uses acrylic paints, pigments with acrylic resins as binders, which acquire increased importance and favour among painters thanks to their peculiar characteristics: they are water-soluble, dry quickly and remain stable in any atmospheric situation, they are smooth and opaque, but may become more transparent if more diluted and can be used on any type of media. They will be the favourite colours of most of the artists of the second generation of Abstract Expressionism.

The eclectic Frank Stella (born 1936), as well as experimenting with new types of media, will use different techniques and more types of pigments in a single work; for instance, in *Gobba, zoppa e collotorto*, 1985, (Art Institute of Chicago) he uses oil, urethane enamel, fluorescent alkyd, acrylic and printing ink on etched magnesium and aluminum. 12

The formula of 'mixed media' is prevalent in the majority of the most famous American artists of this and of the following generation. One last example: the *Portrait of Brooke Hayward* (Tate London) painted in 1973 by Andy Warhol.

" *Warhol created this work by transferring a photographic image of Brooke Hayward to a silkscreen. The commercially prepared canvasses were laid flat and the acrylic emulsion paints were brushed onto the surface. A different colour was used for each of the main elements of the image: the background, skin, lips, irises, eyelids, and eyebrows. The paint was carefully applied within the outlines of these features, but loosely brushed in other areas, with variable thicknesses, incorporating some air bubbles. Next, the silkscreen was placed over the acrylic paint and a black printing ink was forced through the screen with a squeegee, transferring the image to the surface with characteristic dots. The screen was re-used for each of the four pictures and sometimes the positioning of the image did not coincide exactly with the paint. The use of silkscreen by Warhol was not a typical commercial technique. (..) The silk screen (black) areas were all identified as an alkyd medium - an oil-resin binding medium commonly used in house paints and inks. The white priming layer was also identified as an alkyd medium. Warhol's palette included: titanium white; cadmium yellow/orange with associated barium sulphate; cobalt blue; chromium oxide green; possibly Mars red; with calcium sulphate and chalk extenders. The black pigment used in the silk screen ink is probably carbon black and the pink and red pigments were identified as synthetic quinacridone reds.*" 13

The palette is still growing, though without excluding traditional pigments; artists can now choose between an incredible range of alternatives according to their style and their favourite painting technique. And just browse through the catalog of historical and prestigious companies, such as the English Winsor & Newton or the German Kremer, to fully realize that the choice has really no limits.

NOTES

1) THE SEARCH FOR COLOUR

1) Brunello, F., 1964, 'Colori e pitture della preistoria', in *Pitture e vernici*, n.11, pp. 397-400
Milaneschi, A., 1991, 'Bruni e aranciati', in *La fabbrica dei colori*, pp. 139-150, ed. Il Bagatto
Occorsio, S., 1991, 'Verdi', in *La fabbrica dei colori*, pp. 271-2, ed. Il Bagatto
Pietropaoli, R., e Milaneschi, A., 1991, 'Gialli', in *La fabbrica dei colori*, pp. 197-200, ed. Il Bagatto
Quartullo, G., 1991, 'Terre rosse', in *La fabbrica dei colori*, pp. 94-5, ed. Il Bagatto
Rinaldi, D., 1991, 'Neri', in *La fabbrica dei colori*, pp. 58-67, ed. Il Bagatto

2) ANCIENT EGYPT

1) Ball, P., 2002, *Bright Earth*, pp. 62-3, Farrar, Straus and Giroux, New York

2) Luzzatto, L. and Pompas, R., 1988, *Il significato dei colori nelle civiltà antiche*, pp. 28-9/31-2 Rusconi, Milano

3) Brunello, F., 'Colori e pitture nell'Antico Egitto e in Mesopotamia' in *Pitture e Vernici*, n° 4, 1967

4) Della Torre Arrigoni, D., *"Once upon a time Kermes..."*
https://www.academia.edu

5) Brunello, F., 'Colori e pitture nell'Antico Egitto e in Mesopotamia' in *Pitture e Vernici*, n° 4, 1967

6) Augusti, S., 1986, *I colori pompeiani*, De Luca Editore

7) Clifford Dyer, H., 1909, *The lead and zinc pigments*, p. 2, John Wiley & Son

8) Augusti, S., 1986, *I colori pompeiani*, De Luca Editore
Rinaldi S., 'Bianchi e Neri', in *La fabbrica dei colori*,
pp.19-25, Il Bagatto, Roma

9) Ball, P., 2002, *Bright Earth*, pp. 67, Farrar, Straus and Giroux, New York

10) Brunello, F., 'Colori e pitture nell'Antico Egitto e in Mesopotamia' in *Pitture e Vernici*, n° 4, 1967

3) ANCIENT MESOPOTAMIA

1) Ball, P., 2002, *Bright Earth*, pp. 56-7, Farrar, Straus and Giroux, New York

2) Luzzatto, L. and Pompas, R., 1988, *Il significato dei colori nelle civiltà antiche*, pp.140-3, Rusconi, Milano

3) British Museum: *The 'Ram in a Thicket'*
http://www.britishmuseum.org/explore/highlights/highlight_objects/me/t/the_ram_in_a_th
icket.aspx

4) Brunello, F., 'Colori e pitture nell'Antico Egitto e in Mesopotamia'
   in *Pitture e Vernici, n° 4*, 1967

4) CLASSICAL ANTIQUITY

1) Ball, P., 2002, *Bright Earth*, pp. 19/67-70, Farrar, Straus and Giroux, New York

2) Luzzatto, L. and Pompas, R., 1988, *Il significato dei colori nelle civiltà antiche*, pp.11-12, Rusconi, Milano

3) Ball, P., 2002, *Bright Earth*, pp. 51/67, Farrar, Straus and Giroux, New York

4) Luzzatto, L. and Pompas, R., 1988, *Il significato dei colori nelle civiltà antiche*, pp.13-17, Rusconi, Milano

5) Pastoreau, M., 1987, *L'uomo e il colore*, p.19, Giunti, Florence

6) Augusti, S., 1986, *I colori pompeiani*, De Luca Editore

7) Vitruvio, *De Architectura*, VII, 11, 1

8) Augusti, S., 1986, *I colori pompeiani*, De Luca Editore

5) THE MEDIEVAL PALETTE

1) Luzzatto, L and Pompas, R, 1997, *I colori del vestire*, Ed. Hoepli, Milano

2) Pastoreau, M., 2000, *Blu, storia di un colore*, p.42-4, Ponte alle Grazie, Milano

3) Marco Pierini: *Appunti per una storia dei colori nella pittura medievale*
   (anno III n. 3-4, 1992, pp. 4-5, anno IV n.1, 1993, pp.6-7) Available online:

http://www.accademiajr.it/unicorno/articoli/uni008.htm

4)Pastoreau, M., 2000, *Blu, storia di un colore*, p.44, Ponte alle Grazie, Milano

5) Bomford, D., Dunkerton J.,Gordon D., Roy,A., 1989,
Art In The Making- Italian painting before 1400, p. 21,
National Gallery Company Limited
6) Ibid., pp.24-6

7) Monnas, L., 2008, *Princes, Merchants and Painters*,
pp. 68-73,Yale University Press

8) Brunello, F., 1986, *Marco Polo e le merci dell'Oriente*, Neri Pozza, Vicenza
Lazzarini, L., 1983, 'Il colore nei pittori veneziani tra il 1480 e il 1580,' in *Bollettino d'Arte 1983, suppl. n°5*, Studi Veneziani-Ricerche di Archivio e di Laboratorio, pp.131-144

9) Chiappori, M.G., 1989, 'Riflessi figurativi dei contatti Oriente-Occidente e dell'opera poliana nell'arte medievale italiana', in *Marco Polo Venezia e l'Oriente*, pp.281-9, Zorzi, A. (ed), Electa, Milano
Bussagli, M., 1986, *La Seta in Italia*, pp.124-9, Editalia

10) Brunello, F. (ed), 1992, *De Arte Illuminandi*, p.52, Neri Pozza, Vicenza

11) Dizionario di Chimica, 'Alchimia'. Available online:
http://www.minerva.unito.it/Chimica&Industria/Dizionario/DizA.htm

12) Gage, J., 1999, *Color and Culture*, p.139, University of California Press

13) Ball, P., 2002, *Bright Earth*, pp. 74, 76, 79, Farrar, Straus and Giroux, New York

14) Pietropaoli R. e Milaneschi A., 1991, 'Gialli', in *La fabbrica dei colori*, pp. 227-9,
Il Bagatto, Roma

15) Brunello, F., 'I colori nel trattato Compositiones ad tingenda', in "*Pitture e vernici*", Dic.'74
16) Brunello,F. (ed), 1992, *De Arte Illuminandi*, p. 180, Neri Pozza, Vicenza

17) Devoto,G., 1979, *Avviamento alla etimologia italiana*, pp. 53 and 455, Mondadori
18) Brunello, F., 1991, 'Le fonti medievali per la storia della tintura', in *Laniera, 105* (1991),n. 1, pp.123-6
Brunello, F., 1968, *L'arte della tintura nella storia dell'umanità*, Neri Pozza

19) Ball, P., 2002, *Bright Earth*, p.85, Farrar, Straus and Giroux, New York
20) Ibid., p.85
21) Ibid., p. 97

22) Brunello, F. (ed), 1992, *De Arte Illuminandi*, pp.148-9, Neri Pozza, Vicenza

23) M.Aceto, A. Idone, A. Agostino, G. Fenoglio, M. Gulmini, P. Baraldi, F. Crivello, *Spectrochim. Acta A 117, 34 (2014)*.
http://aperto.unito.it/handle/2318/156673#.VUlcv_ntmko

24) Codex Argenteus online:
http://app.ub.uu.se/arv/codex/faksimiledition/jpg_files/000_intro.html

25) M.Aceto, A. Agostino, G. Fenoglio, A. Idone, M. Gulmini, P. Baraldi, F. Crivello, C. Porter , 2014,
    On the Colouring of Purple Codices. Available from:
http://www.associazioneaiar.com/cms/sites/default/files/Extended_abs_2014/CeD_oral/Aceto%20et%20al.pdf

26) Rodríguez Peinado, L., 2014, 'Púrpura. Materialidad y simbolismo en la Edad Media', in *Anales de Historia del Arte, Vol. 24, Nº Esp. Noviembre*, pp.471-495. Available from: revistas.ucm.es/index.php/ANHA/article/.../45189

27) Ratliff, B. and Evans, C.H. ed., 2012, *Bysantium and Islam:Age of transition*, exhibition catalogue, pp.40-41, The Metropolitan Museum of Art, New York

28) Biggam, C., 2007, 'Knowledge of whelk dyes and pigments' in *The Archaeo+ Malacology Group Newsletter, Issue N.9, March 2006*. Available from:
http://www.archaeomalacology.com/MalacGp09.pdf

29) Bede, *Ecclesiastical History of England*, Book 1, Chap. 1. p. 006 . Available from: http://www.gutenberg.org/files/38326/38326-h/38326-h.html#toc13

30) Verhecken, A., 1993, 'Experiments with the dyes from European purple-producing molluscs', in *DHA (Dyes in History and Archaeology), N.12*, p.34. Available from: www.vliz.be/imisdocs/publications/250789.pdf

31) Bicchieri, M., 'The purple Codex Rossanensis: spectroscopic characterization and first evidence of the use of the elderberry lake in a 6th century manuscript'. Available from:
http://arxiv.org/ftp/arxiv/papers/1404/1404.6414.pdf

32) Aceto M, Agostino A, Fenoglio G, Baraldi P, Zannini P, Hofmann C, Gamillscheg E, 'First analytical evidences of precious colourants on Mediterranean illuminated manuscripts', in *Spectrochimica Acta Part A: Molecular and Biomolecular Spectroscopy, 2012, 95, 235-245*. Available from: https://www.academia.edu/2926538/First_analytical_evidences_of_precious_colorants_o n_Mediterranean_illuminated_manuscripts

33) Brunello,F. (ed), 1992, *De Arte Illuminandi*, pp. 171-2, Neri Pozza, Vicenza

34) Friedman, John B., 1995, *Northern English Books, Owners and Makers in the Late Middle Ages*, p. 235, Syracuse University press, New York

35) Ibid., pp. 228-9

36) *An introduction to illuminated manuscripts*, British Library online: https://www.bl.uk/catalogues/illuminatedmanuscripts/TourIntroGen.asp

37) Zuffi, S. (ed) 2006, *La Storia dell'Arte, vol. 3*, pp.351-94, Mondadori Electa, Milano

38) *Lindisfarne Gospels*, British Library online: http://www.bl.uk/onlinegallery/features/lindisfarne/tour.html

39) Friedman, John B., 1995, *Northern English Books, Owners and Makers in the Late Middle Ages*, pp. 235-6, Syracuse University press, New York

40) *Analysis of the Book of Kells*, Trinity College Library online: https://www.tcd.ie/Library/preservation/research/analysis-book-kells.php

41) *Tractatus de Herbis*, Sloane 4016, British Library Available online from: https://en.wikipedia.org/wiki/Tractatus_de_Herbis

42) Stein, Wendy A. "Patronage of Jean de Berry (1340–1416)". In *Heilbrunn Timeline of Art History. New York: The Metropolitan Museum of Art, 2000* http://www.metmuseum.org/toah/hd/berr/hd_berr.htm (May 2009)

43) The Belles Heures of Jean de France, duc de Berry http://www.metmuseum.org/collection/the-collection-online/search/470306

44)"Jean Pucelle: The Hours of Jeanne d'Evreux (54.1.2)". In *Heilbrunn Timeline of Art History. New York: The Metropolitan Museum of Art, 2000–*. http://www.metmuseum.org/toah/works-of-art/54.1.2 (December 2011)

45) Weinstein, C., 1998, *L'arte dei manoscritti medievali*, Idea Libri

46) Brunello, F. (ed), 1992, *De Arte Illuminandi*, pp. 148-195, Neri Pozza, Vicenza

47) Thompson, D.V., 1956, *The Materials and Techniques of Medieval Painting*, p.144, Dover Publications, New York

48) Thompson, D.V. Jr., translator, 1933, *An Anonimous Fourteenth-Century Treatise. De Arte Illuminandi* , p.7, New Haven. Yale University Press

49) Ibid., pp.8-9

50) Hoeninger, C., *JAIC 1991,Vol. 30, N.2*, pp.115-124
http://cool.conservation-us.org/jaic/articles/jaic30-02-001.html

51) Minunno, G., 1991, 'Azzurri', in *La fabbrica dei colori*, pp.335-9, Il Bagatto, Roma

52) Linzi, C., 1984, *Tecnica della pittura e dei colori*, pp.76-79, Hoepli, Milano

53) Ball, P., 2002, *Bright Earth*, p.102, Farrar, Straus and Giroux, New York

54) Brunello, F. (ed), 2001, *Il Libro dell'Arte di Cennino Cennini*, p. 4, Neri Pozza, Vicenza

55) Ball, P., 2002, *Bright Earth*, p.104-5, Farrar, Straus and Giroux, New York

56) Saldarelli,R., in *Omnibus n.1*- Marzo 2001
http://www.bottega2000.it/computerart/giottobottega.htm

57) Magagnato, L., 2001, 'Introduzione', pp. XV-XVII, in *Il Libro dell'Arte di Cennino Cennini*, Brunello, F. (ed), Neri Pozza, Vicenza

58) Saldarelli,R., in *Omnibus n.1*- Marzo 2001

59) Ibid.

60) Thompson Jr, D.V., translator, 1933, *The Craftman's Handbook.* "Il Libro dellArte". Cennino d'Andrea Cennini, p. 65, Dover Publications, New York

61) Saldarelli,R., in *Omnibus n.1*- Marzo 2001

62) Thompson, D. V., 1956, *The materials and techniques of Medieval painting*, p.85, Dover Publicatons, Inc. New York, N.Y.

63) Thompson Jr, D.V., translator, 1933, *The Craftman's Handbook*. "Il Libro dellArte". Cennino d'Andrea Cennini, p. 22, Dover Publications, New York

64) Ibid., p. 24

65) Quartullo, G., 1991, 'Rossi', in *La fabbrica dei colori*, p.81, Il Bagatto, Roma

66) Thompson Jr, D.V., translator, 1933, *The Craftman's Handbook*. "Il Libro dellArte". Cennino d'Andrea Cennini, p. 28, Dover Publications, New York

67) Brunello,F. (ed) 1992, *De Arte Illuminandi*, p. 222, Neri Pozza, Vicenza

68) Thompson Jr, D.V., translator, 1933, *The Craftman's Handbook*. "Il Libro dellArte". Cennino d'Andrea Cennini, pp. 28-9, Dover Publications, New York

69) and 70) Ibid., p. 30

71) Brunello,F. (ed) 1992, *De Arte Illuminandi*, p. 214, Neri Pozza, Vicenza

72) Rinaldi, S.,1991, 'Bianchi', in *La fabbrica dei colori*, p. 20, Il Bagatto, Roma

73) Thompson Jr, D.V., translator, 1933, *The Craftman's Handbook*. "Il Libro dellArte". Cennino d'Andrea Cennini, p. 36, Dover Publications, New York

74) Ibid., pp. 37-8

75) Ibid., p. 50

6) THE TRADITIONAL PALETTE OF THE LATE 15TH CENTURY FLORENCE

1) Dunkerton, J., Roy, A., 'The Materials of a Group of Late Fifteenth-century Florentine Panel Paintings'. *National Gallery Technical Bulletin Vol 17*, pp 20–31. http://www.nationalgallery.org.uk/technical-bulletin/dunkerton_roy1996

2)*The Raphael Cartoons*, V&A Museum
        http://www.vam.ac.uk/content/articles/t/raphael-cartoons-what-is-a-cartoon/

3) Bensi, P., 1980, 'Gli arnesi dell'Arte. I Gesuati di San Giusto alle Mura e la pittura del Rinascimento a Firenze', in *Studi di Storia delle Arti, N. 3*, pp.33-47, Università di Genova

4) Travaini L., 2005, 'Monete, battiloro e pittori. L'uso dell'oro nella pittura murale e i dati della Cappella degli Scrovegni / Coins, gold-beaters and painters. How gold was used in wall paintings: some examples from the Scrovegni Chapel', in *Bollettino d'Arte, Volume Speciale*, ICR Roma. Available from:
http://www.bollettinodarte.beniculturali.it/opencms/multimedia/BollettinoArteIt/docume nts/1424793008637_23_-_L._Travaini.pdf

7) THE CITY OF COLOUR

1) Hills. P., 1999, *Venetian Colour*, Yale University Press New Haven and London

2) Lazzarini, Lorenzo, 1983, 'Il colore nei pittori veneziani tra il 1480 e il 1580', in *Bollettino d'Arte 1983, suppl. n°5*, Studi Veneziani-Ricerche di Archivio e di Laboratorio, pp.131-144

3) Ibid.

4) Ball, P., 2002, *Bright Earth*, p.106-7-8/121, Farrar, Straus and Giroux, New York

5) Ibid., pp.112-115

6) Hills. P., 1999, *Venetian Colour*, pp. 133-6, Yale University Press New Haven and London

7) Lazzarini, Lorenzo, 1983, 'Il colore nei pittori veneziani tra il 1480 e il 1580', in *Bollettino d'Arte 1983, suppl. n°5*, Studi Veneziani-Ricerche di Archivio e di Laboratorio, pp.131-144

8) Quartullo, G., 1991, 'Rossi', in *La fabbrica dei colori*, pp. 102 , Il Bagatto, Roma

9) Lazzarini, L.,1991, 'Indagini preliminari di laboratorio', in *Il polittico Averoldi di Tiziano restaurato*, ed. Ragni and Agosti, Brescia, pp.173-177

10) Ball, P., 2002, *Bright Earth*, p.124-5, Farrar, Straus and Giroux, New York

11) Hills. P., 1999, *Venetian Colour*, p. 150, Yale University Press New Haven and London

12) Lazzarini, Lorenzo, 1983, 'Il colore nei pittori veneziani tra il 1480 e il 1580', in *Bollettino d'Arte 1983, suppl. n°5*, Studi Veneziani-Ricerche di Archivio e di Laboratorio, pp.131-144

13) Hills. P., 1999, *Venetian Colour*, pp. 145-6, Yale University Press New Haven and London

14) Bomford, D., 2000, *Colour*, National Gallery of London

15) Penny, N., Roy, A., Spring, M., 'Veronese's Paintings in the National Gallery, Techniques and Materials: part II', *National Gallery Technical Bulletin, vol. 17*, pp. 32-55
http://www.nationalgallery.org.uk/technical-bulletin/penny_roy_spring1996

16) Berrie, Barbara H., and Louisa C. Matthew. 2005, "Material Innovation and Artistic Invention: New Materials and New Colors in Renaissance Venetian Paintings." In conference proceedings, *Scientific Examination of Art: Modern Techniques in Conservation and Analysis*, pp. 12-26, Washington. Available from:
http://darwin.nap.edu/books/0309096251/html/12.html

17) Berrie, Barbara H., and Louisa C. Matthew. 2006, "Venetian 'Colore': Artists at the Intersection of Technology and History." in *Bellini, Giorgione, Titian, and the Renaissance of Venetian Painting*. David A. Brown and Sylvia Ferino-Pagden, pp. 302-309,
Exh. cat., National Gallery of Art. Washington

18) Bomford D., J. Dunkerton, Gordon D., Roy, A., *Art In The Making- Italian painting before 1400*, London 1989, pp.37-38, National Gallery Publications

19) Matthew, Louisa C., and Barbara H. Berrie, 2010, "Memoria de colori che bisognino torre a vinetia: Venice as a Centre for the Purchase of Painters' Colours." In *Trade in Artists' Materials: Markets and Commerce in Europe to 1700*, eds. Jo Kirby, Susan Nash, and Joanna Cannon, pp. 245 and 248, London: Archetype Publications

20) Freedman , L., 1995, *Titian's portraits through a retin's lens*, pp.125-132, Pennsylvania State Press

8) ANTWERP'S GOLDEN AGE

1) Vermeylen Filip, 'The Colour of Money: Dealing in Pigments in Sixteenth-Century Antwerp', in *Trade in Artists' Materials*, pp. 356, 361, Archetype Publications, London

2) *Portrait of Brigida Spinola Doria*
https://www.nga.gov/collection/gallery/gg45/gg45-46159.html

3) Ball, P., 2002, *Bright Earth*, p.143, Farrar, Straus and Giroux, New York

4) Plesters, J. '"Samson and Delilah": Rubens and the Art and Craft of Painting on Panel'. *National Gallery Technical Bulletin Vol 7, pp 30–49.* http://www.nationalgallery.org.uk/technical-bulletin/plesters1983

5) *Portrait of Elena Grimaldi Cattaneo* http://www.nga.gov/content/ngaweb/Collection/highlights/highlight1231.html

9) THE BAROQUE PALETTE

1) Ball, P., 2002, *Bright Earth*, pp. 129, Farrar, Straus and Giroux, New York

2) Ibid. pp. 130-2

3) Pastoreau, M., *Blu. Storia di un colore*, p. 107, Ponte alle Grazie, Milano

4) Ball, P., 2002, *Bright Earth*, pp. 134-5/145, Farrar, Straus and Giroux, New York

5) Milaneschi A.,1991, 'Bruni e Aranciati', in *La fabbrica dei colori*, p. 174-6, Il Bagatto, Roma

6) Ball, P., 2002, *Bright Earth*, pp. 136-7, Farrar, Straus and Giroux, New York

7) Della Torre Arrigoni D., *Mexico, return to tradition*, http://www.academia.edu

8) Pietropaoli R. e Milaneschi A., 1991, 'Gialli', in *La fabbrica dei colori*, pag. 250-1, Il Bagatto, Roma

10) THE EIGHTEENTH CENTURY PALETTE

1) Zuffi, S. (ed) 2000, *Il Ritratto*, pp. 139-143, ed. Electa

2) Stein, Perrin. "Jean Antoine Watteau (1684–1721)". In *Heilbrunn Timeline of Art History. New York: The Metropolitan Museum of Art, 2000–.* http://www.metmuseum.org/toah/hd/watt/hd_watt.htm (October 2003)

3) *The Reader by Fragonard* http://www.nga.gov/content/ngaweb/Collection/highlights/highlight46303.htm

4) Pastoreau, M., 2002, *Blu storia di un colore*, p.120, Ponte alle Grazie, Milano

5) Kirby, J., 1993,'Fading and colour change of Prussian Blue: Occurrences and Early Reports', *National Gallery Technical Bulletin,Vol.14*, pp. 62-71 http://www.nationalgallery.org.uk/upload/pdf/kirby1993.pdf

6) Pastoreau, M., 2002, *Blu storia di un colore*, p.133, Ponte alle Grazie, Milano

7) Ball, P., 2002, *Bright Earth*, pp. 242-3, Farrar, Straus and Giroux, New York

8) Kirby, J., 1993, 'Fading and colour change of Prussian Blue: Occurrences and Early Reports', *National Gallery Technical Bulletin, Vol.14*, pp. 62-71
http://www.nationalgallery.org.uk/upload/pdf/kirby1993.pdf

9) Bomford D. and Roy A., 1993, 'Canaletto's Stonemason's Yard and San Simeone Piccolo,'*National Gallery Technical Bulletin, Vol.14*, pp. 34-41
http://www.nationalgallery.org.uk/technical-bulletin/bomford_roy1993

10) Bomford, D., Roy, A. 'Canaletto's "Venice: The Feastday of S. Roch". *National Gallery Technical Bulletin, vol. 6*, pp. 40-43
http://www.nationalgallery.org.uk/technical-bulletin/bomford_roy1982a

11) Ball, P., 2002, *Bright Earth*, p. 148, Farrar, Straus and Giroux, New York

11) BETWEEN TWO CENTURIES

1) Ball, P., 2002, *Bright Earth*, pp. 161-2 , Farrar, Straus and Giroux, New York

2) Pietropaoli R. e Milaneschi A.,1991, 'Gialli', in *La fabbrica dei colori*, pp. 248-9, Il Bagatto, Roma

3) Ball, P., 2002, *Bright Earth*, pp.156-7, Farrar, Straus and Giroux, New York

4) Milaneschi A.,1991, 'Bruni e Aranciati', in *La fabbrica dei colori*, p. 184, Il Bagatto, Roma

5) Quartullo G., 1991, 'Rossi', in *La fabbrica dei colori*, p. 135, Il Bagatto, Roma

6) Pietropaoli R. e Milaneschi A.,1991, 'Gialli', in *La fabbrica dei colori*, pp. 242-4, Il Bagatto, Roma

7) 'Emerald Green or Paris Green, the Deadly Regency Pigment', in *Jane Austin's World* blog
https://janeaustensworld.wordpress.com/2010/03/05/emerald-green-or-paris-green-the-deadly-regency-paint/

8) Minunno,G., 1991, 'Azzurri', in *La fabbrica dei colori*, p.372, Il Bagatto, Roma

9) Costantini Scala F.,1991, 'Azzurro Oltremare', in *La fabbrica dei colori*, p. 320-2, Il Bagatto, Roma

10) Brunello, Franco, 1968, *L'arte della tintura nella storia dell'umanità*, p.274, ed. Neri Pozza

11) Ball, P., 2002, *Bright Earth*, p. 182, Farrar, Straus and Giroux, New York

12) Vincent van Gogh. *The letters.*
http://vangoghletters.org/vg/letters/let676/letter.html

13) Renoir, J., 1963, *Renoir mio padre*, p.77, ed. Garzanti

14) Wilson, M. Wyld and Ashok Roy, 1981 in 'Monet's Bathers at La Grenouillere ', *National Gallery Technical Bulletin, Vol.5*, pp 14-25
http://www.nationalgallery.org.uk/technical-bulletin/wilson_wyld_roy1981

15) Roy, A. 'Monet's Palette in the Twentieth Century: "Water-Lilies" and "Irises"'. *National Gallery Technical Bulletin Vol 28*, pp 58–68.
http://www.nationalgallery.org.uk/technical-bulletin/roy2007

16) Reissner, E., 2008, 'Ways of Making: Practice and Innovation in the National Gallery Cezanne's Paintings', *National Gallery Technical Bulletin, Vol.29*, pp 4-30
http://www.nationalgallery.org.uk/upload/pdf/reissner2008.pdf

17) mfa.cameo.org – *Materials Database*

18) Dabrowski, Magdalena. "Henri Matisse (1869–1954)". In *Heilbrunn Timeline of Art History. New York: The Metropolitan Museum of Art, 2000–.*
http://www.metmuseum.org/toah/hd/mati/hd_mati.htm (October 2004)

19) Zuffi, S. (ed) Le avanguardie, in *La Storia dell'Arte, vol 17*, pp. 380-1, Electa

20) *Les Demoiselles d'Avignon.* Conserving a modern masterpiece.
http://www.moma.org/explore/conservation/demoiselles/

21) Casadio, F., Mellom, A.W Conservation Scientist:
Art Scene Investigation: From Can to Canvas, blog. Available online:
http://blog.artic.edu/blog/2013/05/02/art-scene-investigation-from-can-to-canvas/

12) A PALETTE WITHOUT LIMITS

1) Mustalish, Rachel. "Modern Materials: Plastics". In *Heilbrunn Timeline of Art History. New York: The Metropolitan Museum of Art, 2000–.* http://www.metmuseum.org/toah/hd/mome/hd_mome.htm (October 2004)

2) Paul, Stella. "Abstract Expressionism". In Heilbrunn Timeline of Art History. New York: The Metropolitan Museum of Art, 2000–. http://www.metmuseum.org/toah/hd/abex/hd_abex.htm (October 2004)

3) ROTHKO N.13., 1958, 'White, Red on Yellow', Oil and acrylic with powdered pigments on canvas http://www.metmuseum.org/collection/the-collection-online/search/484362

4) Paul, Stella. "Abstract Expressionism". In Heilbrunn Timeline of Art History. New York: The Metropolitan Museum of Art, 2000–. http://www.metmuseum.org/toah/hd/abex/hd_abex.htm (October 2004)

5) POLLOCK, ONE, N. 31 http://www.moma.org/collection/browse_results.php?object_id=78386

6) POLLOCK, N. 28 http://www.metmuseum.org/toah/works-of-art/2006.32.51

7) Torselli Wilma, 26/03/2007, 'Nascita dell'Espressionismo Astratto e dell'action painting'. Available online from: http://www.artonweb.it/artemoderna/espressastratto/articolo2.htm

8) POLLOCK, ONE, N. 31 http://www.moma.org/collection/browse_results.php?object_id=78386

9) Zuffi, S. (ed) 2006, 'L'Arte Contemporanea', in *La Storia dell'Arte, vol. 18*, p. 107, Electa

10) Paul, Stella. "Abstract Expressionism". In Heilbrunn Timeline of Art History. New York: The Metropolitan Museum of Art, 2000–. http://www.metmuseum.org/toah/hd/abex/hd_abex.htm (October 2004

11) Phillips Collection, Rothko Room http://www.phillipscollection.org/collection/rothko-room

12) Frank Stella's 'Gobba zoppo e collotorto'
http://www.artic.edu/aic/collections/artwork/105208?search_id=1

13)TATE LONDON: Portrait of Brooke Hayward
Tate AXA Art Modern Paints Project, newsletter 3, January 2008, available online:
http://www.tate.org.uk/download/file/fid/4498

BIBLIOGRAPHY

ACETO, M., AGOSTINO, A., FENOGLIO, G., BARALDI, P., ZANNINI,P., HOFMANN,C., GAMILLSCHEG, E., 2012,
First analytical evidences of precious colourants on Mediterranean illuminated manuscripts.
Available online:
https://www.academia.edu/2926538/First_analytical_evidences_of_precious_colorants_on_Mediterra nean_illuminated_manuscripts

ACETO, M., AGOSTINO,A., FENOGLIO, G., IDONE,A., GULMINI,M., BARALDI,P., CRIVELLO,F., PORTER,C., 2014,
On the Colouring of Purple Codices. Available online:
http://www.associazioneaiar.com/cms/sites/default/files/Extended_abs_2014/CeD_oral/Aceto%20et %20al.pdf

ACETO, M., IDONE,A., AGOSTINO, A., FENOGLIO, G., GULMINI, M., BARALDI, P., CRIVELLO, F., 2014,
Spectrochim. Acta A 117, 34 (2014). Available online:
http://aperto.unito.it/handle/2318/156673#.VUlcv_ntmko

ART INSTITUTE OF CHICAGO (AIC):

1) Casadio, F., Mellom, A.W Conservation Scientist:
Art Scene Investigation: From Can to Canvas, blog. Available online:
http://blog.artic.edu/blog/2013/05/02/art-scene-investigation-from-can-to-canvas/http://blog.artic.edu/blog/2013/05/02/art-scene-investigation-from-can-to-canvas/

2)*Frank Stella's Gobba zoppo e collotorto*
http://www.artic.edu/aic/collections/artwork/105208?search_id=1

AUGUSTI, S., 1986, *I Colori Pompeiani*, De Luca Editore

BALL, P., 2002, *Bright Earth*, Farrar, Straus and Giroux, New York

BEDE, *Ecclesiastical History of England.* Available online:
http://www.gutenberg.org/files/38326/38326-h/38326-h.html#toc13

BENSI, P., 1980, 'Gli arnesi dell'Arte. I Gesuati di San Giusto alle Mura e la pittura del Rinascimento a Firenze', in Studi di Storia delle Arti, N. 3, Università di Genova

BERRIE, B. H., and L. C. MATTHEW. 2005, "Material Innovation and Artistic Invention: New Materials and New Colors in Renaissance Venetian Paintings." In conference proceedings, *Scientific Examination of Art: Modern Techniques in Conservation and Analysis*, Washington. Available online: http://darwin.nap.edu/books/0309096251/html/12.html

BERRIE, B. H., and L. C. MATTHEW. 2006, "Venetian 'Colore': Artists at the Intersection of Technology and History." in *Bellini, Giorgione, Titian, and the Renaissance of Venetian Painting*. David A. Brown and Sylvia Ferino-Pagden, Exh. cat., National Gallery of Art. Washington

BICCHIERI, M., '*The purple Codex Rossanensis*: spectroscopic characterization and first evidence of the use of the elderberry lake in a 6th century manuscript'. Available online: http://arxiv.org/ftp/arxiv/papers/1404/1404.6414.pdf

BIGGAM, C., 2006,'Knowledge of whelk dyes and pigments' in *The Archaeo+ Malacology Group Newsletter*, Issue N.9, March 2006 . Available online: http://www.archaeomalacology.com/MalacGp09.pdf

BOMFORD, D., 2000, *Colour* , National Gallery London Publications

BOMFORD, D, BROWN, C., ROY, A., 1989, *Art in the Making: Rembrandt*, London: National Gallery Publications

BOMFORD, D., J. DUNKERTON, GORDON, D., ROY, A., 1988, *Art In The Making- Italian painting before 1400,* London: National Gallery Publications

BOMFORD, D., KIRBY, J., LEIGHTON, J., ROY, A., 1990, *Art in the Making: Impressionism,* London: The National Gallery and Yale University Press

BOMFORD, D., ROY, A. 'Canaletto's "Stonemason's Yard" and "San Simeone Piccolo"'. *National Gallery Technical Bulletin Vol 14,* pp 34–41. http://www.nationalgallery.org.uk/technical-bulletin/bomford_roy1993

BOMFORD, D., ROY, A., 'Canaletto's "Venice: The Feastday of S. Roch"'. *National Gallery Technical Bulletin Vol 6* http://www.nationalgallery.org.uk/technical-bulletin/bomford_roy1982a

BOSTON FINE ART MUSEUM ONLINE: *Material Database online*: mfa.cameo.org,

BRITISH LIBRARY :

1) *An introduction to illuminated manuscripts.* Available online: https://www.bl.uk/catalogues/illuminatedmanuscripts/TourIntroGen.asp

2) *Lindisfarne Gospels*. Available online:
   http://www.bl.uk/onlinegallery/features/lindisfarne/tour.html

BRITISH MUSEUM: *THE 'RAM IN A THICKET'*. Available online:
http://www.britishmuseum.org/explore/highlights/highlight_objects/me/t/the_ram_in_a_thicket.aspx

BROWN, D.A., FERRINO PAGDEN, S. (ed) 2006, *Giorgione, Bellini, Titian and the Renaissance of Venetian Painting*, National Gallery of Art Publications, Washington

BRUNELLO, F., 1973, *L'Arte della Tintura a Venezia nel Rinascimento*, Ed. Laniera, Biella

BRUNELLO, F., (ed) 2001, *Il Libro dell'Arte di Cennino Cennini*, Neri Pozza, Vicenza

BRUNELLO, F., (ed), 1992, *De Arte Illuminandi*, Neri Pozza, Vicenza

BRUNELLO, F., 1964, 'L'arte della tintura a Venezia nel Settecento', in *Cultura e Scuola*, Year III, # 10
BRUNELLO, F., "I coloranti nei più antichi statuti dei tintori" in *Laniera*, Year 84 - No. 4

BRUNELLO, F., 1974, "I colori nel trattato dell'VIII secolo Compositiones ad tingenda" in *Pitture e Vernici, n12*

BRUNELLO, F., 1964, 'Colori e pitture della preistoria', in *Pitture e vernici, n.11*

BRUNELLO, F., 'Colori e pitture nell'Antico Egitto e in Mesopotamia'
   in *Pitture e Vernici, n° 4*, 1967

BRUNELLO, F., 1991, 'Le fonti medievali per la storia della tintura', in *Laniera*, 105 (1991) n. 1

BUSSAGLI, M., 1986, *La Seta in Italia*, Editalia

CANNON, J., NASH, S., KIRBY, J., (ed), 2010, *Trade in Artists' Materials*, Archetype Publ., London

CENNINO D'ANDREA CENNINI, *The Craftman's Handbook*, "Il Libro dell'Arte",1960, translated by Daniel V. Thompson, Dover Publications, Inc., New York

CHIAPPORI, M.G., 1989, 'Riflessi figurativi dei contatti Oriente-Occidente e dell'opera poliana nell'arte medievale italiana', in *Marco Polo Venezia e l'Oriente*, Zorzi, A. (ed), Electa, Milano

CLIFFORD DYER, H., 1909, *The lead and zinc pigments*, John Wiley & Son

CODEX ARGENTEUS online
   http://app.ub.uu.se/arv/codex/faksimiledition/jpg_files/000_intro.html

COSTANTINI SCALA F.,1991, 'Azzurro Oltremare', in *La fabbrica dei colori,*

218

Il Bagatto, Roma

DABROWSKI, Magdalena. "Henri Matisse (1869–1954)". In *Heilbrunn Timeline of Art History.* *New York: The Metropolitan Museum of Art, 2000–.* http://www.metmuseum.org/toah/hd/mati/hd_mati.htm (October 2004)

DELLA TORRE ARRIGONI, D., *Once upon a time Kermes,* http://www.academia.edu

DELLA TORRE ARRIGONI, D., *Mexico, return to trdition,* http://www.academia.edu

DEVOTO,G., 1979, *Avviamento alla etimologia italiana,* Mondadori

DIDEROT and D'ALEMBERT, *Encyclopedie des sciences des arts et des metiers,* Tables, Vol.X

DIZIONARIO DI CHIMICA, 'Alchimia'. Available online: http://www.minerva.unito.it/Chimica&Industria/Dizionario/DizA.htm

DUNKERTON, J., FOISTER, S., GORDON, D., PENNY, N.,1991, *Giotto to Dürer, Early Renaissance Painting in The National Gallery,* London, National Gallery Publications

FREEDMAN,L., 1995, *Titian's portraits through a retin's lens,* Pennsylvania State Press

FRIEDMAN, J. B., 1995, *Northern English Books, Owners and Makers in the Late Middle Ages,* Syracuse University press, New York

GAGE, J., 1999, *Colour and Culture,* University of California Press

HARLEY, RD, 2001, *Artsts' Pigments,* c.1600-1835, Archetype Publications, London

HILLS, P., 1999, *Venetian Colour,* Yale University Press, New Haven and London

HOENINGER, C., 1991, 'The Identification of Blue Pigments in early Sienese painting by color infrared photography', in
Journal of the American Institute of Conservation 1991, Vol. 30, No. 2. Available online: http://cool.conservation-us.org/jaic/articles/jaic30-02-001.html

JANE AUSTIN'S WORLD blog:
'Emerald Green or Paris Green, the Deadly Regency Pigment', posted by Vic https://janeaustensworld.wordpress.com/2010/03/05/emerald-green-or-paris-green-the-deadly-regency-paint/

KIRBY, J., 1993, 'Fading and colour change of Prussian Blue: Occurrences and Early Reports', *National Gallery Technical Bulletin,Vol.14,* pp. 62-71
http://www.nationalgallery.org.uk/upload/pdf/kirby1993.pdf

LAZZARINI, L., 1893, 'Il colore nei pittori veneziani tra il 1480 e il 1580', in *Bollettino d'Arte 1983 Supplemento No. 5*, Studi Veneziani- Ricerche di Archivio e Laboratorio

LAZZARINI, L.,1991, 'Indagini preliminari di laboratorio', in *Il polittico Averoldi di Tiziano restaurato*, ed. Ragni and Agosti, Brescia

LINZI, C., 1984, *Tecnica della pittura e dei colori*, Hoepli

LUZZATTO, L., and POMPAS, R., 1988, *Il significato dei colori nelle civiltà antiche*, Rusconi Editore

Ibidem, 1997, *Il colore del Vestire*, Hoepli

MAGAGNATO, L., 2001, 'Introduzione', pp. XV-XVII, in *Il Libro dell'Arte di Cennino Cennini*, Brunello, F. (ed), Neri Pozza, Vicenza

MATTHEW, L. C., and BERRIE, B.H., 2010, "Memoria de colori che bisognino torre a vinetia: Venice as a Centre for the Purchase of Painters' Colours." In *Trade in Artists' Materials: Markets and Commerce in Europe to 1700*, Jo Kirby, Susan Nash, and Joanna Cannon (ed) , London: Archetype Publications

METROPOLITAN MUSEUM OF ART:

1) "Jackson Pollock: Autumn Rhythm (Number 30)" (57.92) In *Heilbrunn Timeline of Art History*. *New York: The Metropolitan Museum of Art, 2000–*. http://www.metmuseum.org/toah/works-of-art/57.92. (June 2007)

2) Rothko N 13
http://www.metmuseum.org/collection/the-collection-online/search/484362

3) The Belles Heures of Jean de France, duc de Berry
http://www.metmuseum.org/collection/the-collection-online/search/470306

4) Pollock, Number 28
http://www.metmuseum.org/toah/works-of-art/2006.32.51

5) "Jean Pucelle: The Hours of Jeanne d'Evreux (54.1.2)". In *Heilbrunn Timeline of Art History*. *New York: The Metropolitan Museum of Art, 2000–*http://www.metmuseum.org/toah/works-of-art/54.1.2 (December 2011).

MILANESCHI, A., 1991, 'Bruni e aranciati', in *La fabbrica dei colori*, ed. Il Bagatto

MINUNNO, G., 1991, 'Azzurri', in *La fabbrica dei colori*, Il Bagatto, Roma

MUSEUM OF MODERN ART (MoMA):

1) POLLOCK, ONE, N. 31
http://www.moma.org/collection/browse_results.php?object_id=78386

2) Les Demoiselles d'Avignon. Conserving a modern masterpiece.
http://www.moma.org/explore/conservation/demoiselles/

MONNAS, L., 2008, *Princes, Merchants and Painters*, Yale University Press

MUSTALISH, Rachel. "Modern Materials: Plastics". *In Heilbrunn Timeline of Art History. New York: The Metropolitan Museum of Art, 2000–.* http://www.metmuseum.org/toah/hd/mome/hd_mome.htm (October 2004)

NATIONAL GALLERY OF ART, WASHINGTON:

1) Portrait of Brigida Spinola Doria.
https://www.nga.gov/collection/gallery/gg45/gg45-46159.html

2) Portrait of Elena Grimaldi Cattaneo
http://www.nga.gov/content/ngaweb/Collection/highlights/highlight1231.html

3) The Reader
http://www.nga.gov/content/ngaweb/Collection/highlights/highlight46303.html

OCCORSIO, S., 1991, 'Verdi', in *La fabbrica dei colori*, ed. Il Bagatto

PASTOREAU, M., 2000, *Blu, storia di un colore*, Ponte alle Grazie, MI

Ibid., 1987, *L'uomo e il colore*, Giunti, FI

PAUL, STELLA. "Abstract Expressionism". *In Heilbrunn Timeline of Art History. New York: The Metropolitan Museum of Art, 2000–.* http://www.metmuseum.org/toah/hd/abex/hd_abex.htm (October 2004)

PENNY, N., ROY, A., SPRING, M., 'Veronese's Paintings in the National Gallery, Techniques and Materials: part II', *National Gallery Technical Bulletin, vol,. 17* pp. 32-55
http://www.nationalgallery.org.uk/technical-bulletin/penny_roy_spring1996

PHILLIPS COLLECTION, Washington
The Rothko Room. Available online:
www.phillipscollection.org/collection/rothko-room

PIERINI, M., 'Appunti per una storia dei colori nella pittura medievale', in *L'Unicorno.* Available online: http://www.accademiajr.it/unicorno/articoli/uni008.htm

PIETROPAOLI, R. and MILANESCHI, A.,1991, 'Gialli', in *La fabbrica dei colori,* ed. Il Bagatto

PLESTERS, J. '"Samson and Delilah": Rubens and the Art and Craft of Painting on Panel'.
National   Gallery   Technical   Bulletin   Vol   7
http://www.nationalgallery.org.uk/technical-bulletin/plesters1983

QUARTULLO, G., 1991, 'Terre rosse', in *La fabbrica dei colori*, ed. Il Bagatto

RATLIFF, B. and EVANS, C.H. ed., 2012, *Byzantium and Islam: Age of transition*,
     exhibition catalogue,The Metropolitan Museum of Art, New York

REISSNER, E., 2008, 'Ways of Making: Practice and Innovation in the National Gallery Cezanne's
Paintings', *National Gallery Technical Bulletin, Vol.29*, pp 4-30
     http://www.nationalgallery.org.uk/upload/pdf/reissner2008.pdf

RENOIR, J., 1963, *Renoir mio padre*, ed. Garzanti

RODRIGUEZ PEINADO, L., 2014, 'Púrpura. Materialidad y simbolismo en la Edad Media', in
Anales de Historia del Arte, Vol. 24, N° Esp. Noviembre. Available online:
     revistas.ucm.es/index.php/ANHA/article/.../45189

RINALDI, S., (ed), 1986, *La fabbrica dei colori*, Il Bagatto, Roma
RINALDI, S., 1991, 'Neri', in *La fabbrica dei colori*, ed. Il Bagatto

ROY, A. 'The Palettes of Three Impressionist Paintings'. *National Gallery Technical Bulletin Vol 9*
     http://www.nationalgallery.org.uk/technical-bulletin/roy1985

SALDARELLI, R., in *Omnibus n.1*- Marzo 2001. Available online:
     http://www.bottega2000.it/computerart/giottobottega.htm

SANDBERG, G., 1997. *The Red Dyes: Cochineal, Madder, and Murex Purple*, Lark Books

STEIN, Perrin. "Jean Antoine Watteau (1684–1721)". In *Heilbrunn Timeline of Art History. New
York: The   Metropolitan   Museum   of   Art,   2000–.*
http://www.metmuseum.org/toah/hd/watt/hd_watt.htm (October 2003)

STEIN, Wendy A. "Patronage of Jean de Berry (1340–1416)". In *Heilbrunn Timeline of Art History.
New   York: The   Metropolitan   Museum   of   Art,   2000*
http://www.metmuseum.org/toah/hd/berr/hd_berr.htm (May 2009)

TATE LONDON:
Portrait of Brooke Hayward
Tate AXA Art Modern Paints Project, newsletter 3, January 2008, available online:
http://www.tate.org.uk/download/file/fid/4498

THOMPSON, D.V., 1956, *The Materials and Techniques of Medieval Painting*, Dover Publications, New York

THOMPSON, D.V. Jr., translator, 1933, *An Anonimous Fourteenth-Century Treatise. De Arte Illuminandi* , New Haven. Yale University Press

THOMPSON Jr, D.V., translator, 1933, *The Craftman's Handbook*. "Il Libro dellArte". Cennino d'Andrea Cennini, Dover Publications, New York

TORSELLI W., 26/03/2007, 'Nascita dell'Espressionismo astratto e dell'action painting'. Available online from: http://www.artonweb.it/artemoderna/espressastratto/articolo2.htm

TRACTATUS DE HERBIS, Sloane 4016, British Library
Available online from: https://en.wikipedia.org/wiki/Tractatus_de_Herbis

TRAVAINI, L., 2005, 'Monete, battiloro e pittori. L'uso dell'oro nella pittura murale e i dati della Cappella degli Scrovegni / Coins, gold-beaters and painters. How gold was used in wall paintings: some examples from the Scrovegni Chapel', *in Bollettino d'Arte, Volume Speciale,* ICR Roma. Availanle online from:
   http://www.bollettinodarte.beniculturali.it/opencms/multimedia/BollettinoArteIt/documents/142479
3008637_23_-_L._Travaini.pdf

TRINITY COLLEGE LIBRARY:
Analysis of the Book of Kells. Available online:
https://www.tcd.ie/Library/preservation/research/analysis-book-kells.php

V&A MUSEUM:
   The Raphael cartoons. Available online:
   http://www.vam.ac.uk/content/articles/t/raphael-cartoons-what-is-a-cartoon/

VERHECKEN, A., 1993, 'Experiments with the dyes from European purple-producing molluscs', in *DHA, N.12.*
   Available online: www.vliz.be/imisdocs/publications/250789.pdf

VERMEYLEN, F., 'The Colour of Money: Dealing in Pigments in Sixteenth-Century Antwerp'
 in *Trade in Artists' Materials*, Archetype Publications, London

VINCENT van GOGH. *The letters.* Available online:
http://vangoghletters.org/vg/letters/let676/letter.html

WATT JAMES, CY and WARDWELL A. E., 1997, *When Silk was Gold,* The Metropolitan Museum of Art, New York

WEINSTEIN, K., 1998, *L'arte dei manoscritti medievali*, Idea Books

WILSON, M. WYLD and ASHOK ROY, 1981 in 'Monet's Bathers at La Grenouillere ',
  National Gallery Technical Bulletin, Vol.5
http://www.nationalgallery.org.uk/technical-bulletin/wilson_wyld_roy1981

ZUFFI, S., (ed), *La Storia dell'Arte*, 2006, Mondadori-Electa

ZUFFI, S., (ed), *Il Ritratto*, 2000, Electa

INDEX

Antonello da Messina 120
Apelles 31
Bacon Roger 57
Bede 74, 75
Bellini Gentile 129, 130
Bellini Giovanni 135, 136, 137, 139, 140, 141
Bellini Jacopo 140
Bernard Emile 187, 188
Borso d'Este 91
Botticelli 121-124
Boucher 159, 160
Canaletto 165, 166
Caravaggio 154
Charlemagne 63, 82, 83
Charles the Bald 82
Carpaccio 129, 130
Cennini Cennino 61, 103, 118-120, 124-126, 141
Cimabue 100
Cima da Conegliano 139
Cione (di) Nardo e Jacopo 145
Cassatt Mary 160
Cézanne 175, 185, 187, 188
Chevreul Eugene 180-182
Clement F. 178
Constable 165, 170
Correggio 154
Crivelli Taddeo 90
David Gérard 135
De Kooning 153, 195
Del Cossa 123
Del Piombo Sebastaiano 130
De Mayerne Théodore 148
Desormes J.B. 178
Diesbach 163
Dioscorides 31, 56, 62, 77
Dippel 163
Duccio di Buoninsegna 100, 101
Duke of Berry 89-91
Eadfrith 85
Fauves 189
Federico da Montefeltro 90

Ferbach Franz 164
Field George 164, 173
Fragonard 159, 160
Gaddi Agnolo 103
Gainsborough 169
Gauguin 174, 189
Gentile da Fabriano 50, 145
Ghirlandaio Domenico 121, 125
Ghirlandaio Davide 121
Giorgione 130, 137
Giotto 55, 103, 104
Goethe 178
Gozzoli Benozzo 125, 145
Grossatesta Roberto 49
Guimet Baptiste 178, 179
Hellot Jean 163
Hogarth 165
Ingres 165
Kandinsky 189, 190
Leonardo da Vinci 121, 124, 125
Limbourg brothers 89
Lippi Filippino 121, 122, 125, 145
Lippi Filippo (follower of) 121
Lippi Filippo 124
Lorenzetti Ambrogio 56, 101
Lotto Lorenzo 144
Louis Morris 191, 194
Marc Franz 190
Martini Simone 50-52, 100, 101
Matisse 174, 189
Memmi Lippo 52
Michelangelo 125, 140
Monaco Lorenzo 145
Monet 160, 175, 185, 186
Morisot Berthe 160
Neri di Bicci 124, 125
Perugino 124, 125
Picabia 191
Picasso 165, 190, 191
Pietro di S. Omer 67
Pissarro 185, 187
Pliny 16, 20, 21, 28, 31, 32, 37-41, 43-45, 62
Plutarch 34, 36

Pollaiolo 121
Pollock 191, 193-197
Polo Marco 54, 67
Pucelle Jean 90
Raphael 10, 135, 145
Rand John 185
Renoir 160, 180, 182, 185
Reynolds 155, 169
Rembrandt 153-155
Rinman Sven 176
Rood Ogden 182
Rothko Mark 194, 195, 197, 198
Rubens 142, 148-151, 159, 160
St. Augustine 48
St. Bonaventura 49
Siqueiros 191, 193, 195
Sisley 185
Spinello Aretino 111
Stella Frank 193, 198
Tassaert M. 178
Theophrastus 20, 31-33, 39, 56
Thénard L.J. 177
Theophilus 68, 69, 105, 120
Tiepolo 160
Tintoretto 131, 135, 144, 146, 148
Titian 10, 13, 131, 134, 137-140, 142, 146, 148
Tura Cosimo 123, 133, 145
Turner W.J.M. 169, 170
Van Dyck 142, 148, 151, 155
Van Eyck Jan 89, 120, 133
Van Gogh 183-185
Vasari 120, 124, 126, 129, 152
Vauquelin 171, 172, 174
Veneziano Domenico 145
Veneziano Paolo 140, 141
Vermeer 157
Veronese 130, 131, 135, 143, 148, 152
Vibert 187
Vitruvius 16, 18, 20, 31, 33, 39, 40, 43, 45, 46, 62
Vivarini Antonio 130, 139, 140
Warhol 193, 194, 199
Watteau J.A. 159
Witelio 49

MATERIALS

Acrylics 191, 193, 194, 197, 198, 199
Aerugo> see Verdigris
Alexandria frit> see Egyptian blue
Alizarin lake 63, 190
Alkyds 191, 193, 199
Alum 22, 56, 63, 64,67, 78, 95, 96, 97, 141, 188
Amatisto> see Red jasper
Antimony yellow 19, 29, 112, 158, 160, 165, 166, 188
Arabic gum 13, 15, 17, 21, 23,42, 71, 78, 79, 119, 123
Armenian bole 114
Artificial basic copper carbonate> see Azurite, synthetic
Artificial orpiment 59, 61
Arzica 113, 114, 125
Asphalt> see Bitumen
Atramentum> 22, 42
Aureolin > see Cobalt yellow
Azo pigments 192
Azurite 24, 35, 54, 78, 98, 99, 100, 101, 113, 114, 115, 118, 122, 123, 125, 135, 136, 138, 141, 154, 163
Azurite, synthetic 162
Azuro de la Magna> see Azurite
Barium chromate 170
Basic copper acetate> see Verdigris
Biacca> see Lead white
Bistre 17, 155
Bitumen 137, 155
Blue black>see Vine (shoots) black
Blue verditer> see Azurite, synthetic
Bone black > see Ivory black
Brazil wood 54, 67, 95, 96, 97, 118, 131, 164
Brasilin 67
Brasilium 67
Brown earths 8, 10
Brunswick green 175
Burnt ocher 7, 15, 42
Burnt Sienna 137, 138, 154, 160
Cadmium orange 171, 172, 187, 199
Cadmium red 174
Cadmium yellow 172, 174, 186, 187, 190, 199
Caeruleum aegyptium> see Egyptian blue
Caeruleum scythicum> see Lapis lazuli

228

Caeruleum Cyprium> see Azurite
Caeruleum vestorianum> see Pompeian blue
Caesalpinia sappan 66
Car paints 193
Carbon black 11, 76, 85, 86, 122, 123, 188, 199
Cerulean blue 177, 190
Ceruse> see Lead white
Cerussa> see Lead white
Cerussa usta> see Red lead
Charcoal black 10, 11, 107, 150, 153, 166, 188
Chrome green 186, 199
Chrome orange 170, 171, 172, 182
Chrome yellow 170, 171, 172, 182, 183, 184, 185, 187, 188
Chrozophora tinctoria 66, 72, 74, 79, 80, 85, 94, 97
Chrysocolla 39, 46, 63, 114
Cinabrese 109, 118
Cinnabar, natural 21, 39, 40, 54, 60, 64, 76, 77, 95, 102, 137, 165
Cinnabar, artificial> see Vermilion
Cinnabaris indicus> see Dragon's blood
Clothlets 79, 93, 94, 97
Cobalt blue 170, 177, 180, 182, 185, 187, 190, 199
Cobalt green 176, 187
Cobalt violet 185, 186, 187, 190
Cobalt yellow 178
Cochineal (lake) 110, 131, 142, 154, 156, 160, 163, 164, 187, 188
Coelon 44
Cologne earth 153, 154, 155
Copper resinate 123, 131, 134, 135, 139, 143
Creta viridis> see Green earth
Dragon's blood 41, 63, 66
Earths and ochres 7, 8, 9, 10, 16, 102, 110, 118, 135, 138, 150, 154, 160, 166, 190
Egyptian blue 16, 18, 19, 20, 43, 46
Egyptian yellow> Antimony yellow
Elephantinum> see Ivory Black
Emerald green 170, 175, 176, 186, 188, 190
Folium> see Chrozophora tinctoria
French ultramarine > see Synthetic ultramarine
Gamboge 156, 165
Geranium lake 183, 184
German yellow(Lead-tin yellow type I) 125, 145
Giallorino 95, 111, 113, 118, 119, 125
Goethite 8, 76

Gold 26, 27, 30, 49, 50, 51, 54, 58, 61, 69, 71, 75, 76, 77, 78, 85, 93, 94, 123, 126, 127, 130, 132

Gommagutta> see Gamboge

Grains d'Avignon 95, 97

Green chrome oxide hydrate> see Viridian

Green earth 9, 11, 38, 54, 62, 113, 114, 115, 118, 122, 123, 139, 165, 166, 187

Green frit, artificial 19

Guignet green > see Viridian

Guimet blue> see Synthetic ultrmarine

Gum lac 110

Hematite 8, 9, 119

Indian lac 54, 110, 118, 122, 125

Indian Yellow 157

Indigo 46, 53, 54, 66, 72, 76, 78, 86, 95, 98, 112, 114, 142, 162

Iris germanica 95

Ivory/Bone black, 43, 150, 153, 190

Kermes 15, 63, 64, 72, 110, 118, 125, 131, 141, 142, 150

Kerria lacca Kerr 110

Lakes 15, 63, 131, 132, 135, 137, 138, 139, 140, 141, 142, 146, 150, 154, 156, 166, 182, 183, 187

Lamp black 11, 21, 42, 97, 102, 107, 108, 138

Lapis lazuli 16, 25, 26, 27, 28, 29, 38, 54, 55, 56, 62, 66, 76, 93, 98, 115, 118, 135, 136, 178, 179, 180

Lead antimonate> see Antimony yellow

Lead oxide yellow 19

Lead / tin yellow 111, 122, 131, 135, 138, 139, 143, 148, 150, 154

Lead-tin yellow type I 122, 123, 125, 144, 145

Lead-tin yellow type II 122, 144, 145

Lead white 19, 20, 21, 42, 62, 63, 76, 95, 97, 114, 115, 118, 119, 122, 123, 135, 136, 137, 138, 143, 148, 150, 160, 165, 166, 167, 182, 185, 187, 188, 190, 192

Lemon yellow 173, 182, 185, 190

Limonite 8, 9

Litharge 44, 62, 78, 170

Lomentum 44

Luza>see Reseda luteola

Madder (lake) 15, 22, 47, 53, 63, 72, 78, 125, 131, 142, 150, 154, 160, 187, 188

Malachite 16, 18, 24, 39, 56, 100, 114, 122, 123, 125, 134, 143

Mars red 156, 199

Mars violet 156

Mars yellow 161

Mineral yellow 170

Minium > see Cinnabar

Minium secondarium> see Red lead

Mosaic gold 59, 79
Murex purple 36, 61, 64, 72, 74, 79, 81
Naples yellow> see Antimony yellow
Nucella lapillus 75
Oak-galls 64, 76, 85, 86
Orchil> see Rocella tinctoria
Orpiment 15, 16, 21, 40, 41, 54, 61, 66, 76, 78, 85, 86, 94, 95, 112, 114, 118, 119, 131, 139
Ostrum 45
Pandius 64
Parchment 64, 70, 71, 72, 73, 76, 81, 95
Paris green 175
Permanent blue> see Synthetic ultramarine
Phthalocyanine 192
Pompeian blue> see Egyptian blue
Prasinus 62
Prussian Blue 160, 161, 163, 164, 165, 166, 183, 185, 187, 190
Purpura haemastoma 72
Purpurissum 38, 45, 110
PVA (polyvinyl acetate) 191, 193
Quinacridones 192, 199
Realgar 16, 21, 40, 41, 54, 61, 94, 112, 113, 139, 171
Red bole 49, 50, 52
Red earth 42, 54, 118, 187, 188, 190
Red eosin> see Geranium lake
Red jasper 54, 56, 93, 109
Red lead 19, 21, 29, 30, 42, 62, 64, 76, 78, 85, 86, 95, 102, 118
Red ocher 7, 9, 14, 42, 61, 62,109
Reseda luteola 46, 53, 63, 94, 95, 113
Rhamnus catharticus 95
Ripolin paints 191
Risalgallo or Risigallo> see Realgar
Rocella tinctoria 72, 74, 76, 81, 85
Rose madder 188
Rosetta 95, 96
Rubrica> see Red earth
Saffron 53, 94, 113
Sambucus nigra 76
Schweinfurt green>see Emerald green
Sheele's green 175
Sienna 10, 17, 154
Sil atticum 41, 46
Sinoper > see Red earth

Sinopis pontica 39
Smalt 101,102, 103, 125, 131, 135, 137, 138, 148, 160, 162, 177
Soot of charcoal 151, 155
Spuma argenti> see Litharge
St. John's white 115
Synthetic resins 193, 195
Synthetic ultramarine 179, 180, 186, 187, 190
Syricum 61, 62, 64
Terre-verte > see Green earth
Titanium white 192, 199
Turmeric 94
Turnsole> see Folium
Tyrian purple 72, 73, 74, 78
Ultramarine 16, 28, 54, 55, 69, 70, 77, 98, 99, 100, 101, 114, 115, 118, 122, 123, 124, 125, 132, 134, 135, 136, 137, 139, 140, 142, 162, 178
Umber 10, 17, 54, 150, 154, 165
Uvatum 62, 63
Verdigris 20, 44, 46, 66, 85, 86, 113, 114, 118, 122, 123, 131, 132, 134, 135, 139, 142
Verditer 162 >see Azurite, synthetic
Vergaut 66, 78, 85
Vermilion 21, 35, 58, 61, 76, 108, 109, 118, 122, 123, 131, 134, 135, 139, 142
Vermillion orange 170, 173
Verona earth > see Green Earth
Verzino > see Brasil wood
Vine (shoots) black 11, 107
Viridian 176, 182, 183, 186, 187, 188, 190
Whelk-dye 74, 75
White clays (Paraetonium, Melinum, Selinusia, Cimolia, Eretria, Argentaria) 37, 38, 42, 45, 46, 64
Woad 53, 62, 85
Yellow ochre 7, 9, 14, 16, 20, 25, 42, 54, 66, 78, 94, 110, 123, 135, 139, 150, 160, 165, 187, 188
Zinc white 167, 187, 190
Zinc yellow 174, 186, 187